DELIGHTS
AND
PREJUDICES

JAMES BEARD

DELIGHTS AND PREJUDICES

DRAWINGS BY EARL THOLLANDER

KONECKY&KONECKY

Konecky & Konecky
156 Fifth Avenue
New York, N.Y. 10010

This edition published by arrangement with Scribner,
an imprint of Simon & Schuster, Inc.

ISBN: 1-56852-108-1

Printed in the United States of America

TO

MARY PATRICIA HAMBLET

DELIGHTS
AND
PREJUDICES

CHAPTER

1

When Proust recollected the precise taste sensation of the little scalloped *madeleine* cakes served at tea by his aunt, it led him into his monumental remembrance of things past. When I recollect the taste sensations of my childhood, they lead me to more cakes, more tastes: the great razor clams, the succulent Dungeness crab, the salmon, crawfish, mussels and trout of the Oregon coast; the black bottom pie served in a famous Portland restaurant; the Welsh rabbit of our Chinese cook, the white asparagus my mother canned, and the array of good dishes prepared by the two of them in that most memorable of kitchens.

The kitchen, reasonably enough, was the scene of my

first gastronomic adventure. I was on all fours. I crawled into the vegetable bin, settled on a giant onion and ate it, skin and all. It must have marked me for life, for I have never ceased to love the hearty flavor of raw onions.

Another taste memory, my earliest, comes from the age of three. I lay abed with malaria and without much appetite, refusing all food except spoonfuls of the most superb chicken jelly that ever existed. For a time nothing counted in my life but chicken jelly. Either because it constituted my sole diet day after day or because it *was* magically good, chicken jelly and the flavor of perfectly prepared chicken have also remained a stimulant to my palate ever since.

This particular jelly was cooked slowly and carefully, beginning with two to three pounds of necks, gizzards, feet, heads, backbones, etc., covered with water to which an onion stuck with cloves, a piece of celery and a sprig of parsley were added. This was cooked slowly for an hour, then salted well. It was cooked again for two to three hours and strained. In this bouillon a good-sized fowl, cut into pieces, was cooked long and slowly until the meat fell from the bones. The whole was tasted, the seasoning corrected, and then it was strained and sometimes clarified. If clarified, the broth was poured through a linen napkin, then the white of an egg together with the shell was stirred in, and the broth was brought to the boiling point and strained again through a linen napkin. Finally it was cooled and then chilled. The resulting jelly had the true essence of chicken and a texture that was incredibly delightful.

I doubt if many people today want to eat chicken jelly unless they are ill or on a diet—the calorie count is low—but good chicken jelly has many uses in cooking. It gives a lift to vegetables cooked in it; it makes a fine Vichyssoise; and it provides the base for many excellent sauces. For a *chaud-froid* sauce it is incomparable.

Nowadays I find that a more practical approach to this delicacy can be achieved as follows:

Superb Chicken Jelly

Place 5 pounds backs and necks in 3 to 4 quarts water, together with 1 onion stuck with 2 cloves, a sprig of parsley, a bit of celery and a few peppercorns. Let this cook for about 3 hours—*à faible ébullition*. Then salt it well to taste. (I use coarse salt— Malden or kosher.) Now add 3 to 4 pounds chicken gizzards wrapped in a piece of cheesecloth after they have been washed. Add another quart of water and let them cook for 2 hours. Remove and save the gizzards. Then if you want a sensational dinner dish, add a good-sized capon or roasting chicken and poach it in this rich broth till it is just tender and cooked through. Be very careful not to overcook it! Serve with a little of the clarified broth and either rice or some crisp sautéed potatoes. Here you have superbly flavored chicken and so simply done. All it takes is the patience to watch the broth. If you have an electric oven, leave it at a low temperature with the automatic control on and forget about it.

If my earliest love in food was chicken jelly, my earliest hate was milk. I loathed milk, cold or hot. It simply couldn't be made attractive to me as a drink. And if occasionally a zealous adult with standard notions about growing children forced me to drink a glass, I promptly became sick. It has never failed to be an effective emetic for me, and I am still revolted when I see people drinking milk with a good meal. Eventually, though, I came to accept milk when it was combined with other ingredients and turned into a modest but delectable dish, clam soup. I grew to love this soup, served with great toasted soda crackers. (For dessert we often had more of the crackers spread with butter and good bitter marmalade.) Here are three different ways of preparing it.

Clam Soup

Razor clams are a must for this dish. You may purchase the minced clams from most good grocers, and
if you care to write to Seaside, Oregon, you can get
whole ones in tins. Heat 1 pint light cream and the
juice from two 7-ounce cans minced clams to the
boiling point. Add salt and pepper to taste, a dash of
Tabasco sauce and 2 tablespoons butter. Now add the
clams and just heat them through. Serve the soup at
once with a dash of paprika or chopped parsley. This
recipe will serve four lightly or two well.

Clam Soup II

In a blender, blend two 7-ounce cans whole razor
clams in juice till the mixture is thick. Remove it to
the top of a double boiler. Add 1 pint heavy cream, 2
tablespoons butter, and seasonings to taste. Heat the
soup to the boiling point over hot water, and serve it
with a dash of paprika.

Corn and Clam Soup

In a blender, blend two 7-ounce cans whole razor
clams and 1 cup whole-kernel corn (or one 12-ounce
can) and place the mixture in the top of a double
boiler over hot water. Add 1 cup light cream, ½ cup
milk, 2 tablespoons butter and seasonings. Heat the
soup to the boiling point, add ¼ cup bourbon, and
serve it with a bit of chopped parsley.

While I'm on the subject of clams, I might as well
produce the clam chowder recipe which my mother
always prepared at the beach. It was very popular with
our family and friends, and it resembles only faintly the
chowders of other sections of the country.

Clam Chowder

Cut 3 to 4 thick rashers lean bacon into rather small
pieces and try out in a heavy skillet. Remove the
bacon to absorbent paper and pour off all but 2
tablespoons of fat. Sauté 1 fairly large onion,

coarsely chopped, in fat till it is just transparent. Add 4 smallish potatoes, peeled and diced, and enough clam broth, about 2 cups, to cover. Bring this to a boil. Cook until the potatoes are soft and almost disintegrated. Add salt and pepper to taste and a dash of Tabasco sauce. Heat 1 quart light cream and add potato-onion mixture, bacon bits and lastly 1½ cups chopped fresh or canned razor clams. Correct the seasoning. Add ¼ cup cognac, and when clams are just heated through, serve the chowder in hot cups with a dash of chopped parsley. This same chowder may be mixed in an electric blender and served cold with chopped chives and parsley.

The ability to recall a taste sensation, which I think of as "taste memory," is a God-given talent, akin to perfect pitch, which makes your life richer if you possess it. If you aren't born with it, you can never seem to acquire it. Great wine palates must depend on taste memory for the sureness of their judgment, and a Lichine or a Schoonmaker without this memory would never be able to perform the almost overpowering task of comparing vintages and selecting wines.

Cheese tasters, tea tasters, cognac tasters—all must depend for a living on the keenness of their taste memories. Great gastronomes also have a highly developed sense memory, or they would not make such a ceremony of tasting and enjoying food. And naturally good chefs and cooks must depend upon memory when they season or when they are combining subtle flavors to create a new sauce or a new dish.

Not all taste memory is accurate. Many people think of Mom's apple pie or Grandmother's dumplings as delicacies that cannot be equaled today. These memories are associated with happy times, and to the untrained palate the pie or the dumplings seemed delicious. If the same dishes were re-created and presented to a sophisticated palate, they would probably belie their reputations. Most of the home cooking one enjoyed in his youth was not as good as one remembers it.

I think I developed an accurate taste memory early in my life. I was not sentimentally attached to the cooking of any one person at home, and we ate in restaurants a good deal. I tried to be as objective as possible about taste and was somewhat precocious in appreciating the pleasure of blending satisfying flavors. While this meant that I learned to enjoy the delights of a good meal, it also meant that I soon grew intolerant of mediocre food. More than once, I'm afraid, my candid appraisals embarrassed a hostess or friends with whom we were sharing a meal. I often wonder why I didn't have a pie thrown at me!

Both my parents had sensitive palates, my father to a lesser degree, although Mother tended to disparage his knowledge of food. In later years he looked forward to the periods when my mother was away at the beach so he could live on his own cooking. Aside from this, he had a favorite late Sunday breakfast menu, which he produced every week, save in winter, consisting of deliciously sautéed chicken served with a bacon-and-cream sauce made in the sauté pan. With this dish there were generally hot biscuits, toasted crumpets or just good toast. In winter the menu changed to sausage, smoked fish or country ham. These expressions of my father's culinary skill were memorable indeed, and whenever friends stayed with us on weekends, they used to request his breakfast.

Mother had an uncanny sense of food and the talent to show others how to prepare it. She loved to cook, eat and talk food more than almost anyone else I have known. At the turn of the century she had an international approach to food that would have been considered revolutionary in the last ten years. She was ahead of her time socially as well. When women were still subordinate and modest, Mother was forceful and fearless. She swept through a room or down the street with an air of determination and authority, and she met men on their own terms. In any social gathering men surrounded her, and on outings she was among them, clamming, fishing, berrying. She could talk their language and used profanity on occasion, though without vulgarity. Women, as could be expected, were less drawn to her, except for those who gave her the boundless devotion often felt by the weak for the strong. Her circle of friends was colossal. Her counsel was constantly sought, and her know-how saved many an occasion.

She was always ready for an adventure—prepared to pack her bag and be off on a journey (she had never been seasick, she boasted, never missed a meal at sea). And it was probably in this same spirit that she had packed up and left England years before.

She was born Elizabeth Jones in the beautiful countryside of Wiltshire and adopted by a childless aunt and uncle who lived in London.

At sixteen she was already eager to see the world and jumped at the opportunity to tour the United States as governess with a Canadian family. She sailed for America unchaperoned, met her employers and then for two years traveled throughout the States. This was in the late 1870s when transportation was not at its most comfortable, but Elizabeth loved adventure and enjoyed every minute of it.

At the end of the two years they happened to be in Portland when the family was suddenly called back to Toronto. Elizabeth decided to remain in Portland. She found work, saved her money and then went to live in New York, where she met many people in the theater and made lifelong friends. Then after a time she returned to England, thinking she might marry a young man she had known earlier. A fresh look at this candidate changed her mind, and she scurried back to America—this was in 1886—continuing to the West Coast and Portland, which was now becoming a point of focus for her. But she was far from settling down!

In Portland she took a position with a Mrs. Curtis, who had several small residential hotels on the Coast. For the next few years she worked contentedly but managed to take a leave of absence from Mrs. Curtis two or three times to visit California and tour Europe, and she also explored the Central American countries with a close friend of hers, a well-known actress of the day, at the time that de Lesseps was in Panama.

Back in Portland, Elizabeth settled down to marry a man named Brennan, whom she had known earlier, and she lived very happily with him. But he died suddenly, after they had been married only a year. The shock of this event sent Elizabeth—now Elizabeth Brennan—traveling again. She returned to England once more and then went to the Continent, where she visited in France and Italy, ate well, and made up her mind to become a successful businesswoman.

She knew attractive people everywhere and could have lived in any one of a half-dozen cities quite comfortably with a lively social life for herself, but again it was to Portland she went and in doing so committed herself to a future that was both happy and bitter.

This was in 1891. She stopped off for a time in New York to visit friends, dine out and see some theater; then she wrote to Mrs. Curtis asking for another job. She said that the European trip had refreshed her culinary lore and that this, plus her gastronomical experiences in New York, gave her a unique background. Evidently Mrs. Curtis thought so too, for Elizabeth was invited to return as manager of the Curtis Hotel in Portland, which was at 12th and Morrison Streets in those days.

Here she spent four years or so while she gradually developed the desire for a place of her own. With characteristic efficiency she began to make plans, and by 1896 she was able to buy a four-story Victorian building two blocks away from the Curtis, which she named the Gladstone.

Portland at that time was a rich city with magnificent houses and a tightly knit society composed largely of New Englanders, English and Scots. As the center of the shipping, lumber and fishing industries, it had the raw vitality that characterized large port cities of the era. Robust waterfront workers, successful madams, even more successful employees of madams (quite a few of whom eventually reached the social register), and operators of "sailors' boardinghouses" were all helping to build Portland's wealth. Meier & Frank had become established as one of the great stores on the West Coast, and a luxury-loving public enjoyed a continuous interchange with the East Coast and Europe. Good food abounded. The great houses maintained fine cooks, society matrons filled their daybooks with treasured recipes, and the ladies of Trinity Church, the plushy Episcopal house of worship in Portland, published the *Web-Foot Cook Book*, one of the best of all cookbooks in its genre, and today a collector's item.

Here are two of its recipes, which illustrate the simplicity of taste, charm and occasional social pretension to be found in the book:

Very Old Recipe for Custard

Used in England before the Revolution by the ancestors of the family that now have possession of it.

One quart of rich milk. Boil well with whole spices, which remove when the flavor is extracted. Then add yolks of six eggs and beaten white of three. Stir until thoroughly hot (do not allow to boil or it will curdle), about five minutes will do. When nearly cold flavor with rose water. It may now be turned into custard cups and a meringue spread over when cold, and slightly browned in the oven. [This recipe has never been made public before.]

12

Trinity Church Salad

The chicken should be put in water which is very salt and cooked until thoroughly done, and let them lay [*sic*] in water until cold. Pull into shreds (which may be cut if too long), remove all skin and bone. Use two eggs for every chicken; beat the yolks a little, then stir in French salad oil very slowly, a few drops at a time. If the oil begins to separate add a few drops of lemon juice. Add a little Cayenne pepper, two salt spoons of salt, a teaspoonful of mustard dissolved in hard boiled yolk of one egg, which has been beaten to a paste with a little oil. When the yolks have been beaten to a stiff batter with the oil, mix the cold water in which the chicken has been boiled and enough vine-

gar to make a dressing rather thicker than rich cream. Taste it to see if seasoned aright. If the dressing should curdle, put the yolks of one or two eggs on another platter and add the curdled dressing by degrees, seasoning to taste. Take a bowl of chopped celery to a bowl of chopped chicken. If you like, beat the whites to a stiff froth, mix with a little dressing, stir into the salad oil and put the rest on top. Good for grouse, quail or pheasant. One grouse goes as far as two chickens.

Mrs. J. Myrick

It was in a food-conscious city, then, that Elizabeth Brennan ran her hotel. Her day would begin at five in the morning. She rose, attired herself smartly in a divided skirt, well-starched blouse, fedora hat, fashionable gloves and shoes, and set off for a three- or four-mile bicycle ride, arriving back fresh and pink, in time to greet many of her guests at breakfast. Then over a cup of tea she planned the day's menu with the chef. Like a director prepared to assume any role in his play, she never put a dish on the menu which she couldn't execute herself, should her chef fail her at the last minute.

She was wary. Experience with imported French and Italian chefs taught her that they grew restless after a time. The lure of the beautiful city to the south, San Francisco, with its tales of glamour, money and women, tempted them to the extent that they would one day slip away via the Southern Pacific Shasta Limited or one of the ships plying the route down the Columbia—a trip, incidentally, once you passed the Columbia River bar, that could be as delightful as a Mediterranean cruise or as rough as a North Atlantic crossing.

After one especially accomplished chef, having saved all his money, had taken off with his sous-chef to the fleshpots of San Francisco, Elizabeth decided such an annoyance would never happen again. She would train —and, what was more, keep—her own staff. She had a

14

shrewd plan. First of all she hired another French chef and a pastry chef as replacements. Then she turned her back on Europeans and began a search for Chinese with deft hands and good references. She found them, trained them—and kept them. (Let as chef, Gin as his assistant, and Poy as pastry chef.) And when they had learned the repertoire, they became the resident company of stars, and the French artists were invited to proceed to the more fascinating, more Latin atmosphere of the Bay Area.

Let was a remarkable person who was later to become a part of our family. He was the one person Mother never could dominate. Whenever she violated the subtle balance of their relationship, it led to a raucous East-West conflict. Once Let threatened Mother with a knife, and once she tried to attack him with a great stick of stovewood. On each occasion the skirmish ended in fits of laughter. The greatest arguments were caused by the smallest of disagreements—usually about an item on the menu or the preparation of a dish. Somehow their volatile friendship prospered over the years, and Let, in his oblique way, even adored my mother.

So the kitchen at the back of the Gladstone ran smoothly, and the dining rooms at the front flourished. It was an age when no one worried about cholesterol; everyone ate and drank without stinting himself. There were often champagne parties, bridge parties, whist drives, smart luncheons, and it was the fashion to entertain at supper after a concert or the theater.

One late supper favorite was *vol-au-vent* with creamed Olympia oysters—surely the most heavenly dish ever created. Let would make the *vol-au-vent* with old Gin, who was as miraculous a pastry chef as Poy. The baked shells were carried hot to the supper room, where a sauce—made of white wine mixed with the oyster liquor, cream, eggs, a little *roux* and a dash of Madeira—was ready in chafing dishes. Just before serving, the oysters went into the sauce to be held till they were just warmed through. Then the glorious mixture was heaped into serving portions and each plate garnished with watercress. This was followed by cold chicken, ham and tongue, perhaps, good rolls, a salad, and either fruit or some cheese and a white wine.

Another supper dish for which the Gladstone was famous was a sauté of wild mushrooms and chicken, to which cream and eggs were added, served with bread *croustades* sprinkled with cognac, and garnished with asparagus—fresh or canned white asparagus—and a touch of drawn butter. Hard rolls, toasted and buttered, accompanied this, and dessert was frequently a delectable fruit combination served with small cakes, *madeleines* and lady fingers.

When spring came there was often a salmon masked with a sensational Russian dressing, made with caviar, herbs and seasonings, and mayonnaise. Followed by a string bean and cucumber salad, a cold meat course and some hot dessert, this made a popular menu. Usually tiny cups of broth or consommé were served as a first course. Mother felt it primed people to enjoy a good meal.

At other times there would be a stupendous chicken or crab salad made by Let. The chicken salad had no celery in it—merely chicken in pieces of generous size, tossed with homemade mayonnaise, capers and some almonds or walnuts, and garnished with more nuts and additional mayonnaise well flavored with mustard.

Mayonnaise, as I later came to know, was always something of a performance for Mother. If a small amount was to be made for a particular dish, it was carefully done with a large silver dinner fork in a dinner plate. Two egg yolks were broken into the plate and worked well with the fork. Then olive oil was added by the spoonful, and the mixture was emulsified with a clockwise movement of the fork till its consistency was thick. A few drops of lemon juice or vinegar—and it had to be tarragon vinegar—were added and a touch of mustard and salt to taste. This mayonnaise was thick enough to cut with a knife or use in a pastry bag.

If a large quantity of mayonnaise was called for, Mother had another special method, which she had learned by watching one of her chefs. It took a great deal of practice, but she finally mastered it herself. First she assembled a rotary beater, a half-gallon tin of oil with two small holes punched in it, a large bowl, and a box that was about one inch higher than the bowl. After placing whole eggs in the bowl, she turned the can on its side, on the box, so that the oil trickled into the bowl in a steady thin stream. Then she began to beat until she had a bowlful of delicious golden mayonnaise. Her dexterity as she went through this performance was nothing short of virtuosic! After the mayonnaise had thickened, mustard, lemon juice, tarragon vinegar and salt were added, and a touch of Tabasco. And oftentimes it was supplemented with chopped eggs, capers, onion and parsley.

If you would like to try homemade mayonnaise for yourself, here is the recipe:

Mayonnaise

Today, of course, this may be put together in an electric mixer or blender. Begin with 2 eggs, 1 teaspoon salt and 1 teaspoon dry mustard, and add 2 to 3 cups oil slowly, a few drops at a time. If the mayonnaise starts to curdle, you are adding the oil too fast. Start over with another egg and a little oil, gradually beating the curdled mixture into this. When the mixture is thick and stiff, flavor it with 1 to 2 tablespoons tarragon vinegar, a few drops of lemon juice and a dash of Tabasco sauce. This mayonnaise will keep for several weeks under refrigeration.

Let distinguished himself by doing as fine a terrapin stew as anyone could make, taught not by my mother but by Mrs. Summers, the wife of my godfather. Clara Summers was a Southerner and an excellent cook, and she and General Summers took a great fancy to Let. One day Clara led him to a corner of her kitchen and went through the intricacies of preparing terrapin. Thereafter, Let's stew was superb—redolent with good sherry and filled with butter and other ingredients to make it deadly rich and deadly appealing to anyone who liked good food.

The terrapins were plunged live into boiling water to blanch for five minutes or so. Then they were lifted to a dry Turkish towel, and the skinning process began. After they were well skinned, the carcasses were placed in a court bouillon, made with one carrot, an onion, a *bouquet garni*, a little white wine and salted water, and the animals were cooked for thirty-five to forty minutes. Next they were cleaned—the nails, gall and large intestine removed, the liver and the small intestine retained. If there were eggs, these too would be used in the stew.

Here is Let's terrapin stew, as it was served by the Gladstone.

Terrapin Stew

Add meat of 2 terrapins to 1½ cups chicken stock and allow it to cook down. Add salt and pepper to taste and a dash of Tabasco sauce. Combine yolks of 4 eggs with 1 cup cream and ⅓ cup cream sherry and stir this into the mixture. Continue stirring until it is slightly thickened. Add the terrapin liver and eggs (if there are any) and correct the seasoning—a dash of lemon is sometimes good. Serve the stew with toast points or *croustades*.

Another famous dish of Let's was his Welsh rabbit. In Oregon we were blessed with fine natural cheeses. The Cheddar of my childhood was delicious, well aged and sharp to the taste. It had a fine texture and tingled the tongue. We often used it in rabbit for an evening party, and at the beach the same dish was very pleasant for supper when the air was brisk or the fog swept in from the sea. It was often made in a chafing dish and sometimes over a low wood fire in a heavy casserole or saucepan. With it went quantities of hot, hot toast, well buttered and crisp, and enormous amounts of beer. Knowing that some delicate appetites were not equal to so heavy a dish for late supper, Mother and Let always provided an alternate dish of chicken with a light cream sauce and mushrooms, flavored with a good deal of sherry. This was served either in patty shells with a little rice on the side, or on well-buttered toast spread with a touch of herb butter, made with parsley and tarragon. As a conclusion to this supper a light fruit dessert was served—sometimes fresh fruit, sometimes a delicate concoction of sliced oranges, fine-cut rind, cinnamon and sugar, and a touch of liqueur—possibly cognac or kirsch—added at the last minute.

Let's Welsh Rabbit

Melt 2 tablespoons butter, and when it is just melted add 1 pound sharp Cheddar cut in small pieces or coarsely grated. Season with a small amount of salt, depending upon the saltiness of the cheese, 1 teaspoon dry mustard, a dash of Tabasco and 1 teaspoon Worcestershire sauce. As the cheese begins to melt, stir in 1 pint good beer, then stir in 1 egg, lightly beaten. When the mixture is creamy and soft, serve on toast or crackers. Do not allow it to get stringy or leathery. Sprinkle with paprika and serve with glasses of beer. If you keep this over low heat, you may dip pieces of French bread in it as you do with a Swiss fondue.

The hotel cuisine followed the classic menu-building processes, and there was a variety of special dishes apart from the standard fare. I can give a firsthand report on many of these, since they were served to me at home years later, after Mother had sold the hotel. Other dishes I only heard about.

Let made a celebrated *pot-au-feu* with beef, chicken and tongue, which was served with broth, horseradish sauce and boiled potatoes, leeks and carrots. And he did a really superior chicken pie, topped with a puff paste crust, which contained a rich cream sauce, tiny onions, peas and seasonings.

Mother had several good curries in her repertoire, which she would vary. Sometimes it was a curry in the French manner with a béchamel sauce to which curry was added; sometimes it was a true curry, with onions, apples and carrots added to the basic mixture, and along with this went bowls of still hotter curry sauce. A favorite way of serving the hot sauce was with hard-boiled eggs sautéed in butter and curry powder and garnished with shrimp and sometimes mushrooms. This made a wonderful luncheon speciality and proved suitable for supper parties as well.

Let did two curry dishes of his own, which must have been a mixture of the Orient and the Occident. Mother was so openly critical of people who served a watery lamb curry that Let developed a fine curry of braised shoulder of lamb with all sorts of enchanting additions to the sauce. The brisk curry flavor blended with the flavor of browned lamb, and it was sensationally successful from its first performance. It has had a continuous run in my own kitchen.

The other curry, which Let said was originally northern Chinese, contained tomato, ginger, turmeric, kumquat and many other things. I shall attempt to re-create this recipe for you. It was Let's secret, but I think I have solved the mystery, and I find that when it is served on noodles instead of rice, it becomes a gloriously new dish.

20

Let's Secret Curry Sauce

Grind or chop fine 4 medium-sized onions, 2 cloves garlic, 6 tart apples cored but not peeled, 1 pound Virginia ham scraps with fat, and ½ cup parsley (Chinese parsley if available). Sauté these ingredients in a little oil until slightly golden in color. Blend in ¾ cup flour and stir until it is lightly brown. Add ¾ cup curry powder, 2 tablespoons turmeric, and 1 crushed hot chile pepper. Stir in 1 cup tomato paste, 2 quarts veal stock, and ⅓ cup lemon juice, and cook the sauce for 1 hour. Correct the seasoning. Add ⅓ cup soy sauce and simmer for another 30 to 40 minutes, stirring frequently so it doesn't scorch. This will make a little over a half-gallon. It will keep for some time in the refrigerator and may be frozen. It is a good base for almost any curry dish. You may make it hotter or blander as you wish.

In summer there was often an aspic on the menu. Let made a veal in aspic, with eggs and capers and other ingredients, which became one of Mother's most famed dishes for hot-weather eating. And there was a chicken aspic, hearty and filled with good flavor, which I can remember having on picnics and at parties on the beach, served with a French potato salad and string beans or peas vinaigrette.

In winter, and sometimes in summer, a stuffed poached chicken became a regular feature. This was no ordinary chicken but a great fowl of distinctive age and size and background. Like as not there would be loads of unshelled eggs inside, which were saved and poached in broth at the last minute. This noble bird was stuffed with one of Let's really splendid stuffings—delicate and rich when hot, firm as a good poundcake when cold. After it was stuffed and trussed, the chicken was put into well-seasoned water, along with the feet and giblets (except the liver), and cooked slowly until the meat was tender but not mushy. If it was served hot, there might be rice and a cream sauce or onion sauce with it. The eggs of the chicken, if any, went into the sauce, as did a little wine. If it was served cold, Let would make a superb rice salad and a good dressing to go with it. And there would be the cold stuffing, as rich as a *pâté* or terrine, though meatless.

Let's roasted capons and chickens with or without stuffings were renowned. I remember parties when I was young at which a roast stuffed chicken or two of Let's was the *pièce* of dinner. These were never cooked dry but always had a moist breast and moist dark meat.

There were many dishes which I suspect Mother picked up from her previous chefs, gave a twist of her own, passed on to Let and then took back again. One was a luncheon dish which created a loyal following and which long after business was forgotten by my mother (if it ever was) continued to elicit an ardent response any time she made it. This was breast of lamb poached in a well-flavored bouillon, and when tender, pressed between plates and the bones removed. For lunch or dinner it was dipped in flour, egg and crumbs, sautéed to a golden brown in butter, and served with a soubise sauce. It was delicately tender, and the crunchy exterior contrasted nicely with the subtly flavored lamb. With this were served tiny potatoes *au beurre* and peas.

One holdover from England which Mother never quite relinquished and which caused her no end of disagreement with Let was mint sauce. As mint sauce goes, it was a good one she made. But Let insisted, and Mother in the right mood agreed, that mint sauce really ruined lamb. She had only to see fresh mint, however, and she weakened. Her mint sauce was redolent with the herb and included brown sugar, hot vinegar and water. No matter how good it smelled, it certainly did nothing to enhance the flavor of young lamb. I recalled this controversy the other day when, in one of the great restaurants of the world, I heard an Englishman ask for bottled mint sauce to put on his baby lamb, which was cooked to absolute perfection. It was, I am sure, flavorful and tender and hot and needed nothing but the eating!

Very often Let boned the shoulder and roasted it in place of the leg, claiming it had better flavor and was more tender. This gave rise to another battle, which continued years after Let had returned to China. Father insisted on the shoulder, Mother on the leg. It was a draw, and sometimes Mother gave in and offered the boned shoulder without any discussion beforehand. I suspect she secretly liked it as well as the leg.

About beef there was no argument. That was clearly Mother's domain. She picked the beef and had it hung. She would use the ribs at one time, the sirloin at another, holding it a bit longer if it was to be used for steaks. The filet was saved for *tournedos* or was roasted whole. Less tender cuts were used by Let to make a beautiful beef stew—not a *bourguignon* or a *daube*. It had an Oriental quality to it, inasmuch as the meat was heavily browned in fat and cooked for a long time before the vegetables were added. These were often prepared separately and added when the meat was about three-quarters cooked. The juices from the vegetables combined with the juices from the meat to make the sauce, which was often thickened with grated potatoes, cooked in the juices, and flavored with a variety of seasonings, including a good dose of soy sauce. Let's stew was immensely popular with Mother's paying guests, I was told, and it later became a favorite of my father's and was served from time to time at home.

Prior to my father's arrival on the scene, Mother went on stimulating the eating habits of Portland at the Gladstone. I am sure that the alligator pear, available very seldom in that part of the country, was first served to the Portland public by my mother. Years later I recall going to a rather new hotel with her one afternoon where tarts of alligator pear in a sticky syrup were served on the tea tray! My mother summoned the chef and told him unsparingly what she thought of them. The shamefaced man had to admit to a misconception about the alligator pear, and he had never bothered to taste his ghastly creation.

When Mother was confronted with a mishap in her own hotel dining room, she was a master of tact. One of her more successful ways of soothing angry guests was to offer to go to the kitchen and do a dish herself. Sometimes she actually prepared the dish and sometimes she only pretended to. She knew the importance of catering to individual tastes and was ready to produce anything the instant it was demanded, from fresh muffins for afternoon tea to "well-curled" bacon for a particular Anglophile. She even went to the trouble of constructing a small shelf under one table for a lady who tippled on the sly. From there the lady could retrieve tiny glasses of her favorite liquor, which she drank discreetly behind a napkin or handkerchief.

Mother enjoyed this kind of conspiracy because of her own rebellious nature. But if anyone tried to hoodwink her, she was a formidable antagonist. Once she caused a scene by "accidentally" knocking against a woman who had stolen some glasses and stuffed them into her toilette. In the encounter they shattered.

Elizabeth Brennan might have continued to run her establishment with great flair and energy for the rest of her days if it had not been for matchmaking friends, the Summerses, who thought she should marry. She was a lovely woman with a good figure for those days, and she carried her pounds with grace and aplomb. Her complexion was the pink-and-white of the English, and her black hair was extremely fine, worn in a French roll from the top of her head to the neck, where curly wisps called "scolders" were arranged. The man her friends urged her to consider for a husband was a lonely widower, though something of a dandy, with a daughter of eighteen. His name was John Beard. He was the son of a pioneer and was only five when he crossed the West in a covered wagon to settle in Linn County, Oregon. He was a brilliant man and the only one of sixteen children to get to college. He became a teacher, then a pharmacist, and eventually he left the town of Silverton to accept a political appointment as assistant appraiser of the Port of Portland. He was a man with charm and good looks, generally well thought of, and like Mother he loved good food. Only his was a less sophisticated palate. He knew good food with a Southern accent, and he knew the pleasures of fresh berries, wild fruits, good game and the delicacy of fish caught in cold mountain streams.

At any rate, the Summerses thought it was a good match, and I'm afraid that John Beard thought it was a good opportunity. He had a daughter to raise, he was in debt, and Elizabeth Brennan was an attractive, successful woman. With continued encouragement from the Summerses, they were finally married, in 1899.

It was only after the honeymoon that Mother learned about Father's debts. Her feelings for him—never too strong, I have since felt—diminished. His daughter Lucille wished to be waited upon, which tested Mother's patience, and when she made it clear that she had no intention of pampering her stepdaughter, Lucille had her revenge by putting stockings in the chef's stock pot—black ones! Then there were my father's relatives—and they were legion—who decided that the hotel made a pleasant rest spot. When Mother offered them bills, they never returned, and they hated her always.

She paid off Father's debts and resolved never to admit to the world she had made a mistake in her marriage. But her well-ordered life began to crumble, and in a weak moment she decided to sell the Gladstone. A good offer had come along from a Miss Murphy and a Mrs. Cornell. These two ladies rechristened it Alexandra Court and built it into a highly lucrative enterprise, prospering with much of the personnel Mother trained. Had she remained sensible, she might have done a great gastronomic service to the entire Northwest.

Now that she was no longer in business, she was determined to live in semiretirement and have a child.

CHAPTER

2

The first to hear of the sale of the hotel was Let. He came to my mother and said, "Missy, do you have all your money?"

"Let," my mother replied, "I have every damned cent, but that's for your ears only. Why?"

Let explained that he was tired of hotel work and would prefer not to work without her. If she had been paid in full by the new owners, he would help Mother in her own house; if not, he would stay on at the hotel, upholding its standards, until she did have her money. So Let was able to depart from the Gladstone along with Mother, leaving Poy and Gin and several others to take over the kitchen.

To my father my mother had announced, "I'm selling.

27

I've built and furnished a house in Hawthorne Park near the Summerses. I want a child. After that's achieved you have a home in my house but it's not your house. Live your life and I'll look after mine. Lucille will be under my supervision."

So at forty-two Mother produced me—a new venture. She was in business again. When I first brightened the Beard household, in 1903, I was golden-haired, fair and plump (there has always been enough meat on the bones for two). I have always said that Mother brought me up in the same way she ran her hotel—more manager than mother. She gave instructions on how I was to be fed, what I was to wear, what I was to see and do, and somebody else—at first a nurse, then a Chinese amah, whom I adored—carried out her plans. Later in life, she guided my taste in the theater and music, and for this I will be eternally grateful, for I heard and saw all the "greats" of their day, and my love of the theater and music endures.

I grew up in the helter-skelter of her life. For periods I saw her constantly, and at other times she disappeared for a long stretch into one of her projects. I was alone frequently, but I was enterprising, and I read a good deal, far beyond my years. And perhaps I spent too much time in the company of Elizabeth Beard's guests, for I listened to a lot of adult talk, adopted snobbish ideas and expressed myself freely on almost any subject. I could toss a remark into mixed company that unnerved the entire gathering, which, I have always imagined, secretly delighted my mother. I soon became as precocious and nasty a child as ever inhabited Portland. Even my mother's closest friends ran and locked their children away when I appeared. At home everyone spoiled me, and I was a special favorite of Let's.

He came frequently to the house, but he refused to live there. He knew better. Mother, much to her annoyance, never quite knew where he lived, although she knew where to leave messages that would bring him running. All through Chinatown I am certain we were observed continually and Let was given full reports of our comings and goings. He gave himself away several times. When he was angry with Mother he would punish her by staying away and by just not being found. The two still had their battles—and continued to produce food wonderful beyond belief. And with my appearance, they developed new pride in the mastery of their art. Both wanted to instill in me a love for food, and together with the cook of Mrs. Summers, the wife of my godfather, General Summers, they offered me the most varied gastronomic experiences any child ever had.

Very early in life I came to adore the smell of good things baking. In the morning there were the light rolls made by Let. My father's roll was always baked in a one-pound baking-powder can and blossomed over the top. I remembered it years later when I first came to know *brioche mousseline*, also baked in its own cylindrical tin. Let's rolls were superb hot or toasted. For dinner, the dough was shaped into Parker House rolls, and sometimes it was rolled into cinnamon buns or cinnamon bread, with pecans, hazelnuts, raisins, butter and brown sugar. These cinnamon delights were sought after by all our friends.

Parker House Rolls

Combine 2 cups scalded milk, 4 tablespoons butter, 2 teaspoons salt and 2 tablespoons sugar; and when cooled, add 1½ yeast cakes or 2 packages dry yeast dissolved in ½ cup warm water. Make a sponge with 2 to 3 cups flour and when it is blended, allow it to rise for 1 hour in a warm place. Punch down the sponge and beat in enough flour to make a light dough that may be kneaded with ease on a floured board— it will take about 5½ cups in all—a bit more or less according to the quality of the flour. Allow it to rise again until almost doubled in bulk. Punch down the dough and roll it out to ½-inch thickness on a lightly floured board. Cut it in rounds with a cutter about 4 inches in diameter. Make a heavy indentation with a pencil or the handle of a knife and fold each round one-third over. Dip the rolls in butter and arrange them on a buttered baking sheet. Let them rise again until just doubled in bulk. Brush them with egg wash (1 egg beaten slightly, blended with 2 tablespoons milk or water) and bake at 350° for about 15 minutes or until delicately browned and nicely risen.

They may be reheated in foil or toasted.

This same dough may be rolled, made into circles, then cut into triangles, and shaped into crescents; or rolled into thin rounds, cut into long sections, braided, and sprinkled with poppy seeds.

Sweet Rolls

Roll Parker House dough into a ½-inch sheet. Brush it lavishly with melted butter, sprinkle with sugar and dot with butter. Then sprinkle it with cinnamon, chopped walnuts, and raisins that have been soaked in a little cognac. Roll up the sheet of dough, cut the roll into slices about 1½ to 2 inches thick, and arrange them in a baking pan, previously buttered. Allow them to rise until double in bulk. Brush the rolls with egg wash (above) and bake at 350° until nicely browned and crisp on the outside. The rolls may be iced with a plain sugar icing if you wish.

Our daily bread varied. Let made a bread which was best eaten fresh. Mother made a more stalwart bread—I am certain she rid herself of much personal anguish in the kneading—which used hard wheat flour and no sweetening. Mother maintained that it should be eaten when slightly stale, and I discovered that its flavor did improve after it had rested and firmed. At times, however, it seemed impossible for me to resist it hot from the oven and gloriously yeasty. It sliced to perfection, and when paper-thin and spread with good fresh butter, for tea or for breakfast, or for picnics or train rides, few things have tasted better. I especially liked sandwiches of this bread made with thin slices of onion, salt and plenty of butter, and served with cooled broiled chicken. And sandwiches of thin-sliced chicken or turkey between buttered slices of this bread were unequaled by any combination, including three-deckers, ever dreamed of.

Mother's bread also made wonderful cinnamon toast: slices of bread toasted, then spread well with butter, brown sugar and cinnamon and placed under a hot broiler until the coating melted. Eaten with cups of rich and creamy hot chocolate on a winter's afternoon or evening, this was an unforgettable feast.

Our Regular Bread

Dissolve 2 yeast cakes or 2½ packages dry yeast in ½ cup warm water and add 1 tablespoon sugar and 1½ tablespoons salt. Or, if fresh yeast is used, you may make a syrup of the yeast, sugar and salt. Add 2 cups hot potato water, or 1 cup boiling water and 1 cup hot milk, to the yeast mixture, and add 2 tablespoons butter and 6 to 8 cups flour to make a stiff dough. Blend ingredients thoroughly and knead dough well on a floured board. If you have an electric mixer with a dough hook, knead partially in the mixer, and then turn dough onto a floured board. Knead it thoroughly until the dough is satiny and blisters easily, turn it into a buttered bowl, brush it with butter, and allow it to rise in a warm place until double in bulk. Remove dough to a floured board, knead it lightly, and cut it into portions for loaves. Knead and shape each loaf and place it in a buttered mold. Allow the loaves to rise until doubled in bulk. Brush them with egg wash—1 egg beaten slightly, blended with 2 tablespoons milk or water. Bake them at 400° until nicely browned and the loaves sound hollow when tapped with a finger. Remove to racks to cool.

VARIATIONS:

1. You may bake one loaf and a pan of rolls. Rolls should be formed into small balls, flattened lightly and placed on a buttered baking sheet. If placed close together, they will make light fluffy rolls with top and bottom crusts. If placed far apart, they will be crustier and less soft. Allow them to rise until double in bulk, brush them with melted butter or egg wash and bake at 400° until they are nicely browned and risen.

2. *Cottage Loaf.* Make two-thirds of the dough into a round loaf and place it on a buttered baking sheet. Make an indentation in the center and brush with butter. Make the other third into a round ball and press it into the indentation. Make a deep indentation with your finger and let loaf rise until double in bulk. Brush it with egg wash and bake.

3. *Braided Loaves.* Cut dough into six equal pieces. Roll each one into a sausage-shaped roll, and make two braids. Tuck ends under each loaf and set loaves on a buttered baking sheet. Allow them to rise until double in bulk. Brush them with egg wash and sprinkle with poppy seeds. Bake at 400°.

Cheese Bread

Cream 2 yeast cakes and 2 tablespoons sugar, and add 1 tablespoon salt and 2 cups warm water. Combine with 3 tablespoons melted butter and about 6 cups flour, and mix thoroughly. When the dough is perfectly blended, toss it on a floured board and knead it until it is satiny and blisters easily. Place it in a bowl in a warm place to rise and double in bulk.

Remove dough from bowl and cut it into two parts. One loaf may be baked plain and the other should be rolled out to about ½-inch thickness. Sprinkle this with 1 cup grated Cheddar cheese, roll it tightly, place it in a buttered loaf pan, and allow it to rise to double in bulk. Brush it with melted butter and bake at 400° for about 20 minutes or until it is cooked through and nicely browned. This bread is delicious when served hot with loads of butter and honey or jam!

The making of bread then was more of a struggle than it is today. Sponge used to be set with potato water and yeast and then left to rise overnight. The next morning it was beaten down, kneaded, formed into loaves, left to rise again and then baked. With our modern electric mixers, dough hooks and improved methods, baking need not be a daylong chore. However, finding the right flour is sometimes a problem. I am a great devotee of hard wheat flour and I send to the far corners to try new flours. I am convinced that the average all-purpose flour we find in the shops will not make the same bread as the heavier, rougher flour which I knew as a child and which many of the French and Italian bakers in and around New York use. For light rolls and for brioche the usual all-purpose flour seems to suffice and, in fact, to be extremely good. Don't let the lack of heavy flour discourage you from making bread, which can be one of the most satisfactory accomplishments in the kitchen. If I were you, I would first try sour-dough bread. Begin with a sour-dough starter and perfect your technique until you can turn out beautiful loaves. This will be a bread of which you may well be proud.

We didn't always eat plain homemade bread in our house. It was often varied with rye, whole wheat and graham bread. And, of course, the quick breads, so popular in America, were part of my mother's baking repertory. She made light biscuits with heavy cream, cut, dipped in butter and baked, which were like floating bits of cloud. They disappeared as fast as they could be brought to table and were often served on Sunday morning with wonderfully flavored comb honey that seemed a perfect match. The honey might be of a clover flavor one week, a buckwheat the next and perhaps a superb wild huckleberry the next, which Mother found somewhere and contracted for each year.

Let's Wonderful Sweet Cream Biscuit

Sift 2 cups flour, 1 tablespoon sugar and ½ teaspoon salt with 3 teaspoons baking powder. Fold in heavy cream until it makes a soft dough that can be easily handled. Turn the dough out on a floured board and pat to about ¾-inch thickness. Cut it in rounds or squares, dip them in melted butter, and arrange them in a buttered baking sheet or pan. Bake at 425° for 12 to 15 minutes. Serve the biscuits hot.

Elizabeth Beard's currant teacakes were acclaimed far and wide, and no tea she offered was complete without them. They were baked in the oven until light, brown and pungent with fruit flavor, and were served either piping hot with butter or cooled, toasted and lavishly buttered. I have seen several pans of these delicacies disappear within a very short time.

My mother and Let had their own opinions of each other's ability with teacake recipes, but I rather think Let was the champion, for I know that after he returned to the country of his birth, when I was about ten, I never again tasted a teacake with as much character and as delicious as his.

Our Famous Teacakes

Sift 2 cups flour, ½ teaspoon salt, 3 tablespoons sugar and 3½ teaspoons baking powder together and blend in ⅓ cup butter and ½ cup heavy cream. Flour lightly ⅓ cup currants, which have been soaked in cognac and dried, and toss them with the dough. Lastly, fold in 2 tablespoons chopped candied orange peel, slightly floured as well. Pat the dough into a square baking pan and cut squares with a silver knife. Brush squares with an egg wash (1 egg beaten with 2 tablespoons cream) and sprinkle them with sugar. Bake at 400° for about 15 minutes or until cakes are nicely browned and delicately risen. Serve them hot with butter and black currant or raspberry jam.

34

VARIATION: These may be patted out and cut in small squares or rounds, brushed with butter, and arranged on a baking sheet.

A well-laden tea table was always offered in our house, and special teas on a Sunday afternoon oftentimes were monumental. My father would never attend these, and I think sometimes my mother outdid herself to spite him for this eccentricity. In addition to the bread and butter and the teacakes, there were often delicious muffins. We had a collection of muffin and crumpet rings Mother had brought back for the Gladstone on one of her trips. Let used these to perfection. I loved the muffins and crumpets dripping with butter and daubed with our strawberry jam, and reveled in their being a Beard household exclusive. They were different in texture from most of the commercial ones found today, and they absorbed butter in shocking amounts.

Crumpets

To make these you will need special crumpet rings—metal hoops that are placed on the griddle to hold the crumpet batter in shape. Dissolve 1½ cakes (or packages) yeast in 1 cup warm milk. Sift 8 cups flour and 1 teaspoon salt into a warmed bowl and stand in a warm place for 15 to 20 minutes.

Make a well in the center of the flour. Combine the yeast and milk with 3 more cups warm milk and pour this into the well. Stir it into the flour, mixing thoroughly. The batter should be thin. If the flour absorbs the milk too much, add more warm milk. Cover the batter with a clean towel and set it in a warm place to rise for about 45 minutes to an hour.

Grease a griddle and place the crumpet rings on it. Heat them well. Fill each ring with a batter to a depth of about ½ inch. Cook until the crumpets are nicely browned on the bottom, then turn them to finish cooking on the other side. The second side will be spongy in texture and not as brown.

To serve, heat or toast the crumpets, and butter them lavishly on the spongy side.

We often had a superb currant bread with tiny clippings of orange peel thrown in. Let had been taught to soak the currants well in cognac before folding them into the dough. What a flavor this gave, and how it puzzled many of the friends who came to tea and tried to uncover the simple secret.

Currant Bread

Cover 1½ cups currants with rum, cognac or sherry and set them aside to soak for about 1 hour or more.

Scald 1 cup milk and stir in 3 tablespoons sugar, 2½ teaspoons salt and 6 tablespoons butter. Let this cool to lukewarm. Meanwhile, dissolve 1½ cakes (or 2 packages) yeast in 1 cup warm water. Add this to the lukewarm milk mixture and stir in 3 cups sifted flour. Beat mixture until thoroughly smooth, and gradually add another 3 cups (approximately) flour or enough to make a smooth, kneadable dough. Turn dough out onto a lightly floured board and knead it until it is thoroughly blended and elastic. This will take about 10 to 12 minutes. If you have an electric mixer with a dough hook, use this for the job and it will take 5 to 6 minutes. Put the dough in a buttered bowl, cover it with a clean towel or napkin, and set it in a warm place to stand until double in bulk.

Punch the dough down, turn it out onto the board again and knead in ½ cup sugar, ½ cup softened butter and the drained currants lightly floured. Form the dough into 2 loaves and put these into buttered bread pans. Brush loaves with melted butter and let them stand in a warm place until they have increased about 60 per cent in bulk. Bake in a fairly hot— about 400°—oven for 50 minutes, or until loaves are done and nicely browned.

Girdle scones and oven scones Mother adapted from recipes of our close neighbor, Mrs. Stewart, who came to live near us long after the Let period in my life. Mrs.

Stewart cooked for a tremendously large household, including a number of relatives outside her immediate family, and had the Scottish baking habits down to a science. Mother worked hard to fathom the secrets of the Stewart kitchen. She would analyze, ask questions in a veiled way and then produce a creditable facsimile. Sometimes it was better than the original, sometimes not nearly as good. But the scones I think she excelled in—both the oven and girdle varieties. The oven scones, hot from the pan, split and generously spread with butter and fine raspberry jam, made a teatime or Sunday morning treat that was sensational. I find my hands deep in scone dough once in a while nowadays, nearly always motivated by the finding or making of a good raspberry jam.

Girdle scones, to my mind, are good only when they are really hot. If served cold, as they often were at the Stewarts', they lose their appeal. However, as we sometimes had them for breakfast or tea, split, toasted and buttered, they were another thing. Mother used to enjoy offering them to her Scottish friends with the idea that she had mastered their native delicacy better than they.

Girdle Scones

Sift 2 cups flour, 1 teaspoon cream of tartar, ½ teaspoon salt, 1 teaspoon soda and 1 teaspoon sugar together. Take a cupful and mix it with enough buttermilk or sour cream to make a soft dough. Pat it with the hand on a floured board. Form it into a circle ½ inch thick. Cut it in triangles or squares with a knife and bake them on a floured griddle (girdle) over a medium heat, turning them to brown both sides. They may be split and eaten hot, or, if cooled, split and toasted. (Note: Many people serve them cold but we always felt that heated scones made a much more appealing dish with jam.)

Oven Scones

(At many county fairs and food shows one of the big
flour mills had a jovial and justifiably famous Negro
chef who produced these scones by the hundreds and
served them piping hot with butter and raspberry
jam.) Sift together 2 cups sifted flour, 2 tablespoons
sugar, 3 teaspoons baking powder and ½ teaspoon
salt, and add 6 tablespoons melted butter and 1 egg
lightly beaten. Stir in approximately ⅔ cup cream,
enough to make a soft dough. Turn dough on a
floured board, pat it into a large circle or square, and
cut it into triangular pieces. Arrange these on a buttered baking sheet. Bake at 425° for about 12 to 14
minutes. (Note: They are best when eaten directly
from the oven.)

Although she made good scones, Mother failed miser-
ably when she tried making Mrs. Stewart's version of
potato scones. These were limp, thin and divinely fine
little cakes with a pervading flavor of the potato. Probably Mother tried improving on them. At any rate, she
failed disastrously and after a few tries she gave up
potato scones for good. Nor could she make the good
crisp and bitter oatcakes, incredibly thin, which the
Stewart kitchen turned out in batches.

Potato Scones

Mix 1 cup warm mashed potatoes with ⅓ cup melted
butter, 1 teaspoon salt and ½ cup sifted flour until
thoroughly blended. Divide the dough into thirds and
roll out each third into a circle about ¼ inch thick.
Cut each circle into sixths and bake the scones on a
hot floured griddle, or in a hot floured skillet, for
about 5 minutes, turning them once so that they cook
on both sides.

Oatcakes

For this recipe you must use the Scotch or Irish oatmeal, not the regular rolled oats commonly found in
our groceries. Mix 1 pound Scotch or Irish oatmeal,

⅔ teaspoon salt and ½ teaspoon soda, and add 2 tablespoons melted fat (butter, beef drippings or bacon fat) and 1 cup hot water. Blend dough with a wooden spoon until it is moist and will hold together. Sprinkle a board with a little oatmeal and roll out the dough into thin round cakes. Dust the tops of these with a little oatmeal and cut each cake into small triangles. Bake them on a hot griddle dusted with oatmeal, turning the cakes several times to cook them on both sides. They should be very crisp.

Oatcakes may be baked in the oven, but they are better if made the old-fashioned way. If you bake them in the oven, arrange them on an ungreased cookie sheet and bake at 350° for 20 minutes, turning them several times as they cook.

Pastries and cakes were not really my mother's forte, but Let taught her how to produce certain typically English cakes. A good poundcake was one of these, and I will say it has seldom been equaled in my experience. It was flavored well with mace, or a bit of citron, or with sultana raisins soaked in sherry, or sometimes with candied cherries, which added great distinction. I have found that the addition of nuts to the batter does a great deal more.

Another of these cakes was seedcake. No tea table, in my opinion, is complete without a good seedcake. We nursed one all the time. It was always there, diminishing, until a brand-new one replaced it. When it was too stale, it was sometimes served toasted and buttered. The soft, strange flavor of caraway left a pleasant taste in the mouth.

Seedcake

Cream 1 cup butter and 2 cups flour together. Add 5 eggs, one at a time, beating the mixture thoroughly after each addition. Add 1 cup sugar, ½ teaspoon salt, 1 teaspoon baking powder, 1 teaspoon vanilla and 1 to 2 tablespoons caraway seeds, and beat for 4 or 5 minutes by hand, or if you have an electric mixer beat the mixture with this for 2 minutes. Butter and flour a 9-inch tube pan and pour the batter in this. Bake in a 350° oven for 1 hour or until the cake tests done with a straw.

Let also taught my mother to make ladyfingers as light as ghosts' footsteps, and he himself made an astonishing charlotte russe—really a charlotte russe-Chinese —which I will set down later. It was mostly whipped cream and flavorings topped with currant jelly or black currant paste, and it was sheer heaven. I have since used the recipe for a *pavé au chocolat* with devastating success. I know Let would have approved highly of the invention.

To this day I feel the force of Let's personality, remembering how quietly he instructed my mother, never losing his integrity and strength in the face of her powerful personality. How I wish I had him around still!

Of course, Mother's delight in food was not confined to the oven. She derived an intense pleasure from eating perfectly ripened fruit fresh from the tree and tender vegetables right from the garden. It was a peaceful bower she had fashioned for herself—this restless woman—around the Hawthorne Park house. There were flowers, rosebushes and shade trees. The fruit trees numbered three Gravenstein apples, a Lambert cherry, a Royal Anne cherry and three May Duke cherries. There was also a greengage plum and later an English walnut. These bore magnificent fruit and supplied both the Hawthorne Park house and the house at the beach for the entire summer. Such cherries the Lambert produced—huge, purple, luxuriant!

There was a tidy garden patch at the back of the house where Mother grew chives, shallots, onions, radishes, some herbs and always a few hills of potatoes. She would insist on having these potatoes dug very early.

She felt if you were going to eat new potatoes, you ate them small, cooked them little and gave them plenty of butter. Therefore, we ate potatoes the size of small marbles, and they had a flavor superior to all other potatoes. Recently at the farmers' market in Lausanne, I found enough of these tiny potatoes to feast on with sentimental delight. Some restaurants ruin them by overcooking them in fat until they are hard and leathery. To be at their best, they should be cooked in their skins, which intensifies the flavor. Sometimes we ate them with their jackets and sometimes without. Occasionally Mother combined them with the tenderest of new peas from the garden, cooked for just a few minutes in a little water with lettuce leaves and butter. What a combination of flavors!

Just as we had people like Mrs. Harris to bring us butter and eggs, there were others on the lookout for Mother's favorite fruits and vegetables. These scouts would call her the minute a shipment arrived, and she would be on the way to collect it with great dispatch. Thus we had the first artichokes of the season to arrive in Portland, and we had them in quantity while they lasted. The same was true of California strawberries, raspberries, asparagus, beans and many other items. Mother was not a season rusher, but she wanted the first good fruits and vegetables that appeared. She maintained that little fruit which traveled from California had the quality of the well-matured local fruit in season, but she kept trying the imports anyway. She generally rejected them in disgust.

In those days there were a great many Italian truck gardeners who had large plots in town and who, in addition, were hucksters. With horse and wagon they sold in different neighborhoods on different days. We had two such men coming to us two or three times a week. Aside from their own produce, they brought vegetables and fruits from other parts of the country.

Later, of course, they became motorized and had much more of a selection to offer. The one, Joseph Galluzzo, finally moved into the public market, where he had only his own produce to sell and no longer had to endure the hardships of driving through town. The other, Delfinio Antrozzo, came to us for many years and gradually became a part of the family life.

He was not long in falling under the wily spell of Mother and would bring her choice tidbits, bottles of homemade wine and sometimes Italian dishes made by his wife. He and Mother would spend endless amounts of time discussing the quality of his merchandise and the ways of cooking vegetables. When either Joe or Delfinio offered vegetables or fruits new to Mother or suggested new ways of preparing familiar things, she always experimented. If she liked the result, she would keep working to perfect the flavor.

Thus it was that I learned as a child to enjoy many vegetables considered outlandish by most other people—cardoons, broccoli, eggplant, zucchini, mustard greens, baby turnips, fava beans, varieties of shell and snap beans, and every type of melon one could dream of. Delfinio grew beautiful leeks, and we had them often in several different guises, including a wonderful leek vinaigrette. Also from Delfinio we learned the delicacy of Savoy cabbage with its tender, curly leaves. This vegetable became the basis of several fine dishes, including an extremely good stuffed cabbage, made with not the leaves but the whole cabbage, scooped out, filled with a savory mixture, wrapped carefully and baked in broth a very short time—not only incredibly good in flavor but very attractive to look upon when it was brought to the table.

Here are some of Mother's vegetable recipes:

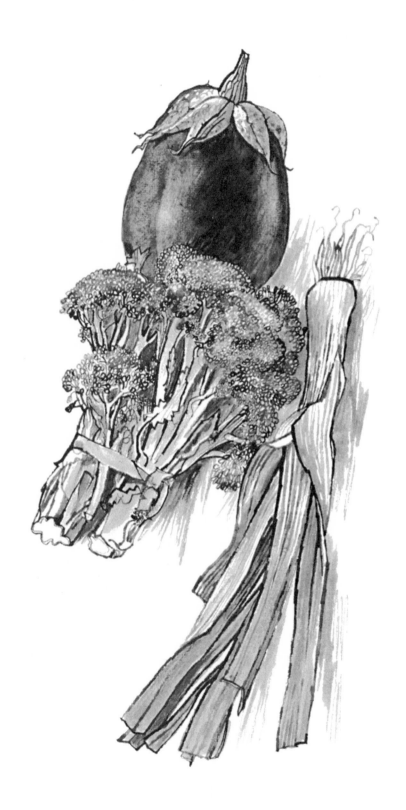

Broccoli Purée

Wash 3 to 4 pounds of broccoli and peel the stems. Cook it in boiling salted water until it is tender and pierceable. Drain it and run it through a food mill or coarse sieve. Season it with 4 tablespoons melted butter, a squeeze of lemon, ⅛ teaspoon nutmeg and 2 tablespoons heavy cream.
(Note: The broccoli must be drained well to avoid a watery purée.)

Broccoli Fritters

For the frying batter, sift 1 cup flour and fold in 3 tablespoons oil, a dash of salt and ⅔ cup water or stale beer. Beat the white of an egg fairly stiff and fold it into the mixture.

Roll broccoli flowerets in flour, dip them in frying batter and fry in deep fat heated to 370° until they are browned and crisp, about 4 to 5 minutes. Drain them on absorbent paper and serve.

Deep-Fried Zucchini

Cut small zucchini into julienne strips. Soak strips in ice water for 1 hour. Dry them. Roll them in flour and fry them in deep fat at 370° until nicely browned. Drain them on absorbent paper. Zucchini may also be cut in paper-thin rounds and treated in the same way.

Artichokes à la Grecque

Use 6 preferably young small artichokes for this pleasant dish. Remove some of the outer leaves, cut each artichoke in quarters, and remove the choke and the tops of the leaves with a sharp knife. To prepare a sauce à la Grecque, combine 1 cup olive oil, 1 cup water, ⅓ cup white wine, 1 tablespoon wine vinegar, 1 teaspoon salt, 1 teaspoon basil, ½ teaspoon freshly ground black pepper and 1 clove garlic, bring sauce to a rapid boil, and add the artichokes. Bring sauce to a second boil, reduce the heat and simmer until the artichokes are just crisply tender. Taste the sauce for seasoning and correct. Let the vegetables cool in the sauce and serve chilled with lemon slices and a sprinkling of chopped parsley.

Mustard Greens with Bacon

Mustard greens when they are fresh have a delicious and pungent flavor not found in any other greens. Wash and trim 2 to 2½ pounds mustard greens and soak them in cold water. Cut 8 slices of bacon into small pieces and try out in a heavy skillet or deep pot until bacon is crisp. Remove the pieces of bacon and drain them. Add 2 tablespoons olive oil to the bacon fat; and when it is heated through, add the mustard greens. Cover the pot and let them cook down until they are just crisply tender, about 5 minutes. Add 1 teaspoon salt, toss the greens well and serve. You may like your greens cooked longer, but I feel they taste much better when just at the crisp, wilted stage. They may also be prepared with oil and lemon juice and a dash of soy in the same fashion.

Leeks à la Grecque

We often prepared leeks, which had been thoroughly soaked to remove all the sand, in the same fashion as artichokes—in a sauce *à la Grecque*. For 12 to 14 leeks you would use the same proportions as for the artichokes on Page 44. Cook the leeks until they are just tender. Do not overcook.

Dandelion Greens with Pork and Fresh Mint

Cut 6 rather thick slices of bacon—not the paper-thin breakfast slices one gets in packages—into quarters and cook them until they are just translucent. Add 2 cloves of garlic chopped fine and continue cooking for 3 to 4 minutes. Add ¼ cup olive oil and ¼ cup wine vinegar, and salt and freshly ground black pepper to taste. In the meantime, you will have soaked and cut in 2-inch lengths 1½ pounds dandelion greens. Add these to the pan in which you have cooked the bacon and the garlic, and toss them as you would a salad over low heat. At the last minute, add 3 tablespoons fine-chopped fresh mint. Correct the seasoning and serve.

Vegetables and fruits were not the sole items discussed with our two gardeners. Mother once gave

Delfinio one of her light, buttery codfish cakes, made with salt codfish, potato, butter and ginger, and cooked in butter until crisp on both sides. Delfinio felt that Mother should extend her repertoire of salt codfish dishes, so he came one day and prepared polenta and codfish for us and gave the recipe for another Italian dish—codfish with garlic, tomatoes, onion and leeks—which we treasured and used often, sometimes adding a variation with black olives and herbs.

Mother's Famous Codfish Cakes

Soak 1½ pounds salt codfish for 8 hours or overnight, changing the water once during the soaking. Drain fish and cover with fresh water, bring it to a boil, and let it simmer until codfish is just tender. Drain fish and let it cool. Flake it very fine. Measure, and combine with an equal amount of whipped mashed potatoes which have been seasoned with freshly ground black pepper and 1 teaspoon chopped fresh ginger or ¼ teaspoon ground ginger. Add 2 egg yolks and 2 teaspoons heavy cream, and blend thoroughly. Form mixture into round flat cakes and dust them with flour. Cook them in heated melted butter until they are nicely browned and crisp on both sides.

Mother had always grown vegetable marrows, which she had brought back from England. But when Delfinio showed her the difference in texture and flavor between the tiny ones which we know as zucchini and the larger ones she had been using, she was astonished and ever afterward served the delightful smaller squash in different styles. Years later, living in Spain, I learned how to prepare blossoms of this squash in wonderful ways and had feasts of them every few days.

Delfinio grew quantities of sweet basil, and he would bring us armloads of it. Mother learned from him how to use the basil in *pesto*, the wonderful green sauce made with this herb, olive oil, garlic, grated cheese, salt and pepper and sometimes pine nuts; and she learned another heavenly sauce which was simply a blend of basil, tomato, salt and pepper and a touch of garlic. She was taught to put the herb to still another use by adding strips of it to a tomato salad, giving it a glory it had never known.

Recently I found recipes of Mother's inspired by the visits of Joe and Delfinio. I tried them and found many of them good enough to repeat here:

Delfinio's Fresh Tomato Sauce with Basil

Peel, seed and chop 12 to 14 really ripe tomatoes. Melt 6 tablespoons butter in a heavy skillet. Add 1 clove garlic chopped fine, 1 small onion chopped fine, and cook them until they are just transparent. Add the chopped tomatoes and let them barely simmer for 20 minutes. Add ½ cup beef broth or stock and ¼ cup white wine. Cover the pot and simmer 1 hour. Stir in 1 teaspoon salt and 2 tablespoons fine-chopped fresh basil, and continue cooking uncovered until the sauce has cooked down. Force it through a fine sieve and return it to the pan. Correct the seasoning and continue cooking down the sauce if it is not thick enough for your taste. This should not be a thick, gooey Neapolitan-style tomato sauce. It is rather a delicate essence of basil and tomatoes which flavors and barely colors *pasta* and which may be used in other dishes.

Delfinio's Pesto

In my childhood, there was no such thing as a Waring Blendor, so the *pesto* was made with a mortar and pestle. We are much luckier nowadays. Place in a blender container ½ cup olive oil, 1 cup basil leaves tightly packed, ¼ cup parsley sprigs, 2 cloves garlic, 1 teaspoon salt, ⅓ cup pine nuts, and blend at high speed until they form a thick paste. This is ample to serve with *pasta* for 2 to 4 persons or for a *pistou*. If you wish to make larger quantities, the sauce may be stored in the refrigerator in jars with a thin film of oil poured over the top and sealed with foil or oil paper.

Portland had a great public market which was originally built along Yamhill Street for about five blocks, on both sides of the street part of the way and on one side the rest. Farmers and producers took stands, which they rented from the city at nominal sums, and filled them with seasonal display, beginning in the spring with the earliest asparagus and berries and continuing through into the winter with celery bleached to an ivory whiteness by the Foltz family, all the winter root vegetables, late cauliflower, apples and pears, nuts and wild mushrooms—in effect, the round of the earth's gifts to the palate. In addition, there were poultry, pork and pork products, dairy products, eggs, honeys and some prepared foods. Certain people were the sole vendors of some items. One woman always had fine lemon cucumbers, for instance, and she was inundated with orders when they were in season. Another woman specialized in the heaviest cream imaginable, and this was as much in demand as anything on the market, requiring orders two or three days in advance. The cream was as close to great French cream as one could find, and the flavor was superb with fruits or in sauces, or whipped as a topping for puddings and soufflés. Some people had better corn than others, and one could buy tiny ears of Golden Bantam picked in the morning to be eaten at night.

Apples were a round of delight in themselves, from the early Gravensteins through the Baldwins, the Rambeaux, the Kings, the Spitzenburgs, the Northern Spies, the Winesaps, the Fall Bananas, the Winter Bananas, and the Newtown Pippins. Each apple had its distinctive flavor, texture and color. Each was right for a certain use. The Gravensteins, for example, made perfect pies, baked apples, applesauce and salads, as did the Spitzenburgs, later in the season. My mother loved the scrubby russet look of the Rambeaux, the pungence of the Spitzenburgs and the delicacy of the Baldwin and the Belleflower. All of these had their places in the seasonal schedule and were purchased by the box.

Tomatoes provided a kaleidoscopic array. There were the familiar large and small red ones, huge yellow and whitish ones, and the plum, cherry and pear tomatoes in all colors from pale white-yellow to a pinky red and a deep red.

One could even find morels in the market. I remember the first time I saw them. I was quite shocked by their strange appearance. To me they resembled dried-up brains (they still do) and I couldn't imagine what they were. I had eaten them at home but had never seen them before in the raw state. But how good they were, made into an omelet, added to the sauce for a chicken or served with veal. In fact, when I first had them I thought they were the most delicious morsels I had ever tasted. Later in life I discovered they were as precious as truffles, but I couldn't have enjoyed them any more than I did when I knew them as strange wild mushrooms.

It was an education in food to know the public market as I did, first as a child when I was largely a spectator and then as a young man when I was a customer. From its international roster of producers—Chinese, Japanese, Italian, German, Swiss, English and a few of Czech and other nationalities—I learned the various national vegetables and seasonal specialties. I had my first white raspberries from this market and my first tiny husk tomatoes, also known as ground cherries. The latter come late in the fall and make a superb preserve which is incomparable in flavor and texture. They exist in France in a larger version. I have seen them in various parts of the Northwest and West but never in the East, until the last few years.

I particularly remember one very early visit to the market in the company of my nursemaid. We had just been to the doctor's and on the way back stopped to buy a few things for my mother. When they were wrapped and handed to the maid, she said quietly, "Please charge them to Mrs. Beard." The clerk blanched and said, "For God's sake, give me that package. If I sent that to *her*, she'd kill me."

Despite this account, Mother was not the terror of the Portland market. She was uncompromising in her standards, true, but she could joke with the toughest guy in the market or with the most supercilious shop owner. She would offer advice to farmers on the growing of vegetables, and they, in turn, would counsel her on the cooking of them. It was usually a friendly exchange, but sometimes when Mother was bored by a long-winded purveyor, she would suddenly stride off, muttering a ribald remark under her breath. On the whole, she was the *fournisseurs'* ideal customer. She had her favorite clerks in every store, and they loved her.

Mother was not one who felt that she should limit her patronage to one shop. She distributed her custom and she was constantly on the search for different products, and always the best. One place she patronized—called La Grande Creamery, which is a pretty grand name for anything—was a fascinating shop. It did a great deal of business with restaurants and hotels and had served Mother for years. What a treasure house it became to me! It dealt in fine poultry and game birds and cheese and eggs. Every week when we bought chickens for our regular Sunday breakfast, I would come away with one or two pounds of gizzards and hearts for myself. I had developed a passion for these. I couldn't abide, and cannot till this day, the livers—not even one liver! I can eat anything else in the world, but this texture repulses me for some reason; and once or twice when it would have been embarrassing not to eat them, I have swallowed them practically whole! But the heart and gizzard I preferred to any other part of the chicken; and when my father came to the beach for a weekend he would bring me my quota. I am still fond of them and prepare them in a variety of ways—sautéed, braised with heavy cream, done with barley in a casserole, grilled with crumbs; and the gizzards are delicious when made into an hors d'oeuvre similar to beef salad.

Cheese came into my life through La Grande Creamery also. They had fine Cheddar of varying ages, Switzerland cheese, Roquefort, excellent Brie and Camembert from the Rouge et Noir people in California, and occasionally good French Camembert and Brie—these and something called "cream brick cheese," which reminds me of a Port-Salut or, if it is very ripe, of a great Pont-l'Évêque.

At home we ate some beautifully aged Cheddar and often had it on toast, hot and bubbling, as a supper or luncheon dish. With a curl or two of bacon on it, what a superb snack it was! I developed a taste for Emmenthal—we had no Gruyère in those days in Portland. Each time I went into La Grande Creamery I managed to get a generous slice of it as a premium and marched along the street nibbling it with the greatest relish.

Sometimes unusual types of cheese would arrive at La Grande Creamery, and we were sent bits to sample, for after all, we were pretty good customers, in or out of the hotel business. I am grateful to have learned young that cheese has an important place in a menu. It isn't something to serve with apple pie, and it isn't something to cut into nasty little cubes and serve with crackers. Early in life I learned to see the beauty of great slabs or rounds of cheese on the table, and I still respond to the sight of a well-stocked cheese tray properly presented. Cheese must have warmth and time to soften. Too many households and too many restaurants ruin every bit of their cheese by keeping it under constant refrigeration. Cheese that is served cold and hard is not fit for consumption.

Another exciting marketing experience for me was the butcher shops. Unlike the run-of-the-mill butcher who catered to a small patronage, these were lively wholesale and retail markets. There was sawdust on the floors, and great cooling boxes, as wonderful to me as an art gallery, held a fascinating array of carcasses waiting to be cut up. It was a special treat when I could get into the boxes to look around and emerge munching on sausage or ham or some such delight.

Mother would pick a piece of beef, have most of the ribs and part of the short loin hung for her, and then take away one huge roast and several steaks at the same time. She would also buy plate or brisket for *pot-au-feu*, and she would have the butcher corn certain cuts for her to be used as corned beef.

My Mother's Pot-au-feu

Mother would combine about 5 to 6 pounds of good brisket or short ribs—very lean, with the tiny end bones in—with sometimes a fresh tongue and other times a piece of pickled pork, lean and fat-streaked. To this were added 2 or 3 leeks, 2 carrots, a large onion with 2 cloves and a bay leaf. The meat and the vegetables were covered with cold water and brought to a boil rapidly and allowed to boil for 5 to 10 minutes. At this time there might be some scum which had risen to the top, and this was skimmed off and 2 tablespoons of salt were added. The pot was covered and the contents simmered slightly either on top of the stove or in the oven until the meat was just on the verge of being tender and juicy. To this, additional carrots, leeks and small white turnips were added, and the whole was cooked until the meat was tender and the newly added vegetables cooked through. It was served in soup plates with a slice of each meat, the vegetables and plenty of crisp home-made toast. Freshly grated horseradish cream—fresh horseradish beaten into thick cream or whipped cream —might be served as well as mustard and usually some homemade pickles. Potatoes boiled in their jackets were served separately with butter. It was a most satisfying and delicious meal at that time. Any leftover beef or tongue was put into a bowl and pressed and cooled to be eaten cold or in a salad. At times the marrow bones were added for the last part of the cooking process and a section of bone was served to each person so that he could scoop the delicious marrow on the crisp toast.

Marketing for meat was no easy matter for Mother. She planned days and sometimes weeks ahead, had her list ready, and shopped with great efficiency and care. For instance, she cut through slabs of bacon to see what was best. There is in bacon a great variation, not only in flavor but in texture. Most of the well-streaked is better, to my taste, than bacon that is mostly fat. We used to eat a great deal of what was then called "bacon back" but is now called Canadian bacon. And there were good country hams to buy, and sometimes the shoulder or picnic ham. We had certain hams smoked for us, and we always had a ham to slice for breakfast. (A small saw was kept in the kitchen to cut through the bone, if it was a steak we cut.) And may I say here that no one can reproduce the true flavor of ham-and-eggs, or fried ham with red-eye gravy, by using the tenderized, quick-cured hams we have today. They are generally wet and tasteless, unfit for human consumption; and except for a few persons fortunate enough to have it served them in a discriminating home, there is a whole generation growing up who will never know what ham should taste like! I can assure you that the smell of good smoked country ham sizzling in a black iron skillet in the early morning is as intoxicating and as mouth-watering as the bouquet of a fine Château Lafite-Rothschild or an Haut-Brion of a great year. Ham for sautéing should be cut thick but not too thick and cooked slowly in the skillet until nicely browned and just done through. This, with perfectly fried eggs, can be a dish as memorable as a *poularde à la parisienne* prepared by the most renowned chef. Strangely enough, ham-and-eggs is a product of purely Anglo-Saxon genius. In England I have had fine

gammon-and-eggs, and in America I have had unforgettable ham-and-eggs, but I never had anything approaching this dish in France or any other European
country.

Apart from the marvelous butcher shops, there were
the grand shops of imported delicacies, fine fruits, and
vegetables out of season—hundreds of beautiful things
to beguile the eye and the nose, as well as the palate.
How little these wonderful bazaars have changed from
the days of my youth! Many of the same labels are to be
found on the shelves—not all of them as good as they
were, perhaps. I especially looked forward to the trips to
Mr. Mayers' or to Sealy-Dresser. Needless to say, these
purveyors knew enough to show Mother their best
items. If they succeeded in piquing her palate or her
curiosity, she would not only buy but by word of mouth
sell for them. Therefore, it was not unusual for them to
open a can or a package just to give her a taste. I was
given a taste also and looked forward to a superior
sardine, some *foie gras* or a good herring. I remember
the little kegs of anchovies and other cured fish and how
tingling to the tongue they were. These were good
lessons in tasting for me.

Then there were marvelous excursions to Chinatown
for visiting and buying. We ate Chinese food at home
whenever Let wanted to cook for us—Mother never
mastered the dishes—but we often lunched or dined
with Chinese friends in one of their restaurants. At New
Year's we would be invited into scores of homes, when
the finest of hangings and *objets d'art* would be on
display. I missed some of the great dinners on these
occasions, but I did taste the delicacies from time to
time, for there would always be presents of sweetmeats
and bits of pastry for the younger group when we went
to call, and on shopping days, when we stopped by to
see friends, there was invariably an offering of tea and a
delicious morsel.

We often marketed for jars of preserved ginger, preserved and candied kumquats, canned and fresh lichee nuts and some of the fine Chinese pickles for use in sweet-and-sour sauces and to accompany cold meats. Also, we bought fresh bean sprouts and water chestnuts in season, and when the mandarin oranges arrived by boat from China, this was an event which called for a shopping trip of its own. The oranges were exquisite and delicate in flavor, possessing a quality seldom equaled by any others I have eaten—pure, heavenly sweetness.

I had always loved lichees in syrup, and when I finally tasted a fresh one, I knew why. This is the most exotically flavored fresh fruit in the world and probably the most luscious fruit ever known. Why it has never been more popular is something I cannot understand. It is fragile, yes, and comparatively difficult to come by. In New York we have been blessed of late by having them on the market for a fortnight or so each year. During that all-too-brief period I cannot have enough of them, so remarkably satisfying do I find them.

Whether it was in Chinatown or the public market, my Mother adored shopping. She had a standing order for such things as sausage meat, cured sausages, a liver *pâté* that one woman made each fall, ground cherries, certain beans and tomatoes, radishes, corn and cauliflower, and her own particular choices of Foltz's celery. I sometimes think she enjoyed shopping for these things more than preparing or eating them. Her virtuosity in selecting food few women I have known could match. Years later in Paris, when I went marketing with Madame Gafner, whose small restaurant I frequented, I was reminded of my mother's touch in picking a succulent fish, the perfect cheese, or the tenderest asparagus. I was lucky to have such a tutor.

When I began to travel in British Columbia, and to Seattle and San Francisco, it is not surprising that I was eager to see the markets there and observe people buying food. This habit has continued through my life, and I now feel the most important thing to do upon visiting a new city or town is to search out its markets. In this way one not only learns about new foods but also gains a unique insight into a city's character.

New York, for instance, in the twenties and thirties, when there were pushcart markets everywhere in the European tradition, presented as stimulating a marketing experience as you could find. On Ninth Avenue there were the French, the Greeks, the Irish and the Italians, and people traveled from all over the city to shop there. On Bleecker Street there was an almost exclusively Italian clientele, as there was on upper First Avenue. Along Second Avenue there were the Hungarians, the Germans and the Czechs, all with similar gastronomic interests. On Delancey Street there were Jews and Italians, and on Mulberry Street Italians and Chinese. Even today there is a delightful mixture of Italian and Chinese markets in the Mulberry Street section where I enjoy shopping a great deal.

I have had gratifying experiences with market people all over the world; I have been invited to their homes to taste the specialties of the country, and I have learned some of my best recipes from them.

56

CHAPTER

3

The first foreign market I explored was on St. Thomas. This was during a trip to Europe, my first alone, when I was just nineteen. We were sailing from Portland to San Francisco and the Canal Zone and thence to England by way of St. Thomas and the Azores. We had eaten badly, and by the time we reached St. Thomas I was rather distressed. After we docked, I had an indifferent luncheon at a small hotel, which is

57

still in existence, and on the way back to the ship I happened to pass the native market. Never since then have I welcomed the sight of a market to such a degree or indulged myself in tasting so many foods that could be eaten on the spot.

I remember going back to the ship with two over-flowing baskets—one of tiny tomatoes and cucumbers and the other of finger bananas, limes, pineapples, ca-shews, and a type of melon that grew on the island in profusion. In addition, I carried an assortment of greens. The stock lasted nearly to the Azores and was shared with one or two persons who had complained about the food as much as I but had not been as enterprising.

This was a magnificent introduction to a semitropical market and to a habit I was going to develop more fully in later years. I felt at home at once in that marketplace, as crude as it was, and it was there that I first discovered my affinity for market folk and first sensed the character of a country through its food.

My next great market experience was Covent Gar-den, and this revealing look into the belly of a nation both startled and fascinated me. I think in some ways Covent Garden is more astonishing than Les Halles because one doesn't expect to see the variety he finds. It is a puzzle to think about the destination of all that produce. Where *does* it go? When one eats in English homes and restaurants and is served practically nothing but greens, and those badly cooked, he might well wonder.

It is rewarding to watch the buyers—the middlemen for producer and consumer—choosing food for their particular clientele or district. And it is equally reward-ing to listen to the conversation of men in the market, who have a hearty, coarse quality about them. They have a sense of justice, too, and if a buyer has been

especially disagreeable he is clapped out of the market.
I love the Cockney and his drily bitter attack on things.
In the days when I first knew Covent Garden, surely
this was the greatest concentration of amusing market
people I can remember.

No market is too small to captivate me. In each I
discover new foods, new challenges.

In Lausanne, situated on the northern shore of Lake
Geneva, market day comes on Saturday. The market is
laid out on several streets steeply inclined, and one
ascends and descends quite some distance before com-
pleting his rounds. Farmers and retailers who buy from
farmers have crates or bins set up along the sidewalks
from which they exhibit their vegetables, fruits and
flowers. Far up one hill there is a square where portable
booths are customarily erected for butchers, *charcutiers*
and fishmongers, along with some cheese vendors and a
few bakers, who bring the good bread of the countryside
with them. Some of the finest bread I have eaten lately I
bought there.

The *charcuterie* in the western part of Switzerland is
like the Savoie, and in the eastern part like the German.
In Lausanne there are some fine sausages for roasting
and grilling, one type about two inches in diameter,
permeated with pure pork flavor and accented with a
touch of thyme. There are also quite good cured sausages to eat as hors d'oeuvre or with bread and butter
as a luncheon dish. And I saw ham of such homely
quality I wanted to carry a whole one to my hotel room
to keep for nibbling. Then, of course, there is the
fabulous *viande de Grisons* or *Bunderfleisch*, the dried
beef which is so typical of parts of Switzerland. This
begins as beef with no fat content to speak of. It is
salted, dried in the sun till hard and then cut to order in
paper-thin slices to be served with asparagus or sometimes with melon. Wonderful to the tooth and superb in

flavor, it is far superior to our own dried beef, widely available in jars.

Naturally the cheese stalls here, as in the markets everywhere in Switzerland, display the great cheeses of the country: the creamy Emmenthal, well cured; the salt and the sweet Gruyère; and the pungent Appenzeller. There is also Vacherin in certain seasons, Swiss Reblochon, the Petite Suisse, Sbrinz and many other local or district cheeses. They all make marvelous eating, and my favorite dishes made with cheese are almost entirely those which use Gruyère, Appenzeller or Sbrinz. For me these have a quality of flavor and smoothness that enhances any dish or sauce.

Among the fruits, I particularly remember freshly picked cherries shining with the wonderful quality of newness that cherries can have, and the black currant or cassis, no longer permitted to be grown in many parts of the United States—it is a carrier of the white pine blister rust—but one of the most flavorful of all fruits. A purée of cassis (try making it with some imported black currant jam and a little syrup) can be the most glorious addition to fruit desserts and ices imaginable. In fact, an ice cream of black currants served with the purée and a bit of *crème de cassis* is about as beguiling a dessert as I know. And *crème de cassis* or a purée of cassis on fresh raspberries or strawberries lifts them to new heights.

Strawberries with Raspberry Purée and Cassis

Hull 1 quart lovely ripe berries. Arrange them in a rather shallow glass or silver bowl. Sprinkle them lightly with sugar and pour over them 1½ to 2 cups raspberry purée which has been mixed with ⅓ cup *crème de cassis*.

Raspberry Purée

Put in a blender, or push through a food mill or fine sieve, 2 packages frozen raspberries or 1 quart ripe fresh raspberries. (If you use a blender, strain the berries through a sieve.) Taste them and add sugar if necessary.

Spoon the raspberry purée over the ripe strawberries and chill them 30 minutes before serving.

You may add sweetened whipped cream to this dish, but it is by no means necessary.

If you like cassis exceptionally well, use 1 package frozen raspberries and 1 cup black currant preserves for the purée.

Among the vegetables, I was impressed by the kohlrabi, which I have always preferred to ignore in this country. In Switzerland it grows to beautiful size without the fuzzy texture of our own variety, and it has flavor. Then, of course, there were the potatoes. The Swiss eat a great many of them, and there are now new potatoes in the market (as of this writing) in all sizes from the tiny marbles my mother insisted upon to the average-sized new potatoes. Before reaching the market they are scrubbed, as almost everything Swiss is scrubbed, and when they are cooked and daubed with butter, they offer a perfect meal in themselves. This, of course, represents my own approach to eating. If a seasonal item is freshly picked or dug or gathered and has great flavor, I am apt to make an entire luncheon of that one thing, savoring each bite with pure sensual enjoyment.

I have always been fascinated by the potato—its history, its many varieties, the endless ways in which it can be prepared. It is small wonder that in Peru—this was almost twenty years ago—the markets enthralled me. For there, in the country where they had originated, were two of the world's great staples, one of these, of course, being the potato. It has always been my contention that the people of the Western European countries ate pretty dull food until the discovery of America. We can assume that the ruling classes in Rome, Byzantium and the Mediterranean countries had wonderful food, but the table of peasant and serving classes was no doubt monotonous. The potato helped to enliven their diet.

It was astounding to see the potato's variation in color and shape in Peruvian markets. There seemed to be present the ancestors of nearly every type developed in America by Burbank and others and in France by that genius of the potato, Parmentier—potatoes with skins that were reddish, russet, yellow, and what appeared to be blue. I am told there are about five or six hundred varieties of this amazing vegetable.

It is ironic how far the potato had to travel before being accepted by the world. It first went to Ireland in 1585 or 1586 and was introduced from there into England; Scotland had it years later. Then it was taken up by all of Europe before it came back to the New World, to North America. However, some countries that grew the potato, such as Italy and Spain, took a long time in using it as food. France, too, planted it only in the flower gardens until Parmentier produced the secrets of making potatoes not only edible but a major gastronomic pleasure.

Since those days the potato has had a highly successful career, but not without some setbacks. Whoever invented the deep-fried potato surely didn't realize what a sin he was committing. Granted that once in a while deep-fried potatoes, beautifully brown and crisp and cooked in fine oil or fat, can be a complement to a good chicken or a grilled pig's foot, or a fine steak. But the notion that these bits of potato—when limp, greasy, without flavor or texture and barely warm—should be served with every dish in the world is odious beyond belief. Usually they are unsalted and have been allowed to retain all of the cooking oil. Then to crown all other horrors, people drench them with cold catchup and eat them! I have watched these same people consume nothing but a double order of French fries (and where that name came from, I don't know) for lunch, along with bread and, of course, the catchup.

It is remarkable how the potato was taken up by practically every Western European country, and yet in Latin America it is eaten less than rice. And what is even more remarkable is that it is France, England and Germany that have given the world the greatest potato recipes. The country of its origin has contributed not a single potato dish of any renown. Nor have we developed many good potato dishes in the United States, although what we have can be exciting if done well.

Certainly a baked Idaho potato is a great gastronomic experience if it is rushed from oven to plate and then split, buttered and seasoned with freshly ground pepper and salt. I don't feel the same way about it with sour cream and chives, although it is an agreeable combination. The Idaho can also be taken from the peel, mixed with butter and cheese, returned to the shell and reheated to make one of the most rewarding of stuffed potatoes. And the Idaho, baked and mashed with butter and cheese, can be as rich and delicious a potato dish as it is possible to eat. But try a perfectly baked Idaho with freshly ground pepper and coarse salt—no butter. This has pure potato flavor and is light and delicate.

We perfected the boiled and fried potato here as no other country did. The home-fried or hashed brown potatoes which one found in good steak restaurants in the prewar days were incredibly good. And I can remember visiting an aunt who had a large sheep ranch in Oregon, and there great platters of hashed browns were served at breakfast every morning—there would be a large number of us at table—to go with ham and eggs, chops or steaks. The crust was golden brown and crunchy, and the potatoes had the waxy quality peculiar to refried potatoes. I can also remember a cook in a Western diner who chopped potatoes with an empty one-pound baking powder can and then tossed them into a skillet with bacon fat, browning them quickly and serving them with bacon and eggs.

Hashed Brown Potatoes

This may seem a strange recipe for a book like this, but too few people have ever learned to make hashed brown potatoes properly. Good ones must begin with potatoes boiled with their jackets, peeled and cut either coarse or fine, as you wish. Transfer the potatoes to a heavy iron or cast aluminum skillet in which you have melted and heated enough fat to cover the bottom of the pan generously. The fat can be beef drippings (superb), pork drippings, goose fat, bacon fat or butter. Any of these has flavor and will make the potatoes taste better. Press the potatoes down into the fat and let them cook fairly slowly on the bottom to form a crust. Shake the pan from time to time. With a large spatula or turner try to fold over the potatoes so that you can expose unbrowned ones to the heat. Or invert the pan on a plate, add more fat to the pan and slide the uncooked side into the pan again. At any rate, the potatoes must have a crust and brown crispy bits in them to rate as hashed browns. Salt and freshly ground black pepper are a must.

Usually short-order cooks in diners and greasy spoons do the most superb hashed brown potatoes.

Mother's Beach Hashed Brown Potatoes in Cream

Mother used to chop 8 to 10 smallish new potatoes, which had been cooked in their jackets, quite coarsely. She melted 6 tablespoons butter or beef drippings in a skillet, preferably butter for these, added the potatoes and let them crust on the bottom. She salted and peppered them well, added ¾ cup heavy cream and let it cook down over a brisk fire, then turned the potatoes out in a flat dish and served them with a goodly sprinkling of chopped parsley. Excellent with fish or with cold meats.

Really Good Home-Fried Potatoes

Here again people err and make something sad and horrid out of this dish.

Peel potatoes that have been boiled in their jackets. Slice them about ¾ inch thick. Melt, for 6 medium-sized potatoes, 6 tablespoons butter or goose fat and when it is hot but not smoking add the potatoes and cook them over a fairly brisk heat for about 4 or 5 minutes, turning them carefully with a spatula. Be careful not to break up the potatoes more than you have to. Add salt and freshly ground black pepper. The potatoes must be crisp and not soggy—and as brown as you like them. Do not stir too much, but turn them judiciously.

Americans are responsible for one version of potato salad—that with a boiled dressing or mayonnaise. To be sure, this was created by Middle European immigrants but has become so Americanized that the dish can be attributed to us. And America invented a potato layer cake, which I consider to be one of the best of that type of cake in the whole gamut of pastries. It is light and moist and has a good texture.

Whoever thought of boiling potatoes in their jackets—probably the Irish or the English—has my gratitude. This is the simplest way of preparing potatoes, and they are a triumph of good flavor if properly done. Split them gently with a fork—don't cut—and butter them profusely, add salt and a grinding of fresh pepper, or spoon on sour cream and chives, and eat them while they are hot.

The Swiss have two famous recipes for potatoes to their credit: the *roesti*, the grated potatoes browned like a pancake on both sides, and the *raclette*, which really is as much cheese as potato, but nevertheless is a wonderful dish with a satisfying combination of texture and flavor. For *raclette* the cheese is melted in front of the fire—or nowadays in front of an electric burner—and is then scraped off with a wooden spatula onto freshly boiled potatoes, sprinkled with a little freshly ground black pepper and eaten with the accompaniment of a good white wine. This makes an exceedingly good luncheon dish or first course. There are restaurants in Switzerland where it is served at all times, and one restaurant I know serves it as a first course, followed by a small steak. The *roesti*, on the other hand, is as close to the American hashed browns as one can come, although the Swiss version has a quality not found in the other. This is the pure flavor of potato, which dominates and at the same time blends incredibly well with the other flavors. Except for these two estimable potato dishes, the Swiss, along with the Americans and the French, are inclined to overdo the frying process. It is so hard to get anything in the average restaurant other than greasy little bits of potato, which in summer are worse than in winter.

Roesti Potatoes

These delicious Swiss potatoes are prepared in many ways.

I find that boiling good-sized potatoes in their jackets for 10 minutes, then peeling them, is a fine idea. Grate them coarsely and form them into a large cake. Sauté in 6 to 8 tablespoons butter till they are exquisitely brown and crusty on the bottom. Invert the pan on a plate, add more butter to the pan, and slip the uncooked side into the pan. Cook the potatoes over medium heat till they are crusted on the other side. Add salt and freshly ground black pepper to taste.

These may also be made with raw potatoes or cold baked potatoes grated coarsely. Thoroughly devastating and utterly astronomic in calorie count.

Naturally the English, who were the first to take the potato to their hearts, have contributed some excellent recipes. The greatest is what is called by the French *pommes à l'anglaise* and is nothing more than plain boiled potatoes cooked well and dried in the pan after draining. These may be served with butter and parsley, or with a sauce, and if you have never eaten a perfectly boiled potato with nothing on it but salt and freshly ground black pepper, you have an experience in store for you. The boiled potato with fish or with certain meat dishes is unexcelled, but alas, this too can be a pretty dull bit of eating if the potato stands around and becomes soggy and heavy, offering nothing but starchiness and poor texture.

The English, I think, were also the originators of oven-browned potatoes—tossing the potatoes into the drippings as a roast turned, which gave them the flavor of beef drippings and a crisp outer covering. The French do this in another fashion with *pommes parisiennes*, and the Americans came to the same thing with the beginning of the oven, making what is termed the "browned potato." In any of these versions the fat and potato are a perfect union, the one with so much flavor to bestow and the other so receptive. A good browned potato takes about an hour to cook. If you want to hurry the process, boil the potatoes for a few minutes and then transfer them to the dripping pan. Turn the potatoes and baste them as they cook until they are crusty and brown.

Another superior accomplishment with the potato, probably invented by the Scots, is the potato scone which I mentioned earlier—thin, delicate with potato flavor, and marvelous with tea or toasted for breakfast. It is as simple a scone as it is possible to make, but it has an entirely unique quality.

Of course, the French have taken up the potato as if it had started on French soil, and they have done some incredibly good things with it, as well as a few bad. To me, the various versions of the *gratin savoyard* are sensational. The one done with layers of Gruyère and milk and butter is light and exquisite. By substituting broth for milk in the same recipe, it becomes even better. And the combination of celeriac, celery or sausage with the potatoes and Gruyère is another triumph.

Gratin Savoyard

Peel 1 large or 2 small celery roots and 6 Idaho potatoes. Cut them in even slices about ⅛ inch thick. Butter a baking dish or casserole quite well and alternate layers of potatoes, celery root, grated Swiss Gruyère or Emmenthal, being certain that you have a layer of potatoes on the bottom and the top. Dot the top well with butter. Add 1 teaspoon salt and several grindings of black pepper. Pour over ¾ cup beef or chicken bouillon and bake at 325° for 1 to 1¼ hours or until the potatoes are tender and have absorbed most of the liquid. Sprinkle them with a bit of grated cheese and return the dish to the oven until the cheese melts.

There are two variations of this dish. One is to eliminate the cheese entirely and add buttered crumbs at the last minute to brown on top.

The second variation is to add coarse-textured pork sausages that have been poached in white wine for 10 to 12 minutes. Arrange the sausages on top of the celery root mixture about 20 minutes before the *gratin* is ready to be removed from the oven.

I once had a French-style bubble and squeak, a *gratin* of potatoes with a base of chopped cooked cabbage, which I found to be a robust dish with wonderful flavor, good with ham, pork or boiled meats. And something else the French do: they add vinegar and olive oil and perhaps a bit of chopped shallot to boiled potatoes to be served hot with sausage or *charcuterie* (other pork products) for a first course. This is unbelievably good and so simple it is a wonder we have never discovered it for ourselves. Then there are *pommes fondantes*, steamed in butter without coloring the potatoes, which gives them a luscious texture seldom found in other potato dishes and makes them extremely appropriate for a delicate veal or chicken dish.

Pommes Fondantes

This is a very simple, elegant preparation for new potatoes or waxy potatoes. They should be peeled and trimmed to a uniform size—balls about 1½ inches in diameter—and steamed in butter. This requires a heavy saucepan with butter melted to about ½ inch in depth. The potatoes are put into the pan with a bit of salt and covered and steamed over low heat until they are tender. Shake the pan from time to time.

Whoever she may have been, "Anna" deserves the Legion of Honor. When the potato dish named for her is done properly—with thin-sliced potatoes and plenty of butter in a heavy cooking pot—nothing in the entire potato world can excel them! They emerge crisp and golden and rich with the unadorned flavor of potato and butter. If you choose good potatoes, good butter and the right pot, you should have no difficulty in making perfect potatoes Anna. One can make a similar dish atop the stove, called potatoes Annette, and these can be almost as delicious if done with care.

Pommes de Terre Anna

Pommes de terre Anna, or potatoes Anna, are made in a heavy pan. The potatoes should be cut in even slices ⅛ inch thick.

You will need about 1½ pounds of potatoes for four persons, perhaps more if you are very fond of buttery potatoes.

Butter the mold or pan very well and arrange a rosette of overlapping potato slices in the bottom. Then arrange more layers above these and some around the sides of the mold, overlapping as well. Dot the slices with butter midway in the stacking and on top. Add salt and freshly ground pepper.

Bake at 450° for 45 minutes to 1 hour or until the potatoes have a delicate brown crust on the outside and are tender and buttery all through. Invert the pan on a hot plate and garnish it with parsley. As good a potato dish with beef as one could wish.

The Auvergnats make a potato dish with bacon which begins with a good idea but is not quite successful. It is too floury for my taste. I much prefer to cook some bacon, remove it from the pan, add the potatoes and onion and then replace the bacon for the last minutes of cooking. This way it is a pleasant luncheon dish when served with a salad and some fruit. Top the potatoes with an egg if you wish to make a heartier meal.

Speaking of eggs, an *omelette savoyarde* is an exceptionally fine dish. I have had so many versions of it that I am not certain which is authentic. But the one I like best is a potato omelet, made pancake style, placed on a piece of ham, covered with Gruyère and slipped under the broiling flame for a few minutes. The eggs help the potatoes to blend nicely with the ham and cheese, and the combination has a hearty, savory quality. I have also made the same dish without the ham, sometimes mixing the cheese with the egg and sometimes melting it on top. All of these are superb, although I remain partial to the first of the three, and the first I ever ate. Another version you might like, however, uses rather crisply fried potatoes, eggs and grated cheese.

I am suddenly reminded of the time I saw *omelette savoyarde* on a restaurant menu in New York, ordered it, and received an ordinary omelet with a bit of grated Parmesan cheese on it. Quite a disappointment.

Omelette Savoyarde

For each person, sauté 2 or 3 boiled potatoes sliced ¼ inch thick in your omelet pan. Add 3 eggs beaten lightly with 1 tablespoon water and cook the omelet pancake fashion until it is just set. Sprinkle it with grated Gruyère cheese, slide it onto a slice of grilled ham on a hot plate, and serve at once. This may be varied by using Parmesan or even Cheddar cheese.

No doubt the most epicurean of potato dishes is one called *sarladaise*. Here again there are versions and versions. Basically it is a combination of crisply sautéed potatoes and truffles; and they must be fresh truffles. Some say the truffles must be sliced, sautéed in butter and combined with potatoes which have been sautéed in goose fat. Others say both ingredients should be sautéed in goose fat, and still others say butter only. My advice is, be sure to use the fresh truffles if you can, but use whatever fat you wish. In all versions, *sarladaise* remains remarkable among potato dishes.

There is also a famous salad made with boiled potatoes sliced thin, fresh truffles sliced thin, greens, and either walnut oil or olive oil. The manner in which the truffles perfume the potatoes provides one of the great experiences in eating.

I am not sure to whom credit should go for most other potato salads. I have had very good ones in France, Switzerland and Germany. They resemble each other essentially in the use of hot potatoes treated with oil and vinegar. They differ in seasonings—some have onion and parsley, others have white wine, fine-chopped carrot and almonds, and still others use quantities of chives, parsley and onion. Occasionally bacon and bacon fat are used instead of oil. The number of these salads one finds throughout Europe is unbelievable. In each, the vital quality comes from the texture of the potato itself.

One must not forget the superb soup named for Parmentier—a potato and leek mixture, which has been copied all over the world and which was the inspiration for Vichyssoise, an American derivation with overtones of that master of the kitchen, Diat. And the Scotch cockaleekie must have first been produced by a French chef working in Scotland.

The Germans' major offering to the repertoire of potato dishes is the *Kartoffel Knödel*, a dumpling which I consider an insult to the delicacy of the vegetable. They also make potato pancakes, which are either divinely light or dull and heavy. The Russians used to make them better than anyone else—thin, crisp and light, enhancing the potato flavor rather than smothering it. As a matter of fact, this crisp pancake makes delicious blinis with caviar or herring and sour cream. Caviar is extremely friendly to the potato flavor in this dish, and the Germans also use caviar with a baked potato, along with sour cream, chives and parsley, an interesting combination, although it is a waste of good caviar. If the caviar is of an inferior grade, it is perhaps quite suitable.

The greatest gift of the Italians to potato eaters is *gnocchi:* the Roman *gnocchi*, rather than those of northern Italy, where they are sometimes made with polenta and flour and *pâté*. Roman style, the mashed potatoes are mixed with flour and formed into dumplings, which are cooked in boiling water. Served with a pungent sauce, these are delectable nuggets and have few equals in farinaceous food.

Potato Gnocchi

Peel and quarter 2 pounds potatoes and cook them in boiling salted water until tender. Drain and mash them, or put them through a food mill, and gradually beat in 1½ cups milk. Season them to taste with salt and add ¾ teaspoon ground black pepper and a pinch of mace. Place them over a medium flame and stir in enough fine semolina to make a very stiff mixture. Add ½ cup grated Gruyère cheese and beat in 3 egg yolks. Pour the dough into a buttered tin or dish, allow it to stand until cool and refrigerate it for 24 hours. Form the dough into small balls, drop them into boiling salted water and cook them about 4 minutes, until they are puffy and float. Serve them with melted butter and grated cheese or with a béchamel sauce or with Delfinio's fresh tomato sauce (p. 47).

I have never had what I consider a good original Spanish potato recipe or a good original one from Scandinavia.

Certainly no country can claim potatoes puréed or

mashed as its own. This treatment of potatoes has turned up in every country where the potato is used, in varying styles and with varying degrees of success. I will list a few of the interesting variations I have encountered, assuming you know how to make good mashed potatoes, beginning with dry boiled potatoes. I do not agree with Dumaine that the mashing should be an up and down motion entirely; this way your potatoes get tough. Let and my mother both made them with a whisk, and I have even done them superbly with an electric beater. Cream, milk, cheese, butter, bacon, goose fat, chicken fat, sour cream have all been introduced to the mashed potato. Some other ingredients and combinations of ingredients you can consider are: bacon and cheese; bacon, onion and cheese; chives and parsley; pepper; goose fat and cracklings; celery root; turnips; *duxelles*.

Duxelles

This is the answer to an all-purpose seasoning agent. Its flavor is irresistible. You will want to add it to everything you make. Chop 3 pounds mushrooms fairly fine. They do not have to be of the very top quality. You can use little ones and mixed sizes. Melt ½ pound butter in a very heavy skillet and add the mushrooms. Stir them to blend with the butter and cook them over low heat, stirring occasionally until the mushrooms have thrown off all their liquid and have turned a very dark brown, almost black. It may be necessary to add additional butter, and care must be taken that they do not get crisp. They must remain soft. Add salt and pepper to taste and spoon them into a jar or bowl for keeping.

A little of this preparation added to eggs is delicious. It is an integral part of many sauces and may be used for a quick toasted sandwich or for hors d'oeuvre.

We have come a long way from Lima, but the fact remains that we owe our debt to Peru for the original vegetable. The other great gift of Peru to the world's food was, of course, corn. Here again we find many varieties, many colors, many textures. The United States has the unquestioned lead in the eating of sweet corn. It is a pity that we now live too far from our gardens to have it as fresh as we might wish, but it is being marketed quite efficiently.

Over the past thirty years the strains have been so improved that the eating of corn has spread outside this country. It is getting some attention in France, and there is a restaurant on the avenue Matignon where the specialty in the summer months for hors d'oeuvre is fresh corn, which the *patron* buys from an American who grows it near Paris. Hediard and Fauchon and other greengrocers in Paris handle it, too. I have cooked it in Paris for French friends several times and succeeded at least in making them say they liked it.

The English have taken our canned corn, which is extremely good most of the time, and often use it straight from the can on an hors d'oeuvre tray. However, I am happy to learn that there is soon to be a great corn festival in Brighton, not in honor of cans but of fresh green corn.

Americans dried corn in the early years, using it for meal and for animal fodder, and eating only fresh corn themselves. Then the canning industry came forth with what is known as "cream style corn," and it revolutionized the country's consumption of this vegetable. This was followed years later by whole-kernel corn in a vacuum pack, which is better than some fresh corn and almost as good as the best. Now both whole-kernel corn and corn on the cob are sold frozen, and recently the most advanced of the corn canning companies started the production of canned whole-kernel shoe-peg corn, which is tiny kerneled corn exceptionally good in flavor. Whole-kernel corn is taking hold in Europe, and who knows what another Parmentier may create someday!

We have fine corn soufflés, soups and salads and *gratins* of corn, but there is still a tremendous potential for this vegetable in the world's cuisines.

Corn au Gratin

Butter a small baking dish and add 2 cups corn kernels, either canned or fresh. Add 1 tablespoon grated onion, ½ teaspoon salt and ½ teaspoon freshly ground black pepper, and mix well with the corn. Add 1 cup grated Gruyère or Emmenthal cheese and 1 cup heavy cream. Dot top with butter and bake at 350° for about 20 minutes until the cheese is thoroughly melted.

Corn Chile Soufflé

Whirl in a blender 1 cup whole-kernel corn, canned or fresh, and 3 canned, peeled green chiles. Add to this mixture ½ cup grated Gruyère, Swiss or Emmenthal cheese and 5 egg yolks. Beat 7 egg whites until stiff. Fold in one-third very well and lightly fold in remaining two-thirds. Pour mixture into a buttered 1½-quart soufflé mold. Bake soufflé at 375° for 30 minutes or until it is light and puffy. Serve it at once as a vegetable course with beef or chicken dishes.

One form of corn we think about all too seldom is hominy: corn kernels that have been treated with lye, which causes them to swell and lose their skins. Good hominy is an interesting dish if well prepared; in fact, it can be quite distinguished. It is little known in the East and Middle West, and I don't know when I last saw a dish of hominy brought to table as a garnish for chicken or pork. A nicely fried chicken with hominy and cream gravy, as it was made by good farm cooks, is a menu not to be looked down upon. This is genuinely good, simple fare. Hominy was probably first brought to this country by the Mexicans, but it has remained a staple of the South and Southwest without having had enough attention from the world of cookery to make it a national dish. There are one or two good brands of canned hominy which can be used very successfully.

Menudo

(*From Elena Zelayeta*)

This favorite Mexican dish displays the palate-pleasing delights of hominy as well as any that I know. Wash 2 calf's feet well, then wash 4 pounds tripe and cut it into small squares. Place the feet and tripe in a large casserole and cover them with water or stock. Add 1 onion stuck with cloves, 2 teaspoons oregano and 2 teaspoons crushed coriander seeds, 1½ teaspoons salt and 1 teaspoon freshly ground black pepper. Cover the casserole and let it cook in a 300° oven for 6 to 8 hours or until the tripe is tender. Cool it. Remove the calf's feet, pick off the meat and discard the bones. Add 3 cups canned whole hominy and simmer casserole on top of the stove or in the oven for 30 minutes. When you serve it, pass dishes of chopped green onions and chopped chiles; and, if in season, chopped fresh mint.

The only European country which has accepted corn whole-heartedly, aside from England and France, is Italy, and even there, not the green corn, but cornmeal. Polenta has been for a long time a favorite food in the north of Italy, where it is served as often as potatoes in America or rice in other countries. Great copper pots with wooden paddles are used to prepare polenta, which is cooked for hours and then served hot, or cooled and recooked in several ways—sautéed, baked and sauced. It can be varied as much as potatoes, for the combinations seem endless. One with sausages, tomatoes and seasonings is a favorite of mine; and there is a classic dish with stockfish, polenta and a highly seasoned sauce. You are not apt to find the latter on great menus, but in the right places, with some pleading, you can have it prepared. If you come across it in a small *trattoria* where it is a specialty, it can be a memorable experience.

Polenta goes into *gnocchi* in the north also, and is used in a *galette*, not unlike a corn pone, which I find exciting fare sometimes. One can discover a little of this in Nice and its environs, but not as much as there might be, considering how standard much of the Niçoise cooking is.

Polenta

Combine 1½ cups cornmeal with 1 cup water in the upper part of a double boiler. When it is well mixed, stir in 3½ cups boiling water and continue stirring until the mixture comes to a boil. Add 1 teaspoon salt, place polenta over hot water and continue cooking for 1 hour. Add 4 tablespoons butter and a copious sprinkling of grated Parmesan or Romano cheese, or you may pour the polenta into a serving dish and sprinkle it with the cheese just before serving.

Polenta with Sausages

Prepare polenta as above, pour it into a baking dish and top with previously poached Italian sausages— they should be poached for 5 to 7 minutes and drained. Spoon over some of Delfinio's fresh tomato sauce (p. 47) and bake at 350° for 10 to 15 minutes. Serve with additional tomato sauce and grated cheese.

Our Favorite Polenta with Salted Codfish

Soak 2 pounds salted, boneless codfish in enough cold water to cover for 8 hours, changing the water once. Drain, cover with fresh water, bring it to a boil and simmer it until the fish is tender and flaky. Heat 3 tablespoons olive oil in a sauté pan and add 1 fine-chopped garlic clove and 1 small chopped onion. Add 1½ cups Italian plum tomatoes and a few leaves of fresh basil or 1 tablespoon dried basil. Simmer this mixture for 30 to 40 minutes, and add 2 tablespoons Italian tomato paste. Pour polenta, prepared according to previous directions, in a baking dish and top it with the codfish. Spread tomato sauce over it, sprinkle the top with grated Parmesan cheese and put the dish under the broiler flame for 2 or 3 minutes to glaze.

Again, Peru itself contributed little to the refinement of corn as a food, but what Peru didn't do, Mexico did.

78

Mexican cookery has a great deal of corn in it and is almost unexcelled in its use of corn for flavoring. All tamales have cornmeal as a base, and tamales made from cornmeal and fresh corn and cheese are one great specialty. And the tortilla—what could express the true flavor of corn more robustly than this hearth-baked bread? Served fresh from the griddle or toasted, tortillas are also a basic part of many Mexican dishes.

Corn used to be hand-ground on the metates and made into a paste called masa, from which the tortillas were patted out and baked on a flat griddle. Nowadays there are few made by hand; machines do the work. The tortilla machine at La Fonda del Sol in New York is able to turn out an astronomical number of these small breads each day.

Whereas in Peru one is astonished by the assortment of potatoes and corn, in the markets of Brazil the most fascinating phenomenon is the many varieties of bananas. People delight in choosing their favorite bananas; and no Scotch drinker could be more discriminating about his Scotch than a true Brazilian about his bananas! And I must say, the difference among them is incredible. I became intrigued and tried to learn the character of each before I left. Some are rich and sweet, some are less unctuous and semisweet, and some are bland in flavor without a trace of sugar. And the oranges! What glorious ones I found there, and how many I used!

The cosmopolitan aspect of Rio is reflected in its markets. Besides the native items one sees Italian, Swiss, German produce; and there is, too, an engaging holdover from an earlier era: the purveyors offer for sale, right next to their produce, the trays, boxes, and other objects they carve between business deals.

Fish is an important part of the Brazilian diet, and the varieties differ from those available to us in the

North. However, I felt that the choice was far less exciting than that to be found, say, in Nice, Paris, London, or along the Spanish coast on the Mediterranean. There were wonderful shrimp and crab, but I discovered more interesting fish in the mountains—trout and similar fish, fresh from streams and lakes. The mountain markets also offered wonderful berries—the best strawberries, both cultivated and wild, I think I have ever eaten—glorious cream and fresh regional cheeses, and often the *peru*—the turkey—which appeared to be better cared for in the mountains than below in Rio.

I was first introduced to the exciting markets of Mexico by way of Yucatán, and then later I was guided through the markets of the capital by a great food explorer, Francis Guth. He was so in love with Mexican markets at that time he started a restaurant, and later another, so he could share his enthusiasms with the public. To do the markets with Francis was always a gratifying experience. There were several in and around Mexico City, and oftentimes we drove into the hills in search of a particular item we had only heard about from market people. In this way, we found some interesting cheeses—Mexico has a small and not distinguished dairy industry; and as though on a treasure hunt, we once followed the trail to the source of morels, the wonderful mushrooms sold in the market. And I recall the day we found mountains of cepes, the great wood mushrooms, waiting for us—great, beautiful ones, which we used *à la provençale* and *bordelaise* in a delicious salad.

Cepes Bordelaise

These delicious mushrooms are not generally available fresh in this country but may be purchased in tins from both Italy and France. They should be drained thoroughly and washed before cooking.

For one 20-ounce can of cepes, peel and chop 6 to

8 shallots and sauté them in 6 tablespoons olive oil.
Add the cepes, which may be cut if they are extremely
large, and heat them thoroughly—do not overcook.
Add ¼ cup fine-chopped parsley, a dash of lemon
juice, and salt and freshly ground pepper to taste.

Cepes Salad

Wash cepes thoroughly and arrange them in a salad
bowl or ravier. Add 3 to 4 fine-chopped shallots,
1 tablespoon chopped chives, ¼ cup chopped parsley,
and dress with a good vinaigrette sauce.

We explored among the vegetables, fruits and herbs,
too, and I was particularly struck by the peppers. If I
remember correctly, the best recipe for *mole* I know
contains twenty-three different types of chile blended
together in a metate, or with mortar and pestle. It is
nothing for an ordinary recipe to call for four or five
varieties. To distinguish among the appearances and
textures of the dried ones, alone, is a feat, and then there
are the fresh ones! At any rate, after a few weeks of
application I had developed an index of chiles which
was formidable.

Beans also require some study, they occur in such a
profusion of forms. (The Peruvians, again, may have
had this vegetable originally, but the Mexicans have
been its greatest consumers.) The types of dried frijoles—beans—one finds are staggering in number.
Added to these is an endless assortment of fresh ones.

As is usual in countries with a starchy diet, the meat
in Mexico is not on a par with its other products, with
the exception of pork, which is usually very good. The
beef is, in general, tough and tasteless, although quite
admirable beef has recently appeared in the better restaurants of the largest cities. Turkey and chicken are
extremely good at times.

Fish from the Gulf and from the Pacific are interesting and in great supply. If one has never eaten
seviche—raw marinated fish—in one of its forms, he is

missing something. This is an exceptionally satisfying dish, and although it is supposed to have had its origin in Ecuador, no one could do it more justice than a good Mexican cook.

Seviche

Cut 1 pound white fish—lemon sole, snapper, Rex sole or any delicious white fish—into thin strips. Arrange them in a flat dish and cover them with lime juice. Refrigerate for 1 hour. Drain the fish, reserving the lime juice, and add 1 good-sized onion chopped fine, 3 or 4 canned, peeled green chiles chopped fine, 1 chopped ripe tomato, a pinch of oregano and 2 to 3 tablespoons olive oil. Toss ingredients well. Garnish dish with chopped parsley and, if available, leaves of *cilantro*, also known as Chinese parsley, or fresh coriander.

Seviche is also very good if it is served in avocado halves; but no matter how you serve it, it must be very cold.

The Mexican shellfish—shrimp of all sizes, *langostos* and crab—are all superlative. And I find the oysters from the Gulf surprisingly good and as salty as many of the European ones—and I have eaten a good many oysters in my life. Tiny squid and tiny octopuses occasionally reach the inland markets and are nearly always available along the Pacific. They are, of course, remarkably good fish when properly prepared.

Pomegranates, cherries, berries and the mangoes and other tropical fruits which appear in the markets are extremely good and contribute to pleasant eating. Then there are unusual things like the maguey worms, found in the plant of that name, which are cooked to a crispness that is quite delightful; they are like salted nuts—habit-forming. I know of few foods with such a distinctive quality and flavor, and if one didn't know he was eating worms, he would never guess! But above all in Mexico, there are always, always chiles, always,

always corn and cornmeal, and always, always *cilantro*, the herb common to Mexico and China—exotically flavored coriander with its haunting perfume.

What makes Mexican markets especially delightful is the tasteful way in which the produce is arrayed even when there may be little to sell. I have been to country markets where there were the simplest of things—a few tomatoes, plums, or oranges—and they were arranged as though the market were a showplace in the county fair, and as though there were untold quantities in reserve. And there is always a festive air about these markets, which is as it should be. Hence, the market people sell faster and return home happier. Except for the French, I believe the Mexicans arrange their food more attractively than anyone else, but the French lack the Mexicans' good humor.

Fish markets have always appealed to me because of my great love for fish lore and for fish per se. The market in Venice near the Rialto, the markets in Nice and Marseille and the one in Istanbul have the treasures of their individual seas in profusion. It is beguiling just to wander through these markets, and one is always compelled to rush home and read up on the strange fish he has seen. I have, unfortunately, not been able to cook them all, but I have sampled the Marseille and Venice markets pretty well.

In Spain one summer, also, I had a house in Palamós on the Costa Brava, which I shared with two friends, and our diet was mostly fish. We had an enchanting assistant in the household named Mercedes, who understood that we wanted to know and taste every fish we could find. Thus, she led us off to market sometimes twice a day. To go when the fishing fleet had just returned was an exciting opportunity, because you chose your dinner and rushed it home to cook, practically from sea to table. Our cooking facilities were three charcoal burners in a tile stove and an oven heated with charcoal. We served up some rare good dinners from there, and our reputation grew through the summer.

Our greatest treat was an occasional *dentón*, a Mediterranean fish of exceptional texture, generous in size, which when poached and served cold is astoundingly good. (Our striped bass is an equivalent delight when served cold with a good sauce and a cucumber salad.) *Rougets* grilled over charcoal proved extraordinary. And fresh sardines and anchovies grilled to a crispness outside were fabulous! Tiny squid (*calamares*) cut in small lengths, dipped in flour and cooked quickly in oil till crisp were as delicious as any dish from the sea. Squid have a quality which I find completely winning. We sometimes stuffed them with other fish and rice and braised them, but most memorable were the sliced squid we had *a la Romana*.

Calamares a la Romana

One should use only small *calamares* for this. They should be cleaned and cut into 1-inch pieces, flavored well and cooked very quickly in hot oil, salted and peppered and rushed on hot plates to the table. Lemon is obligatory with this and a cucumber salad most agreeable.

We also had *gambas*, the bright-red shrimp abounding in those waters, which have a sweetness few fish ever develop. These, charcoal-broiled in their shells, made a fine luncheon. And we ate quantities of *langostos*, like the *langoustines* of France, and occasionally superb *langoustes*, which were hard to come by but worth waiting for. Served cold, this sea crayfish is extraordinarily good, and combined with chicken in a sauté, it has some qualities which I find in no other crayfish or in lobster. In many ways I find a good *langouste* a far more rewarding dish than lobster, especially cold. It has a sweeter meat and seems to be more tender.

84

We shopped once in a while for fish to use in a *suquete*, which is a typically Catalan dish made with white wine and oil. It is not as liquid as a bouillabaisse—it is more like a braised dish than a chowder—and is far more exciting. That celebrated dish I can take or leave; certainly I won't weep if I never have another one! You can't make a real bouillabaisse in this country anyhow. A true *suquete* you *can* make here, and I think you might come to favor it too.

Suquete, Catalan

Sauté 2 large onions, chopped fine, in ½ cup olive oil. Add 2 fine-chopped garlic cloves, 6 or 7 ripe tomatoes peeled, seeded and chopped, or 1½ cups canned Italian plum tomatoes, 1 cup white wine, 1 bay leaf, and salt and pepper to taste. Simmer 1 hour or until the ingredients achieve a smooth consistency. Strain the sauce through a fine sieve and combine it with 1 cup blanched almonds pounded in a mortar or whirled in a blender until they are practically a paste. Bind the sauce with 1 ounce (2 tablespoons) semisweet chocolate, melted. Correct the seasoning. Simmer 4 fillets of any whitefish—sole, lemon sole, flounder, etc.—in the sauce until the fish flakes easily when tested with a fork or toothpick. Serve the *suquete* on saffron rice or fried toast.

When we weren't shopping for fish, we went to another market in Palamós, far removed from the fish market. Mercedes had relatives here, and friends, so marketing was more or less a family affair. Like my mother, she got the best the market had to offer. Certain choice items were kept under the counter, or under the skirt, if need be, till Mercedes appeared.

Thus, we had wonderful squash blossoms for omelets much of the time (Spanish omelets are done in pancake style and called "tortillas"). We had the tenderest little *chuletas*, tiny cutlets of lamb, practically the only good meat in that part of Spain. These we broiled very quickly and served with a selection of wonderfully fresh vegetables, which were always available. Sometimes we found a good piece of veal and made a *vitello tonnato* with it because the meat was better braised, and because we wanted to have a cold dish. Our Spanish version of this classic Italian recipe had a variation or two suggested by the locale. If you'd like to try this superb veal dish with a dash of Spain in it, here is what we did.

Vitello Tonnato Spagnolo

Have your butcher bone and tie a piece of veal from the leg, about 4 to 5 pounds. Place it in a deep kettle or casserole with 3 or 4 cloves of garlic, a veal bone, two 7-ounce cans top-quality tuna, 12 to 14 anchovy fillets, 3 or 4 pieces of parsley and a tiny sprig of fresh rosemary. Add ⅓ cup olive oil and 1 cup white wine. Cover and bake in a 325° oven for 2 to 2½ hours or until veal is tender. Cool and chill overnight in the refrigerator. Remove any fat that rises to the top of the dish, which should be jellied. Remove meat, discard bone and strings, and return the veal to the refrigerator. Whirl the other ingredients in a blender, and taste for salt content. If you feel that the flavor of this sauce is too intense, you may add a little mayonnaise or sour cream to it. If, on the other hand, you feel it has not enough of the tuna flavor, you might add more fish. Slice the veal very thin and arrange the slices on a serving platter or dish, and spoon the sauce over it. Chill until serving time.

We always enjoyed a French-style potato salad with this, although many people prefer a rice salad.

An occasional chicken or duck would come our way if one of Mercedes' relatives revealed he had a good one, and we were always blessed with remarkably good eggs as well as Spanish bacon—salt-cured and lightly smoked—which I found to be delightful.

I have never eaten such *fraises des bois* in my life as came into that little market. Usually, nowadays, I find them rather dull, but these were like the wild strawberries gathered in the mountains above Rio or at the beach in Oregon. Mercedes would take a bowl to market with her and return with it filled with these incredible berries. Sometimes that very bowl was carried off into the wilds by the berry pickers and returned later in the day.

Another great delight of Palamós was our baker. He aspired to be an artist as well as a baker, and he would often do the most amusing chickens, rabbits, or other shapes, in bread, which he displayed in his window, hoping others would enjoy his talent. I did, and I am sure others did, and I especially liked having these museum pieces in bread on my table when guests were arriving. Our baker also made some extraordinary deep-fried cakes with a pastry-cream filling, which came hot from the caldron about five o'clock every afternoon. If you happened to be in the neighborhood at the right time and were fortunate enough to taste one of these juicy cakes, you were lost; for you wanted more, and they were devastatingly rich!

The native *charcuterie* was quite interesting, and Mercedes had her special sources for this. We often had a luncheon of *jamón serrano*, the ham which differs from all others, together with sausages, a salad and fruit—thoroughly good, simple food, which contradicts the notion that one cannot eat well in Spain.

Once in a great while Mercedes would make her version of *paella*, and to satisfy me would put extra gizzards into the dish. This was made entirely atop the stove and took not too long to prepare. It was triumphal, and each time we had it (usually when foreign guests were there, who expected to have *paella* in Spain), it was eaten to the last grain of rice.

Mercedes' Paella

When we made this dish in Spain, we always used the second joints of chicken and the gizzards and kept the breasts for another dish. I think it is a much more pleasant arrangement this way.

For six people, you will want the second joints and legs of 3 chickens and 1 pound or so of gizzards. Heat ½ cup olive oil in your *paella* or in a large skillet. Brown the chicken pieces and gizzards in this and salt and pepper them to taste. Remove the legs and thighs to a hot plate when they are nicely browned, but allow the gizzards to remain in the pan. Add 2 cloves of garlic and a very large onion, all chopped fine, and cook them for 2 to 3 minutes. Add 1½ cups rice and let it brown lightly. Add to this 1 pinch of saffron and 1 cup white wine and let it cook down. Add 1 cup stock or water and continue adding and reducing until the rice is almost tender. Return chicken pieces to the dish. Add ½ cup chopped ripe tomatoes, 12 washed and shelled shrimp, some thin-sliced Spanish or Italian sausages and 12 to 18 clams, which have been well scrubbed. Continue cooking until shellfish is ready, the rice tender and the chicken cooked.

Serve with a garnish of pimiento and pepper strips.

The Spanish, contrary to a widespread misconception, do not eat hot, heavily seasoned food. They use very little pepper and very few herbs. I believe this conception of the Spanish diet must have originated in Texas, where they do Mexican and Spanish dishes in the hottest manner I know. Garlic and saffron are used a good deal in Spain, and paprika in some places, but the herbs and spices we take for granted are not to be had. In fact, all about us in Palamós there were great bushes of rosemary, and oregano and other herbs grew wild. But I never saw these in the market nor saw anyone pick them. They appeared to grow solely for the delectation of Spanish birds.

In American towns and cities, markets, except in a few localities, have given way to supermarkets. There are even fewer country markets than there used to be, and the whole experience of meeting in the market, exchanging pleasantries and doing the shopping in leisurely fashion, belongs to an era now past. The custom today is to whiz to the shopping center by car, transfer to a shopping cart, which you whirl through the store, past the cashier and out to the car, and then have a quick drive home. It is even the practice to do an entire week's shopping at one time. This, of course, is easier on the housewife, but it does not mean that the best of food will reach the table. Naturally, vegetables that wait for a week to be cooked won't have the same quality as those freshly picked, even with the help of modern refrigeration.

Supermarkets could be improved if we could only induce them to show more imagination and offer greater choice in their fresh foods. I know that some of the chain stores do carry the finest available meats, and in the metropolitan markets they are prepared to cut according to your tastes, if you order ahead. Surely one can't complain about the lack of variety in supermarket merchandise, generally; what doesn't one find there?

There are still a few places in this country, however, where marketing is pleasant. Of course, the Farmers' Market in Los Angeles is among them. But it is anything but a farmers' market these days. The produce one finds is chosen by a few dealers, and only show pieces are offered for sale. These are displayed imaginatively, which makes for fun, but there are also hordes of tourists, and the dreariest of prepared food is sold in stalls that purport to be Mexican, Chinese, Italian and Spanish. There are superb fruit and vegetable stands, good poultry and fish markets, some outstanding delicacy shops, and a fine bakery with as great a variety of good breads as you'll find in any shop in the United

89

States. This is by no means a great public market, but the quality of its produce is consistently higher than in any other market in the country and it may well be the last of its kind.

Nowhere in America does one see finer vegetables than on the West Coast, in Los Angeles, San Francisco and Portland. In Los Angeles the tiny green squash, the asparagus, beans and salad greens are absolutely splendid and spotless. Vegetables of all kinds are in abundance, and fine small fruits. There are also beautiful outsized apples and pears, so perfect as to appear made of wax; but wax has more flavor than some of these, and they are apparently grown to look pretty in the markets.

San Francisco always cheers me, for there is such an array of produce in the markets. There is no longer a great central market, but the markets along—yes—Market Street and in some of the residential districts are quite stimulating. There is one especially good one on Market Street where the quality and variety of merchandise are beyond belief. Outside of France—Marseille, Nice and Paris—I have never seen better fish or more types: sand dabs, whole and ready for the pan, salmon, skate wings, abalone, Alaska black cod and Rex sole. (This last is a great Pacific Coast fish with wonderful texture and flavor. If you have never eaten it and happen to find yourself in San Francisco, go at once to Jack's on Sacramento Street and ask to have it *meunière*.) There are also Dungeness crab, Pacific Coast crawfish or rock lobster, sometimes bass, and occasionally turbot. All these are spotlessly clean and handsomely displayed.

The same market has one of the best meat sections I have ever seen on the West Coast, featuring not only a good grade of meat but interesting bits of variety meats and some French cuts, unusual to find in the run of American markets.

The vegetable section is equal to the fish and meat departments, and I will not enumerate the beautiful

specimens to be found there, but a selection of them was provided for a special food demonstration I did in San Francisco last year. They were so handsome and so photogenic I have been grateful ever since to the gentleman in charge of vegetables.

Fisherman's Wharf, of course, is one of the most publicized markets in the United States. It is good for a few varieties of fish but unique for the great vats of crab one sees being freshly cooked in season. Only sampling will tell you which crab dealer to patronize.

Small farmers' markets still appear in the countryside, offering fresh local produce and some cooked foods. These seem to prosper in Pennsylvania as in few other places, and in some towns and cities there are famous markets where Pennsylvania Dutch specialties, prepared by the farmer's wife, are sold along with produce of the soil, raised by the farmer himself. The old Reading Market in Philadelphia has lost a great deal of its patronage, and there is, sadly enough, no longer the excitement of earlier days. Only a few of the old-timers remain there. Like most other central markets, it is the victim of the supermarket.

Americans who have the opportunity to travel abroad ought to acquaint themselves with the market tradition, lost to us now for all time. And if I had to send everyone to one market only, I would send them to Paris. For there is nothing in the world to equal Les Halles!

CHAPTER

4

There is the threat that within the next two or three years Les Halles will be decentralized. If you have never spent a night there, by all means go. Stay through from about midnight until seven in the morning. Then go a second day from about ten in the morning till lunch and eat in one of the excellent restaurants which abound there. Naturally these *bistros* have as their custom the men who are the heart and brains of the market, and they buy the finest of produce to satisfy them. Here you will find great regional dishes from nearly every province.

I have eaten *omelette au lard* in the early morning and returned for lunch, when there were such seasonal items on the menu as larks or a fabulous dish of chicken and eel sautéed together, which is a specialty of lower Burgundy. In one of the small restaurants, where there are seats for only about twenty-four, the *pièce de résistance* is probably the best sole anyone ever eats anywhere. The *patron* chooses large sole, which invariably seem to hang off the plate, head and tail, and sautés them in just enough butter to color them without having them swim in it. In the same restaurant one pastry is served. This is a *gâteau de Pithiviers*, which consists of layers of fine puff pastry with cream of almonds sealed in it—a dessert that leaves me limp, I enjoy it so.

In another of the restaurants there is a *patron*—his name is Monteil—who delights in his Rabelaisian wit. However ribald the talk, the food is impeccable and the variation of dishes something rare. Here one of the features is a duck with tarragon which I consider superlative, being devoted as I am to that herb. I believe if ever I had to practice cannibalism, I might manage if there were enough tarragon around!

At night there are a few places where one may eat well, but beware the tourist traps with their watery onion soup. I am of the opinion that in all Les Halles there is not one place left where one can find a good onion soup. Anyway, it is far better at home than in a restaurant. I suggest you dine late in the neighborhood, perhaps at L'Escargot or at La Grille, and linger over your coffee and cognac. Then start a trek around the market before the arrival of the farmers, who swarm in from the provinces to set up their fare in the streets. You will have a chance beforehand to see beef being hung and fruit and flowers being set up.

Wander in and out of the shops. No one will bother you.

Finally the vegetables will be arranged. You will see enormous pyramids of cauliflower or cabbages, endless baskets of watercress packed in spirals to keep the leaves fresh, piles of onions and potatoes, and crates of asparagus, in season. It is fascinating to see whence comes so much that feeds France—Israel, Algeria, the United States, Chile, Italy, Spain, to name only a few countries. And the produce of neighboring nations arrives in time to advance the season.

Later the fish and *charcuterie* markets and the cheese and butter shops will begin to open and arrange their wares. Activity continues steadily with trucks arriving, coffee and wine being drunk, and prostitutes picking up sex-hungry farmboys. As you see four or five o'clock approaching, stop and restore yourself in a *bistro* with a good omelet or a *choucroute garnie*, and then go back to watch the buyers arrive. Some restaurateurs come to Les Halles themselves and push their way around to find the choicest of viands and bargain. Some send their emissaries who do the same. I have had the experience of going to market with a number of restaurateurs and have observed them making a first round to collect ideas while they kept a close watch that no one else got something they wanted at a lower price. It is a system of trading that is enchanting in its way but is also really difficult.

There is a great range in the quality of particular products that is evident to the most casual passerby. This is true not only of vegetables and fruits but of fish, fowl, game and meat as well. Some growers come into the market with choice produce for only two or three customers, who contract for their entire output. I know of one such grower with about fifty acres of espaliered trees, which produce some of the best pears and apples one might ever see. Yet these never reach the common trading ground. Butter, eggs and cheese, for the most part, are handled by private purveyors or middlemen, who carry varying grades and cater to varying classes of clientele. The greatest restaurateurs and those who search for the exceptional have, of course, their favorite purveyors to whom they are known. But there is nevertheless a great deal of competitive bidding, and it is fascinating to witness the bargaining and the contest for certain items, which reach a high pitch of excitement but take place with a maximum of hearty feeling.

The fish section of Les Halles alone is worth the entire trip, for there is such a selection as to make you eager to rush to the nearest stove and start cooking. You will see: *rouget*, the delicate pink, almost shocking pink, mullet in its varying types, including the extremely well-meated variety from the Mediterranean; the hake or *colin*, a relative of the eel and a fish not eaten much outside France but tremendously good cold with mayonnaise; the John Dory, the ugliest, boniest fish, which when filleted and cooked offers a rare good flavor; salmon of the Loire in season, delicate, rich and not too large; fresh sardines; salmon trout and brook trout; sole and haddock; and *brochet* or pike, which is certainly as much in demand as any fish in France because it is used in the famous quenelles, standard fare in every section of the country. I feel that the average quenelle is a far overrated dish and that if it had not been publicized so much, many people would find it pretty dull. Even at best it is not much without a sensational sauce. I have eaten quenelles from the best chefs and still think they are a lot of needless toil. I would a hundred times rather have a perfect piece of fish well sauced—such as the superb *omble chevalier braisé au porto*, which is one of the specialties of Père Bise in Talloires on the shores of Lake Annecy, where the omble is caught. Quenelles are amusing as a garnish, yes, but no more.

In season one also finds the great shad from the **Loire** and the Gironde. Strangely enough, the French have never made a pleasure of the roe as Americans have. Cooked with a generous amount of butter and served tender and juicy with a touch of parsley, salt and the butter, it is a memorable plate. Roe is a food which we take for granted should be parboiled and broiled or sautéed or creamed—but it can be used in other ways. I once had it prepared by Pierre Franey, one of the greatest chefs in the world, who combined it in a fish forcemeat as a stuffing for shad, which was braised and served with a white wine sauce. This was an imaginative use of shad and its roe to create a fish dish without peer.

Shad Stuffed with Sole Mousse

Preheat the oven to 400°.

Place two fillets of shad (1 whole boned shad), skin side down, on a flat surface. Since the two fillets will eventually be tied together with string, five or six lengths of string may be placed at one inch intervals beneath one of the fillets. Sprinkle both fillets with salt and freshly ground black pepper. Spread the center of each fillet lengthwise with mousse of sole (recipe below). Do not spread it too thickly.

Separate 1 pair shad roe and lay the halves the length of one of the fillets spread with mousse. Sprinkle the roe with salt and pepper. Bring the two shad fillets together sandwich-fashion so that the sole mousse envelops the roe. Tie the stuffed fish with several strings.

Generously butter the bottom of a baking dish and sprinkle it with 2 tablespoons fine-chopped shallots or onion and ½ teaspoon thyme. Add 1 bay leaf and the stuffed shad. Butter the shad. Scatter 2 large mushrooms, sliced thin, around the fish and add 1½ cups dry white wine. Cover the dish with aluminum foil. Bake 45 minutes, lifting the foil and basting occasionally.

Remove the fish to a warm platter and keep it warm. Strain the sauce into a saucepan and reduce it over high heat to half its original volume. Add 2 cups heavy cream and reduce slightly. Blend 1½ tablespoons flour with 1½ tablespoons butter (at room temperature) and add the mixture bit by bit to the simmering sauce, stirring constantly, until the sauce thickens slightly. Remove the strings from the fish and serve it with the hot sauce and buttered potatoes. This yields six to eight servings.

Sole Mousse

Prepare fresh bread crumbs by tearing or cutting 2 slices day-old bread into bits and whirling them in an electric blender. Add ½ pound fillets of sole cut into small cubes, 1 medium-sized fresh mushroom sliced, 2 sliced hard-cooked eggs, 2 tablespoons fine-chopped shallots or onion, ¼ cup chopped parsley, salt and freshly ground black pepper to taste, and ⅓ cup heavy cream. Blend on medium speed. A rubber spatula will facilitate the blending. Use the spatula to stir the ingredients as they blend. Use caution, however, and do not let the spatula come into contact with the blades. The ingredients must be thoroughly blended and smooth. Yield: about 2½ cups.

Eels are found in Les Halles in abundance. Several years ago *Life* had a picture story on how to skin an eel, which was a practical lesson. I trust everyone cut it out and put it in his files. Eel has such a poor reputation that few people ever get around to eating it. Yet how utterly delicious it can be! Grilled over charcoal it is as fine as anything one can grill; and the *matelote* of eel so popular in Alsace is another excellent dish. I have already mentioned the chicken and eel combination from lower Burgundy, and the addition of eel to a bouillabaisse or *bourride* gives both a lift. Smoked eel is a fine appetizer, and jellied eel with a good rémoulade sauce or mayonnaise is a highly satisfying summer lunch dish. And the superb green eels of Belgium!

Matelote of Eel

Prepare a mirepoix by cutting 3 onions, 2 carrots, and 3 stalks celery into very fine julienne strips. Peel 24 small white onions and put them to cook in salted water. Fry 12 small croutons in butter. Skin and clean 2 to 3 pounds of eels and cut them into 3-inch pieces.

Put the mirepoix on the bottom of a saucepan and top with the pieces of eel. Season them with salt, pepper, thyme and tarragon. Pour 1½ cups cider over this and simmer until the eel is tender. Remove it to a hot dish or tureen.

Prepare a béchamel sauce with the broth: reduce the broth to 1 cupful and strain it. Blend 3 tablespoons flour with 3 tablespoons butter and stir the broth into it. Continue stirring until the sauce is thickened. Mix 2 egg yolks and ½ cup heavy cream and stir this into the sauce. Continue cooking and stirring until the sauce is smooth and well blended, but do not let it boil. Add a few leaves of chopped fresh sorrel, if it is available.

Pour the sauce over the pieces of eel and surround it with the small white onions and the fried croutons.

Green Eels

Skin and clean 3 pounds of eels and cut them into 3-inch pieces. Brown them in 6 tablespoons butter, and when they are just colored add ¼ pound chopped sorrel or spinach, ½ cup chopped parsley, ¼ cup chervil, 1 tablespoon fresh or 1 teaspoon dried tarragon, and a pinch each of savory, rosemary, sage and thyme. Mix the herbs well with the pieces of eel, add salt and freshly ground black pepper to taste, and cover with white wine. Cover the pan and poach the eels just until they are tender. Remove the fish to a large earthenware or glass dish.

Stir 4 slightly beaten egg yolks into the broth, and continue stirring and cooking until it is lightly thickened. Be careful not to let the sauce boil. Taste for seasoning, add 1½ tablespoons lemon juice, and pour the sauce over the pieces of eel. Chill the dish and serve it cold.

The lordly turbot, a fish practically unknown
to Americans, although it exists on the West Coast,
comes into its own in Les Halles. Such great and perfect
specimens are on display that one no longer wonders
why chefs designed a special cooker for this fish—a
turbotière, made in the shape of the fish and large
enough to accommodate a specimen of no mean proportions. Sauced with a fine hollandaise, a white wine
sauce, a *beurre noir* with capers, or just served cold with
a good mayonnaise or anchovy sauce, it is truly a king
of fish. Braised with anchovy butter, turbot can be an
entirely unique tasting experience. The anchovy provides the salt and piquance, heightened with the addition of a little lemon, and the butter is the unctuous
blender of flavors.

I cannot begin to list the shellfish one encounters.
From the tiny cockle and periwinkle to the largest
langouste and *homard*, they are here still alive and
exciting. There are the *palourdes* and the *praires*, the
French varieties of clam, both small and extremely
delicate in flavor. I cannot abide raw clams, generally,
and think that cherrystones, Little Necks and other
types of New England clams are better left in the sea
than eaten uncooked. I am, of course, fond of razor
clams, and I have had the *praires* prepared magnificently in and around Nantes. One also sees *langoustines*,
which are related to the *scampi* of the Adriatic—good
with sauces or in a *gratin;* and crawfish, mussels and
shrimp, ranging from the tiniest to the biggest and
varying in color from an autumnal reddish brown
through scarlet to a delicate pink. The little *bouquets
roses*, the pink ones, served in their entirety, are wonderful in taste and an especially good dish for dieters; for
they take a long time to shell and have hardly any
calories!

If you go into this fish market after rush hours when
there is a chance of buying fish for yourself, most likely

you will soon be exchanging recipes with the fish dealer. I used to know a dealer in the great St.-Germain markets who was quite flattered at the thought of catering to an American delighting in her fish. We often discussed the ways one might prepare a fish I had just bought, and I have in my files some of her best recipes. She could truss a *langouste* or a lobster better than anyone I have ever known. This is a service which makes the cooking of these crustaceans a much easier procedure. They are tied quickly and securely so that when they are dropped in a court bouillon there is no crawling and no clattering, and you can face the stove feeling you have been more humane.

In addition to fresh fish, Les Halles carries smoked fish in profusion, for it is in great demand. Smoked trout, sturgeon and eel come in varying degrees of smokiness from neighboring countries. Salmon comes from Scotland, Ireland and the Scandinavian countries, with some German salmon from the Rhine, as well. These all have differing textures and flavors; some are smoked longer than others, and some have a little more cure before they are smoked. I am partial to the Swedish, Scotch and Irish myself, although many of the other types have proved to be exceptionally good. The trouble with so much of the smoked salmon we get in this country is that it has either been chilled too long or was an inferior fish when it was smoked. Sixty per cent has a mushy texture which I find extremely disagreeable to the tongue. And unfortunately, it is seldom possible in America to get salmon cut as it should be—in long slices diagonally against the grain rather than in thickish slices across the grain. To be perfect, the fish must roll from the knife in thin, almost transparent, slices which are delicate but firm.

Smoked trout, sturgeon, eel, roes, and cured fish, such as finnan haddie, are bountiful in the market too, to say nothing of great bales of salt codfish. I imagine the finnan haddie addiction came from England, possibly introduced by French chefs who spent a long time there. At any rate, this fish works beautifully in a soufflé or in finnan haddie Delmonico, which might be called a *gratin*.

Finnan Haddie Soufflé

Poach 1 pound finnan haddie in milk, or in half milk and half water or in a mild court bouillon. Flake it and combine with ¾ cup heavy béchamel sauce. Beat in 4 egg yolks. Season the sauce to taste with salt and freshly ground black pepper and add a few grains of nutmeg. Beat 6 egg whites until stiff and fold them into the mixture. Pour it into a buttered soufflé dish and bake at 375° for 35 to 40 minutes or until the soufflé is well puffed and brown. Serve it with a béchamel sauce.

Béchamel Sauce

Melt 3 tablespoons butter, add 3 tablespoons flour, and cook, stirring, until the butter is slightly colored. Add ½ cup fish broth and stir until it is smooth. Gradually add 1 cup milk and continue stirring until the sauce is nicely thickened. Cook it 5 minutes and season it to taste with salt, pepper and nutmeg.

Finnan Haddie Delmonico

Poach 1 pound finnan haddie in milk, or in half milk and half water, or in a mild court bouillon. Flake it.

Combine 2 cups flaked fish with 1½ cups béchamel sauce, ¼ cup chopped pimiento, ½ cup chopped olives, 3 sliced hard-cooked eggs, and 2 teaspoons onion juice. Arrange mixture in a baking dish, sprinkle it with grated Gruyère cheese, and brown it under the broiler for a few minutes.

The *charcuterie* section of Les Halles is not to be believed. Every province of France is represented by its typical sausages, and there are hams from France, Italy, Spain and Germany as well. (It is strange that no fresh meat may be imported into France, while offal and cured meats may enter freely.) There is a coarse-meated sausage, lightly smoked, from the Jura, called *morteau*, after the name of the town where it is made. It is about eight inches long and is held together with a small wooden skewer. Braised in Beaujolais or the red wines of the district, it is served with a hot potato salad as an entree or a supper dish. I know of few sausages to equal it when it is prepared in this manner. There are the truffled sausages of Lyon, which when served hot are superb with sautéed potatoes or the potatoes named for Lyon. And they are excellent to use as a stuffing for a boned capon. This combination is particularly good cold, when one may slice the bird and find the handsome pattern of sausage and forcemeat. (If you cannot get the *saucisson de Lyon* for this wonderful buffet dish, you can substitute other good French, Italian or German sausage.) There is another sausage from Lyon which is not truffled and which is often served hot or in buttered brioche, and traditionally accompanied by a hot salad.

Naturally we find the *saucisses de Strasbourg* familiar, for they resemble in appearance and taste our frankfurters. Then there are the huge blood sausages, cured and fresh, which when grilled or sautéed in butter and served with mashed potatoes and applesauce are a supremely good dish. Oftentimes this type of sausage is used as a garnish for certain dishes on rounds of puff paste.

The sausages of Toulouse are also represented, and these are used a good deal in cooking, notably in the famous dish of that region, a *cassoulet*. These sausages are also braised with wine and water, with the addition of herbs, shallots and sometimes a bit of tomato, and served as an hors d'oeuvre.

One of the great sausages of France to be seen is *andouillette*, a tripe sausage encased in a tripe lining. Grilled or braised in champagne and served hot with mustard and *pommes frites*, it is a delicious, but by no means light, luncheon dish. The same type of sausage, when more firmly packed in a larger casing and smoked, is called *andouille*. This is sliced thin and served as an hors d'oeuvre.

From Burgundy come some cured sausages used for slicing and for a *charcuterie* plate—*rosette de Fleurie* is one (*rosette Beaujolais* is another name for it). Then there is a *saucisson à l'ail*, which is sliced and has, naturally enough, a heavy garlic content. It is dried like salami and has a pungence only a real lover of the bulb can welcome. I find it thoroughly exciting with good country bread and a light red wine.

Capon Stuffed with Coteghino or Garlic Sausage

Have the butcher bone 1 or 2 capons for you, leaving the leg bones intact. This is such a good dish hot or cold that you might as well do two at a time. For each capon you will need 2 large or 3 medium-sized coteghino sausages or garlic sausages. These you can find at Italian or French shops where they make them in a variety of flavorings. Poach the sausages for about 2 minutes till they are firm enough for you to remove the skins. Stuff the capons with the sausages, arranging them so that the birds take on some semblance of their original shape. Tie the legs, and close the vent with foil or tie it with string and small skewers. Butter the capons well and place them on a rack in a shallow baking pan. Roast at 325°, allowing about 2½ to 3 hours for the roasting time—until the flesh is tender. Baste from time to time with equal parts of white wine and melted butter. Salt and pepper the birds midway in their cooking.

While the capons are cooking, make a broth from the bones and giblets of the birds with an onion stuck with cloves, a sprig of parsley, a bayleaf, a leek, and salt to taste. Add about 1½ quarts water and cook for 2 hours. Remove the cover and cook the broth down rapidly. Strain the broth through a linen towel.

Remove the capons to a hot platter. Skim excess fat from the pan and spoon the pan drippings into a skillet. Add 1½ cups broth to the skillet and let it all cook down to 1 cup. Correct the seasoning, add ½ cup cream and 3 egg yolks and stir the sauce over low heat until it is slightly thickened. Correct the seasoning, add ¼ cup sherry or Madeira and serve the sauce with the capons. Sautéed potatoes and a salad are excellent with it hot, or a large chiffonade salad and sliced tomatoes with basil if it is served cold. With the hot capon serve a St.-Julien of good year, and with the cold I prefer a good Meursault or a Pouilly-Fumé.

Many of the country sausages which reach Les Halles may be sampled raw. Others require cooking. The latter, encased in brioche and baked, offer as good a first course or luncheon or supper dish as one can find. It is customarily served with a hot potato salad, but it is also good with a green salad, a string bean salad or a cole slaw. The preparation of sausage in brioche is not uniformly good in all restaurants. Some chefs, for example, do not remove the casing, which to me indicates carelessness. It is a simple matter to poach the sausage in advance, remove the skin or casing and roll it in the brioche after it has cooled slightly. Sometimes a rich puff paste is substituted for the brioche—a delicious variation, I admit, but the combined richness of crust and sausage is overwhelming.

Of course the sausages constitute only part of the *charcuterie*. There are also the hams, some to be eaten raw and others to be cooked: *jambons de Parme* (from Italy), *de Bayonne, de Westphalie;* many from various mountain sections, and some from Switzerland, Spain (*jamón serrano*) and Belgium (*jambon d'Ardennes*). These hams vary in their cure and smokiness and are well worth sampling.

As a matter of fact I have done a ham tasting with friends in Paris several times. We purchased as many types as we could find and arranged them as for any other tasting. With bread and champagne, which is the perfect wine for ham, we sat down to a luncheon which was rewarding for several reasons: We did not eat too much of any one ham—we truly tasted; we took our time (there were five of us), discussing and comparing each ham; we did not eat them with *cornichons* or mustard but sought out the hams' pure flavors, which were markedly varied.

Cornichons, the gherkins that are served with all sorts of *charcuterie* in France, are for the most part one of the big mistakes the French make in eating. So acrid, usually, and so lacking in flavor, they destroy the palate for accompanying food and wine. Occasionally one finds *cornichons*, homemade evidently, which are not so poisonously sour, but this is rare.

Those of you who enjoy a good ham without full flavor will enjoy the blandness of the *jambon de Paris*. You will also enjoy the *jambonneau*, which is a prepared ham, presented in a conical form with a bone stuck right in the center. Delicious and mild it is and a perfect picnic ham for a lunch by the side of the road.

One can find such ham specialities in the markets as the superbly flavored *jambon persillé* of Burgundy, but it is often enough the restaurateur who prepares his own special hams and gives them an added touch of glamour. La Bourgogne in Paris makes a sensationally beautiful dish that begins with ham placed in a large bowl lined with parsley and jelly. The small cuts of boiled ham are put in with much more chopped parsley and seasoning and additional jelly. This is next pressed cold and finally turned out on a platter to be sliced extremely thin. It is like a mosaic.

Head cheeses of various types turn up with the seasons. One is made from wild boar; others are made from pork. Some are put into a huge casing and resemble a rather modern mosaic when they are cut in great slices. Others are made in small molds about the size of a bread tin and are suitable for the ordinary household.

Still others are prepared in great bowls, like the Bourgogne ham, to be pressed and unmolded. A particularly favorite restaurant of mine, L'Alliance in Paris, offers its superb head cheese with a vinaigrette sauce, along with sliced onions marinated in a very herbed and oily French dressing and thin-sliced *cornichons*—a most enticing dish.

In addition to these *charcuterie* items one finds such famous dishes as the *rillettes de Tours*. There are many *rillettes* available in France, but those that hail from Tours are indisputably the greatest in flavor and texture. If you make your *rillettes* with loving care, you can give them to special friends as Christmas gifts. The secret of a perfect *rillette* is good leaf lard and good lean pork. I find that the neck and loin offer some of the best meat.

Rillettes

Try out 5 pounds leaf lard, which has been cut into small pieces, in a heavy kettle; and when it is melted, add 5 pounds pork loin cut into small pieces and 1 cup water. Cook, covered, over a low flame or in a 250° oven for 3 to 4 hours or until the pork is cooked very soft. Drain it. Remove the meat to a large bowl or plate; and when it has cooled somewhat, break it into small shreds with 2 forks. Fill small pots or glasses with the meat. Now add a ladle of the lard, which will form a cover over the *rillettes* and help to preserve them for several months. This dish is simple to make and make well, but care must be taken not to let the lard soak into the pork or it will be disagreeable to the tongue.

There are also *rillettes d'oie*, made from goose and cooked long in goose fat, the fat being an utterly delicious by-product of *foie gras*. Then there are *rillons*, which resemble a Mexican specialty, pork *carnitas*. These are pieces of fresh pork cooked long in their own fat till they are thoroughly crisped and dried. In the case of *rillons*, fresh siding is used, and in *carnitas*, usually the loin or shoulder. Both have a particularly delicious pork flavor, due to its fat, which, after all, is what gives the meat its great distinction.

It might be interesting for you to visit a butcher in or around Les Halles who thoroughly knows the meat cuts of France. Learning how meat is cut in other countries can change one's idea of meat cookery sometimes, and it can be valuable to understand the differences between their cuts and our own.

Beef in France is sold almost exclusively with the bones removed. The *côte*, which we know as the ribs, is sometimes sold in thick steaks for two with the bone in. These are meant to be broiled and are considered the best cut of beef aside from the filet. The sirloin, as we know it, is boned and cut in *entrecôte* or *faux filet* for broiling and is often used for roasting. The filet is served in many ways as it is in America. The rump steak is cut from what we call the hip or the rump and is one of the more popular cuts. The plate, or *plat côte*, is used for *pot-au-feu* a great deal, and what we call chuck and the leg are both used for the famous *daubes* and for *boeuf à la bourguignonne*. The quality of French beef differs from our own, as I explained before, and therefore these poorer cuts are cooked much longer than is customary for braised dishes in this country. One should be careful in following French recipes to see that the meat is not overdone—a frequent fault with many cooks anyway. Meat should retain its texture and flavor when it is cooked and should not become stringy and tasteless.

Boeuf en Daube

Choose a piece of rump of beef, about 5 pounds, and have it tied securely. Ask the butcher to split 2 pig's feet or calf's feet for you. If possible purchase a little fresh pork skin, which gives great body to the sauce.

Place the beef in a deep casserole or *braisière*. Add

the pork skin and the feet, 3 cloves garlic crushed, 12 small white onions, 4 carrots, 1 or 2 sprigs of parsley, 2 teaspoons salt, 1 teaspoon freshly ground black pepper. Pour ½ cup hot oil over the meat and place it in a 450° oven uncovered for 25 minutes or until browned. Remove from the oven and reduce heat to 300°.

Add ½ cup cognac, 1½ cups good red wine and a touch of thyme. Cover the casserole and place it in the oven to cook for about 4 hours, or until the meat is perfectly tender and soft. Correct the seasoning and serve this delicious dish with its own sauce and plenty of good boiled potatoes, and perhaps a salad afterwards and some good cheese. Drink an excellent Burgundy with it—a Chambertin or a Vosne Romanée.

This dish is to me doubly good when cold and served with a potato salad, perhaps, and plenty of crusty bread. It has wonderful flavor and texture.

Some of the greatest French chefs use the shin of beef, a cut we usually discard, for some of their succulent stews and ragouts, and others use the round of beef. The cheeks or jowls of beef are used frequently in a cold salad for hors d'oeuvre after being cooked in a court bouillon and then sliced thin as paper. The dish, known as *salade de museau*, is very pleasant in texture to the tongue and, in my opinion, is best made in France. One can buy the German version of it in New York and Chicago, called *Ochsenmaulsalat*, but it is overvinegared usually. You might take this domestic version and try balancing out the vinegar with oil and flavorings.

Even oxtails are sometimes boned in France, a procedure no American butcher is prepared to undertake, and the tails are then stuffed and braised to make a most delectable dish. I once published a recipe for this specialty and had frantic letters from *cordons bleus* who were turned down by butchers in all parts of the country. I want to state once more for historic fact that oxtails can be boned and have been boned for a long time. I do not advise you to try it yourself unless you are especially deft with a knife.

Some cuts of beef are tied and barded with thin pieces of fat. If you find the old-fashioned type of butcher, he may shape the barding into flowers and leaves, which are decorative as well as lubricating. Sets of cutters are made especially for this purpose, just as there are cutters for truffles, vegetables and such.

Marrow bones, another item neglected in this country, are greatly prized in France and are served with *pot-au-feu*. They are frequently covered with cheese-cloth to prevent the marrow from slipping out into the broth. (One can achieve the same end with a strip of foil twisted around the bones, large enough to hold the marrow but not to envelop the bone completely.) Often thin cuts of marrow bone are served atop a steak as a garnish, first being heated through in herbed butter. Marrow is also served this way on fried toast as an alternate to poached marrow. To make the eating of marrow easier at the table, marrow spoons with long bowls are available, designed especially for scraping.

Tripe and *gras-double*, which is the heavy tripe, can be bought in separate markets in France and are usually sold cooked and ready for seasoning and serving. There are so many different ways to prepare this delicious bit of beef that it could make a cookbook in itself.

Tripe Genoise

Have 1 calf's foot split by the butcher. Combine it with 3 pounds honeycomb tripe cut into 2- to 4-inch pieces, 2 teaspoons salt, a grinding of pepper from the mill and enough white wine or broth to cover. Bring it to a boil and cover the casserole or *braisière* and place it in a 350° oven for 1 hour. Reduce the heat to 300° for the next hour and to 250° for the third.

During the last hour's cooking sauté 3 medium-

sized onions, chopped fine, in 4 tablespoons olive
oil. Add 1½ cups tomato purée or 1½ pounds ripe
tomatoes, peeled, seeded and chopped, 1½ teaspoons
basil, a touch of rosemary, salt to taste and 1 teaspoon
freshly ground black pepper. Simmer the sauce for
45 minutes to 1 hour, then increase the heat and cook
it down for 10 minutes. Add this to the tripe at the
end of 3 hours and let it cook for 45 minutes. Add
½ cup chopped parsley and serve the tripe with
ample quantities of freshly grated Parmesan cheese.

The feet of the steer are a fine addition to soup, and
the heavy, rather gelatinous skin and meat surrounding
the bone are good when jellied and made into a somewhat highly seasoned bit for hors d'oeuvre or sandwiches. This is called brawn or potted meat. If you are
as much a devotee of the gelatinous parts of the animal
as I am, this dish is something you will welcome.

Beef heart and kidneys are prepared very much as we
do them.

If you want to try a particularly delicious recipe,
order a boneless sirloin and have it tied well with very
little fat and no barding. This is the cut for a famous
dish—*boeuf à la ficelle.*

Boeuf à la Ficelle

You may use a whole filet or individual filet steaks or a
fine piece of sirloin. The beef should be tied securely
and, as indicated by the name, there must be a long
string attached to the meat for lifting it from the pot
in which it cooks. There must be some type of hanger
above the stove as well, for the piece of beef must be
suspended by the string in a large container of broth
to cook to the degree of rareness you prefer.

First make a strong rich broth with bones, meat,
vegetables and good seasoning. Lower the beef into
this and cook it at high heat for a few minutes, then
simmer it until it is delightfully rare on the inside and
just colored by the broth on the outside. The cooking
time is the same as for roasting a filet: about 25 min-

utes for a good-sized whole filet and about 8 to 10 minutes for individual ones.

Serve this deliciously different dish with coarse salt, boiled potatoes, with or without some of the broth, and mustard or horseradish if you wish. Served with mustard sauce, anchovy butter or béarnaise, it is a splendid treat and one that confounds all people who claim they dislike boiled beef. Try with it a good Châteauneuf du Pape or an Hermitage.

The veal found in French markets is another whole subject for study. Whereas in both France and Italy veal is one of the most delicious of meats, it remains for the most part an indifferent meat in America. The difference lies in the feeding and in the age of the animal when it is slaughtered. Milk-fed veal is taken for granted in Europe. And young veal is more easily purchased than older veal, which prevails in most of our markets. Fine European veal is delicately gray-pink, almost white at times, and the fat is white and flaky, while ours is rosy, similar to young beef, and it loses some of its tenderness in maturing. It seems strange, with all the veal available in this country, that a proportion of fine-quality veal cannot be produced. There is certainly a market for it. This is just another of the unfathomable practices of the meat industry in the United States, which produces the finest beef and the worst hams, veal and lamb in the world.

Veal also is cut differently in Europe than it is here, and if you are prepared to spend a little time with your own butcher, you might be able to secure some of these same cuts.

The shoulder is cut the same, frequently boned, rolled and tied for roasting, or boned for other purposes. The *longe*, or loin end of the saddle, is the choicest part of the veal for roasting. This, too, is boned, rolled and tied, after the kidney fat is removed. It is extremely good served cold. If, on the other hand, you want a *rognon-*

nade of veal, considered to be the choicest of all cuts, you have the saddle boned and the kidneys placed back inside before the roast is rolled and tied. In serving, the kidney is sliced along with the meat. The surrounding wall of veal acts as insulation, and the kidney is usually cooked just to the perfect point. This combination makes an excellent dish for a dinner party or buffet. Veal, cold or hot, should not be cooked till it crumbles. There is a point in cooking where it becomes juicy, firm and done.

There is a famous recipe for saddle of veal Prince Orloff (in this country the cut is called a double loin), attributed to Escoffier, in which diagonal slices are cut from the cooked loin, spread with *duxelles* and then replaced. The whole is covered with a soubise sauce, and put back in the oven to glaze. Thus one can remove his portion easily and have the sauce at the same time.

One of the most delicious parts of the veal, which is particularly delicious when the veal is white, is the breast. Stuffed with a forcemeat and served hot, it is excellent. Stuffed carefully in an elaborate pattern, covered with a *chaud-froid* sauce, decorated and glazed with aspic, and served cold, it is sensational. And it makes an incredibly stunning picture. Stuffed breast of veal was a dish my mother loved to prepare for summer eating. It is a dish which I have seen on elegantly arranged buffet tables in France, and which I often enjoy making for my own guests.

Stuffed Breast of Veal

Have the butcher cut a pocket in a breast of veal. Prepare stuffing with 1 large onion chopped or 12 green onions cut fine and sautéed in 6 tablespoons butter. Add to this 1 pound ground pork and 1 pound ground ham. Cook the mixture, breaking up the meat and mixing well. Add 1 tablespoon fresh basil or 1 teaspoon dried basil, a touch of thyme, 1½ cups crumbs, ½ cup chopped parsley, 2 eggs, and salt and pepper to taste. Stuff the breast and secure the opening. Brush the breast with butter or oil. Brown the meat quickly in hot oil or fat, searing each side well. Place it in a deep baking dish. Add 1 cup hot broth, 1 cup white wine and 1½ teaspoons dried tarragon or 1½ tablespoons fresh tarragon cut in small bits. Cover dish and bake at 325° for 2½ to 2¾ hours. Allow it to rest for 10 minutes. Combine the pan juices with 2 tablespoons tomato paste and cook this down briskly. Add 1 cup green olives to the sauce and correct the seasoning. Serve veal with buttered noodles and drink a Cassis wine or a Muscadet.

This dish is also delicious served cold.

The breast meat, if it is good, makes a marvelous *blanquette*. A *blanquette* is really a white stew or fricassee, but it can be a watery mess when not prepared with care. Sometimes the meat and onion are slightly browned, which in my opinion yields a richer, more definite flavor. Usually it is poached, and frequently too long, so that the veal becomes stringy and tastes like boiled veal and nothing else. The sauce should be made with onion, carrot and lemon, together with bouillon, cream and egg yolks. The dish is garnished with mushrooms and tiny white onions. There is another version of *blanquette* made with the shoulder of veal, which is thoroughly good as well and perhaps a bit more suitable for dinner parties, for when you use the breast there are lovely little bones to pick, a pleasure you may want to reserve for the privacy of the family dinner table.

Another rewarding dish is a slowly broiled marinated breast of veal, which can be done on a charcoal grill. The meat never becomes completely tender but has a wonderful chewy quality and a savory crust; and as I do it, there is a surprise center, for I stuff it with herbs, butter and a bit of ham.

Many people are puzzled by the fact that cutlets and scallops of veal are really the same cut of meat. Both are from the leg and should be quite thin for most dishes. In fact it is very often necessary to pound them out still thinner than the butcher has cut them. When this is done, be certain that any fibrous tissue on the outside of each piece is removed. Otherwise the meat will curl in cooking. The butchers in France always remove the tissue before pounding veal, while here it is seldom done.

Among the veal at Les Halles, one will see the *côtes de veau* proudly displayed. These are the rib chops, delicately white, and excellent for braising and sautéing—and for broiling, if you broil slowly and do not toughen the meat.

The leg, as well as being the source of *escalopes* or *scallopini*, can also produce a *paillard*, which is a large, very thin scallop, broiled quickly and served *au nature*, usually. This is admirable low-calorie fare with a touch of herb added or a bit of shallot or garlic. It is served in many French restaurants, and it will be prepared for you upon request in certain New York restaurants, such as the Italian Pavilion or the Four Seasons.

The leg of veal offers a good roast, too, especially when pleasantly seasoned. Tarragon and basil are both friendly to veal—take your choice. Garlic and anchovy complement veal perfectly also. And, of course, there is the classic tuna-veal combination, *vitello tonnato*—oftentimes disappointing but sometimes perfection. There is a version of *vitello tonnato* prepared with salmon instead of tuna, and delicious it is, too. And there is a recipe for veal in which it is cured and cooked so that it takes on an inky hue. This is called *veau saumoné*.

Veal with Salmon Sauce

This is a very refreshing dish when served in summer.

Choose a 3½-pound piece of boneless veal rump with a veal knuckle bone to go with it. Place these in a heavy casserole with 3 garlic cloves, 1 large onion sliced, 2 slices lemon, 12 anchovy fillets, 1 carrot, 1 teaspoon basil, a sprig or two of parsley, 1 teaspoon freshly ground black pepper and 1½ cups white wine. Pour over the meat ½ cup olive oil and bake, covered, in a 350° oven for about 1½ to 1¾ hours or until the veal is tender.

Remove the casserole from the oven and cool it overnight. Remove the veal from the casserole and chill it. Strain the juices and let them chill.

To serve, slice the veal extremely thin and arrange the slices on a serving dish. Remove all skin and bones from 1 can top-quality salmon, and combine salmon with the jellied juices from the veal. Whirl them in a blender or put them through a food mill. Or combine the salmon with 1 cup mayonnaise and beat well. Beat in some of the jelly from the veal, pour the sauce over the cold meat, and decorate it with capers and chopped parsley.

If you wish more salmon flavor, you may double the amount of fish and combine it with mayonnaise and lemon juice and a bit of onion juice. Beat the sauce well.

The offal of veal and the extremities are surely among the most desirable parts. The feet make a refreshing change of fare when poached and served with a poulette sauce, or when served just cooled with a rémoulade sauce, or when jellied and boned and served with a vinaigrette or a *gribiche*. Naturally the feet, when added to many other dishes, give them a rich gelatinous thickness of sauce, which is remarkably smooth to the tongue and stimulating to the palate. A rich broth of veal, called *fonds de veau*, makes a great addition to many dishes, sautéed, braised or sauced.

The head is versatile and classic in French cuisine. It is usually found boned and tied at Les Halles, ready for cooking. Sometimes you will see a long array of the heads sitting on a counter, all staring at you, of a spotless white from blanching and scrubbing, and standing out from everything else like a series of marble busts. I have heard of some chefs who present the cooked head whole and proceed to carve it for you at table. I have never seen this done myself and consider it a rather macabre performance. My most frequent objection—and I have the concurrence of several chefs and my old butcher in Paris—is that most cooks serve too acid a vinaigrette or *gribiche* with a *tête de veau*. It should be herby, capery and unctuous without being dominated by vinegar. This plate can also be served with a poulette sauce or *en tortue* and is often preferred that way. Traditionally, the meat and tongue are served first and the more delicate brains second, cooked separately. Boiled potatoes, and in some parts of the country hard-cooked eggs, are served with *tête de veau*.

The good butchers in Les Halles save kidneys for their best customers. The number of restaurants where a veal kidney dish is the specialty is endless. The kidneys are prepared whole, sliced, diced and split in a variety of ways, with and without sauces, and with great tableside performances at the chafing dish. (Many restaurants throughout the world pride themselves on their tableside cooks—among them, Boule d'Or, Relais Bisson, La Bourgogne and Lapérouse in Paris, various well-known *auberges* in the provinces, and the Forum, the Four Seasons and Quo Vadis in New York.) My close friend Philip Brown, who travels a good deal through Europe, has a theory that if a restaurant prepares kidneys well, it is probably a first-class restaurant, and his first order in a new place is therefore usually a kidney dish. He has probably eaten more kidneys while traveling than any other living person. And he has uncovered some gems of restaurants along the way.

Naturally the liver and heart of the calf both figure importantly in good cooking. The French butcher will not advise you to do much with liver beyond cooking it *à l'anglaise*, which is sautéing it quickly and serving it with a little bacon; or he might tell you to sauté it—in thin slices, *please*—with shallot and parsley or just a touch of shallot and tarragon. Or he might also

tell you the pan should be *déglacé* with a little Madeira
or cognac, but that is all one does with liver. The idea of
the liver steak, a thick piece of liver broiled over coals
and served with béarnaise, is entirely an American
conception. In France, liver is sometimes served with
raisins soaked in Madeira or cognac and added to the
cooking pan to make a sauce, but this is seldom encountered and is another of those strange sweet-sour combinations that occasionally appear in French cuisine and
remind us of the Orient.

Finally, we have *les ris de veau*—the sweetbreads.
They are used in many fashions, from the superb hot
pâté at Père Bise to the larded and piqued sweetbread
served at La Coupole in Montparnasse. A favorite restaurant of mine in Paris serves them with a sauce so
delicate and so well textured that it is like a delicious
foam in your mouth. It is made with the court bouillon
in which the sweetbreads are cooked, lemon, egg and
cream; and once you have had sweetbreads with this
sauce, you will have experienced the supreme approach
to this delicacy. The restaurant is L'Alliance.

We move along in Les Halles to the specialists in
lamb and mutton, and what is called mutton in France
corresponds to most of the lamb we get in the United
States. French lamb *pré-salé* is much younger and more
delicate (and *pré-salé* does not mean presalted; it means
"salt marsh," and *pré-salé* lamb is fed on the marsh
grass in the north or southwest of France). As you
wander through Les Halles, you will see a great variety
of meat from sheep, and if you're a good judge, you can
see differences in quality from shop to shop. You can
almost guess which lamb will go to which restaurants.

One of the lamb dishes difficult—almost impos-
sible—to find in the United States is the feet, or what the
English love to eat as "sheep's trotters." At Prunier's in
Paris, where fish is supposed to be the specialty, one

finds delicious *pieds de mouton poulette*, and at L'Espa-
don of the Ritz they still make them occasionally, and
superbly, a holdover from the Ritz Grill days. In a small
bistro near the Opéra Comique, À la Lyonnaise, they
make an hors d'oeuvre specialty of *pieds de mouton*
with a rémoulade. The feet are served warm and the
sauce at room temperature, and the spiciness of the
sauce with the gelatinous texture of the feet is a marriage which I find superlative. You might as well treat
yourself to these when you can find them, or get your
butcher to bootleg a few for you. If all else fails, substitute calf's feet, which are not as delicate but are as close
as you can come, and try to get them small, although
this is usually an impossibility!

Calf's Feet Rémoulade or Sheep's Trotters Rémoulade

Sheep's trotters are practically impossible to get in
this country. So substitute calf's feet if you are lucky
enough to know where you can get small ones! Wrap
the feet in cheesecloth and place them to cook in
enough cold water to cover. Add 1 onion stuck with
cloves, 2 or 3 carrots, 1 bay leaf, a sprig of parsley,
1 or 2 leeks and about 1 tablespoon salt. Cook the
feet for about 3 hours. Bring them to a boil and then
reduce heat and simmer them covered for 2½ to
3 hours or until they are tender.

Serve these delicious morsels with a good rémoulade
sauce and boiled potatoes. A good eater can eat three
sheep's trotters, at least, and at least one calf's foot.
If the calf's feet are small, two is a better choice.

Sheep's heads are arranged in some of the stalls, but
they are not as common in Les Halles as they are in the
markets of Mediterranean cities. And they do not have
the lovely gelatinous quality of calf's head, nor the
meatiness, but they are fancied roasted or grilled by the
Balkan and Near Eastern peoples—mostly a task of
picking bones and getting very little to eat.

The tongues of lamb, however, are delicate and tender and a great dish hot or cold. They are often pickled, but here again the vinegar content is usually so violent that there is no flavor save that of the vinegar. If, on the other hand, you prepare the tongues yourself and put them in a well-herbed vinaigrette sauce, you have a delicious plate for summer and one that is unusual enough to delight guests. The tongues are especially good done with a curry sauce or with a Provençal sauce redolent of garlic, olives, a bit of tomato and basil or fennel.

Lamb's liver is a delicacy that most people don't know, and yet it is a most tender and at times wonderfully flavored morsel. It can be roasted whole with bacon, or in a cocotte with butter and a little salt pork, with cream and seasonings added to the sauce afterwards. Like calf's liver, it should not be overcooked, for when it is rare, the texture is succulent. When it passes a certain point of doneness, like calf's liver again, it becomes dull, grainy, and disagreeable. I have already described my aversion for chicken livers. It took me years to be able to eat calf's liver because I once tasted it away from home where it was cooked poorly. The spell was finally broken when a friend served me some perfectly sautéed calf's liver with shallots, parsley and butter. It was pink-rare and incredibly good in flavor. I realized what I had missed all the years before.

Lamb's kidneys are fine if they are soaked in milk, red wine or acidulated water for some time before cooking. For some reason lamb kidneys have a more distinct odor than veal—that is, unless they come from young lambs. Recently we ate a saddle of young lamb at Père Bise in the Savoie, and it was decorated with tiny slices of kidney set in fat in a pattern around the saddle. The kidneys had been put in place for the last few minutes of cooking, for they were tender and fresh-tasting and made a delightful contrast to the subtly flavored saddle. I hope I can get you into the habit of a good saddle of lamb now and again for your own cookery, because I feel it is more delicate than the leg, cuts to great advantage and looks tempting when it arrives at table. For cooks who like to do lamb on a spit, it is a good cut also—probably better than the boned leg.

Beautiful racks of lamb are found in Les Halles, and you can have them from your butcher once you have him trained. A rack for two, three or even four persons, roasted with parsley, butter and a whiff of garlic, if you like, can be pretty ambrosial. It should be roasted until crusty on the outside but rare inside.

Many people have asked why a leg of lamb in a puff paste crust does not taste as good in the United States as it does in Les Baux or in one or two other places where it is a specialty. It is simply because a tiny leg of lamb is used in Les Baux, cooked a bit before it goes into the crust and then finished off in the crust. A greatly over-rated dish, in my opinion, too. I much prefer to have a crisp outer quality to the lamb and a pink interior. On the other hand, I know of a leg of lamb roasted with tarragon, basted with cream and served with a creamy tarragon sauce, which is extraordinarily different. The cream and tarragon combine to make a crust on the meat and a most pleasing flavor.

Leg of Lamb with Tarragon and Cream

A young leg of not over 5 pounds, or a leg of baby lamb about 3 to 4 pounds, is ideal for this delicious dish. Skin the leg and remove as much of the fat as possible. Rub the meat with butter and tarragon and sprinkle it with coarse salt. Fresh tarragon is preferable, but a good dehydrated tarragon is acceptable. You will need a lot—I use 1 tablespoon or so of the dried or several sprigs of the fresh. Rub it in well all over the roast.

Roast the leg on a rack or a spit at 325° for about 1½ to 1¾ hours or until the internal temperature when tested with a thermometer registers about 140°. For the last hour brush the leg with heavy cream several times.

Remove the roast to a hot platter to stand before carving and skim the excess fat from the pan. Pour into the pan 1 cup heavy cream, stir, and add salt and pepper to taste. Bring the sauce to a boil and reduce it over a brisk flame very quickly.

Serve the sauce with the lamb and perhaps some potatoes Anna as a pleasant accompaniment.

Have your leg of lamb boned or not, as you wish, but to my mind, if a roast leg with the bone in is carved by someone who understands anatomy, the performance is more spectacular and satisfying than that of a host who slices a boned leg with no challenge whatsoever. As to garlic, I think it depends upon your taste. With young lamb, all one needs is a touch, whereas with maturer lamb a really heavy dosage results in a surprisingly delicate flavor; garlic used in large quantities as an ingredient is remarkably delicate when cooked. Elizabeth David suggests roasting a young leg of lamb studded with garlic and anchovies, and this proves to be an exceptional change in flavor. The same is true of an older leg that is marinated for several days in red wine, oil and herbs and then cooked quickly and served with a sauce of the marinade. The result is strangely like game and certainly different from the average roasted lamb.

I mentioned earlier that my mother preferred a good shoulder of lamb to the leg. And Let produced a boned shoulder which was extremely good, rubbed with soy and garlic and roasted well, basted during the cooking with soy and oil. The shoulder is also a good cut for braising with the ingredients one uses for *ratatouille*. The lamb should be served somewhat pink, and the *ratatouille* with a lamb flavor is excellent. There are endless ways to braise lamb—with olives, with petits pois, with turnips, with a wealth of things. This is a cooking method that Mother and Let brought me up on, and I suggest you try it if you have never done so.

Braised Shoulder of Lamb, Provençal

Have the butcher bone and roll a shoulder of young lamb for you. Make several incisions in the lamb and insert slivers of garlic and an anchovy fillet in each incision. Rub the roast with salt and a little rosemary.

Brown the lamb on all sides in 6 tablespoons olive oil over a brisk flame. Reduce the heat and add 2 good-sized onions sliced, 1½ cups eggplant cut into small dice, 1 green pepper cut in strips, 1 or 2 cloves garlic, and 4 peeled seeded ripe tomatoes or 1 cup tomato purée. Cover the dish and simmer it over low heat or place it in a 325° oven for 1 hour. Remove the cover and add 1 cup thin-sliced zucchini, ½ cup black olives, and ½ cup chopped parsley. Taste and correct the seasoning. Return to the oven or to the burner for another 30 minutes or until the lamb is tender and the vegetables have combined into a rich blend. Serve the lamb on a hot platter surrounded by the vegetable mixture. Rice seems to be indicated with this pleasant dish.

The breast of lamb we get in this country, unless it is in the spring when the young lamb comes in, is usually so fatty it is unpleasant to eat. Sometimes I find breast of lamb when it is surprisingly lean and amazingly cheap. As a matter of fact, in New York I have found it as cheap as fifteen cents a pound! There are so many delicious dishes to make with the breast, I wish Paris could come to New York. For in Les Halles you find delicate pieces of breast with plenty of lean and some fat, just right for a *navarin* or for a *blanquette* of lamb (which is every bit as good as a *blanquette de veau*) or for grilling or for boning, stuffing and rolling. This is a cut of meat all but forgotten with us, but it sometimes appears in our markets under the precious name of lamb riblets.

Blanquette of Lamb

Have your butcher cut a leg of lamb into small pieces about 2 by 3 inches for you. You will need about 3 pounds of meat, all told, without fat. Peel about 12 small white onions and trim about the same number of mushroom caps of a uniform size.

Salt and pepper the lamb and sauté it in 6 tablespoons butter till delicately browned on all sides. Reduce the heat and simmer it, turning the pieces occasionally, for about 18 minutes.

Sauté the onions in 3 tablespoons butter and dust them with a little sugar to give them a light glaze. Add a touch of salt and the mushrooms. Add this to the lamb with ½ cup Madeira. Cover the skillet and simmer for 10 minutes. Add to this 1 cup velouté sauce, made by preparing a *roux* with 3 tablespoons flour and 2 tablespoons butter. Gradually stir in ½ cup lamb or beef broth and cook the sauce until it is thick. Add to this 1 cup heavy cream and stir until the sauce is nicely thickened and smooth. Stir the sauce into the meat mixture and correct the seasoning. Add another ½ cup heavy cream, cover the skillet, and simmer for about 30 minutes, either on top of the stove or in a 325° oven. Serve the lamb with croutons of fried toast and a garnish of additional mushroom caps, lightly sautéed in butter, and chopped parsley.

I like loin lamb chops, and I also like what the French do with them. They bone the saddle and cut the boned meat into chops or noisettes for grilling, skewering and a variety of sautéed dishes. These chops are delicious charcoal-broiled, and they are excellent sautéed with a *niçoise* sauce, tarragon butter, or an anchovy butter and shallots. The tiny chops—those we call "rib" or "French" chops—are much daintier in Les Halles than in our local supermarkets, and they taste better. However, since we must make do with what we have, trim these little chops well and cook them carefully. Don't let them get well-done or you'll regret it. Served with a kidney, a bit of bacon and a broiled tomato, they make a beautiful plate.

The pig is king in Les Halles! I am sure that the French, what with their *charcuterie* and their fondness for pork, must be the greatest per capita consumers of that animal in the world. And there is a use for every bit of it from head to tail. The head, of course, goes into head cheese, and there are also some recipes in French cookery for using the head in ragouts. The tails are cured and served along with a great deal of other cured pork and sausages as *cochonailles*. These are also braised, and they are crumbed and broiled in the same manner as a pig's foot and served with mustard, *pommes frites* and watercress. In addition to being broiled, the feet are truffled, and sometimes they are braised with Madeira, a favorite European style for ham, too. The ears are used in a variety of ways and are considered delectable by those of the gelatinous school of eating. I like them, naturally, but many people I know shun ears completely.

The loin is the best part for roasting and is prepared in a number of ways. In the French shops it is often boned for you, with the tenderloin wither either tied into the roast or kept separate. In our markets we used to use much more pork tenderloin than we do nowadays. It is such a delicious part of the animal, I find it a pity that it isn't more generally available. Some cities carry it, others don't. I always find pork tenderloins in Chicago, for example, and often on the West Coast, but in New York it is a treasure almost impossible to locate.

In some parts of France a good deal of the pork loin is smoked, especially in Alsace and in the Savoie. This is used in many different dishes, such as *choucroute garnie*, and with beans and other vegetables in a braised dish. Also, much pork is pickled for use in *potée* and other dishes, together with fresh vegetables, lentils and beans. This sort of dish is heavy peasant fare. It is usually a regional specialty, containing whatever vegetables happen to be available. Smoked and pickled pork is used during the winter when fresh meat is less available.

Fresh ham is not roasted in France as much as it is here, but if it is, the skin is scored and roasted with it, and there is great delight in eating the wonderful crackling. The same is true sometimes with the loin: it may be roasted with the skin on and is most choice that way, especially if it is lightly rubbed with garlic and either thyme or basil.

One extraordinary puzzle to me is why some people refuse to eat pork in summer. There are few things as delicious as cold loin of pork with a salad. It is light and extremely pleasant summer fare; so is a hot roast loin, served with an herb sauce or a tomato sauce. I wouldn't want hot roast pork on the warmest days, but the same roast served cold is certainly exquisitely suitable for any day in the summer.

Shoulder of pork and the other cuts are used for braised dishes, pickled pork and some smoked dishes, and of course, they also go into sausages and other items which abound in the *charcuterie* sections. Pork offal, except for use in *pâtés* and other such delicacies, I find unpleasantly strong and overfat, which is precisely why it is good in *charcuterie*.

Now let me here offer a few good recipes for pork which you may not have used, for I would enjoy promoting the use of this meat by making people aware of its great versatility and its delicacy of flavor when properly cooked. One reason for the bias against pork, probably, is that we have had all too many horrible, greasy breaded pork chops with tomato sauce on them, and too many other poorly prepared pork chops, neither tender, flavorsome nor good for the stomach.

A Drunken Roast of Pork

Use 1 fresh ham, weighing 6 to 8 pounds, boned and tied. Place it in a marinade composed of 1 fifth red wine, 2 to 3 crushed garlic cloves, 1 thin-sliced onion, 1 bay leaf, ⅛ teaspoon ground cloves, ¼ teaspoon ground ginger, ¼ teaspoon nutmeg, 1 tablespoon salt, and 1 teaspoon crushed rosemary.

Turn it once, and let it stand, covered, for 3 to 4 days in the refrigerator, turning it every day. The day you roast it, remove it from the refrigerator and let it stand at room temperature for several hours, turning two or three times. Place it in a shallow roasting pan and roast at 325°, allowing 25 to 30 minutes per pound. Baste it frequently with the strained, heated marinade. Remove the pork when it is cooked, and keep it hot. Skim the marinade and if it has cooked down too much, add a little more red wine. Bring it to a boil; and if you would like a slightly thickened sauce, add small balls of *beurre manié* (flour and butter kneaded together), and stir the sauce until it has the proper thickness. Correct the seasoning, and add ½ cup each of sultana raisins and pine nuts and a good dash of Tabasco. Serve the pork with saffron rice.

Roast Pork Loin

Use a loin of pork weighing 5 to 7 pounds. Chop very fine 3 cloves garlic and ½ cup parsley. Blend this with 1 tablespoon olive oil, 1 teaspoon thyme, 1 teaspoon salt and ½ teaspoon freshly ground black pepper. Add more oil if necessary to make a thickish paste. With a sharp knife, slash small incisions in the pork loin, and insert some of the mixture. Rub remaining bits on the outside of the roast. Place the pork on a rack in a shallow pan and roast at 325°, allowing 25 to 28 minutes per pound. Remove the pork, when done, to a hot dish. Pour off all but 2 tablespoons of the fat in the pan. Add to the pan 1 onion and 1 garlic clove, both chopped fine, and sauté gently for 2 or 3 minutes. Add 1 cup tomato sauce made from 8 to 9 fresh tomatoes, peeled, seeded and chopped and sautéed in butter until well blended and thick, or 1½ cups canned Italian-style tomatoes which you have cooked down in butter for 25 to 30 minutes and forced through a food mill or sieve. Blend the sauce with the pan juices, bring to a boil, and allow it to cook down, stirring until well blended. Correct the seasoning and serve the sauce with the pork.

Serve the roast with polenta or fresh hominy.

Pork Chops Normande

Trim 6 thick loin pork chops of any excess fat, dredge them very lightly in flour, and brown them quickly in a mixture of 1 tablespoon oil and 3 tablespoons butter. Let them cook, turning them once, for about 15 minutes. Add salt and pepper to taste, pour ½ cup cider into the pan, and simmer, covered, for 10 minutes. Test the chops for tenderness, and let the cider cook down in the pan. When the chops are tender, remove them to a hot platter, and pour off excess fat from the pan. Stir in 3 egg yolks combined with 1½ cups heavy cream, and continue stirring over a medium heat until the sauce begins to thicken. Pour the sauce over the pork chops. Garnish with a little chopped parsley, and serve with sautéed apples.

Sautéed Apples

Peel and slice thin 3 to 5 cooking apples, depending on size. Sauté them very gently in 4 tablespoons butter. Sprinkle them with 1 to 1½ tablespoons sugar, and turn them very carefully with a spatula. Cook the apples until they are delicately brown.

Pork with Snap Beans

Brown 1½ pounds pork loin, cut into 1½-inch cubes, in a mixture of 2 tablespoons butter and 2 tablespoons oil, tossing them well and shaking the pan. When nicely browned, add 1 medium-sized onion and 1 clove garlic, both chopped fine, 1 tablespoon grated fresh ginger, 2 tablespoons soy sauce and 2 tablespoons sherry. Cook briskly, stirring constantly until the ingredients are well blended and tender. Cover, and simmer over very low heat until the

JAMES BEARD [4]

pork is just cooked through. Correct the seasoning.
Cook 1 pound snap beans until they are crisply tender
in a small amount of salted water. Drain them and
sauté for 2 minutes in 6 tablespoons butter. Correct
the seasoning.

To serve, make a border of 1½ cups rice on a
serving dish. Place the pork cubes in the center. Top
with the buttered beans, and garnish with ½ cup
chopped almonds.

In addition to the standard cuts of pork and lamb, in
season the great purveyors and markets in individual
districts have the tiny *agneau de lait*, the *cochon de lait*,
and the *cabri*—all baby animals to be cooked whole or
halved. They make an arresting array in the markets,
and their meat is pleasant and delicate to the palate.

The chicken, poultry and game one finds in Les
Halles and elsewhere in France are of an extraordinary
excellence. France probably has the best-tasting and
best-textured chickens in the world, if you take the
poulets de Bresse as an example. The Bresse chickens
are all marked with a metal band which distinguishes
them at once from the chickens that are taken to Bresse
for fattening and then sold to the markets. The Bresse
strain is as old as gastronomy and evidently different in
appearance from other chickens. Chicken is much more
expensive than meat in Europe because of the way it is
cared for and handled. Next to the Bresse chickens
come those from Le Mans, which are also extremely
good. These roasters are well fatted and have a skin
which crackles and browns magnificently and gives
flavor to the roasted birds. They also poach very well. It
is interesting to note that some of the greatest specialities in French restaurants nowadays are chicken dishes,
such as the *poulet au vapeur chez Dumaine*, the *poulet
demi-deuil* at Mère Brazier in Lyon and the *poulet à
l'estragon* at Bise. The last two are poached, and the

Dumaine version is steamed over a rich broth. Of course the sauces and stuffing will sometimes make up for the simplicity of preparation, but that is another matter.

There are a number of French names connected with chicken which may be confusing to the untutored, such as the *poussin*, which is our small squab chicken; the *poulet* or the young chicken; and the *coquelet* or young cock (we do not have this distinction); then there are the *poularde* and the *chapon*, the *poularde* being comparable to our roasting chicken and the *chapon* to our capon.

The French are quite sensible about serving chicken. They cut it into quarters and consider a quarter of the average roasting or poaching chicken a good portion for one person. There is no struggle in trying to carve and divide the bird into smaller sections. Quarters are easier to cut, so much neater on the plate, and they assure everyone of having the chicken while it is still hot.

Our duck raisers could also take a fine lesson from France, for the French ducks which you see hanging in the poulterer shops at the central market and in the neighborhood markets are meaty and of different varieties. There is no great layer of fat to cook through before reaching the meat. These ducks—from Rouen, from Nantes, from Bresse—are full-breasted, too, and can be sliced extremely well.

Game is something else again. We, of course, have such tight conservation controls because of the ruthless slaughter of game birds during the last century that it is difficult to come by any game at all, except in the hunting season and unless you are a good shot or have friends who are good shots. I was fortunate when I was younger, but living in New York has its disadvantages. The first of September is usually a happy day for

JAMES BEARD   [4]

Parisians—the first oysters and the first partridges. I
have eaten many different kinds of game bird, but I
think my palate achieves its greatest satisfaction from a
perfect partridge roasted to a turn. And nothing else
tastes quite as good to me as toast with the fine-chopped
trail on it or the giblets.

From the first of September on there is a constant
flow of game of all descriptions into the markets. Some
species are naturally more scarce than others and are
held in reserve for special customers—top restaurateurs
or chefs for great houses. There are the tiny quail, so
good when cooked wrapped in grape leaves; the lordly
pheasant; the old partridge and the larks; the ortolans,
caught in nets and fattened before killing, and as plump
and tasty a bite as one can find—they should be eaten
bones and all down to the beak, which is thrown away!
Then there are the woodcock, figpeckers, wild ducks,
thrush and probably a score more. There are hares and
boar and venison and delicious meats of other furred
game as well. What a land of plenty France is during
the game season! I hope there is some sort of conservation law there, too, so we can enjoy these things for a
long time to come.

Nowadays, with fast transportation and efficient refrigeration, almost all the types of game available in
French markets are brought to New York. They
might be a little difficult to track down, but they are
there, somewhere, for your delectation, if you care to
search . . . and to pay. I can remember back in the
war years when I was in the south of France, we had
black-market game from time to time. I recall feasting
on *grives* in Marseille in a small but excellent black-
market restaurant. It was not unlike speakeasy days in
New York.

CHAPTER

5

Stocking our house for winter was an operation on a scale that would have been appropriate to the hotel business. Mother had really never left the hotel in her own mind, and I can assure you that once she had the larder full, all of Portland could have dropped by for a meal.

Summer and fall the Mason and Economy jars were in constant use. Let was called in at times to assist, and other friends of Mother's were on hand for particular canning events. Once again Mother had a staff at her disposal. The amount of work that was put in from

June through October was staggering, but Mother thought it was a disgrace not to fill the cellar with the good things of life, and by the beginning of November a tour of our winter's food supply was an impressive experience.

She would not dream in those years of using any commercially canned vegetables, except an occasional tin of French peas or mushrooms or truffles. So the first thing put down was apt to be asparagus—but not the green variety, and this was an absolute rule. It was the white we canned, and during the season asparagus was often shipped to us from California in lots of several cases. Mother was famous for her jars of this vegetable, mammoth and ivory-colored, and she was vain enough to spend a great deal of time in its preparation. The stalks had to be matched for size and cut uniformly so that the jars presented a professional appearance after they were processed, and I must say they were as fine as any canned asparagus I ever ate.

In winter they were served as an hors d'oeuvre with a strip of anchovy or pimiento and Mother's incomparable mayonnaise. Or they were served hot with drawn butter or sometimes a mustard butter. Each stalk was treated with the tenderest care imaginable before it appeared on the table.

During the period of asparagus canning, restraint and patience were summoned up by each member of the household, for it was evident that a prima donna was onstage, determined to score a success with every palate.

Next in line for canning were certainly strawberries. And the Marshall or the Everbearing were all that were allowed into the house. Special growers in the nearby countryside were commissioned to have the berries picked for a certain week. Then out came the great brass preserving kettle. A sugar-and-water syrup was made, and the cleaned berries were popped into the syrup with additional sugar and watched with unwavering attention till they were just right. As a result of fine berries and careful timing, these became legendary for their firmness, wholeness and flavor.

Raspberries had their turn soon after this and were done in much the same fashion, but in greater quantity because they were used in so many tarts and desserts as a flavoring agent.

Apricots were sometimes worked into the schedule before we went off to the beach in June or July. These were often combined with canned pineapple—one of the rare concessions to a can my mother would make. "I've traveled in the tropics," she would say, "and had ripe pineapple brought to my cabin every morning for breakfast. And no pineapple that reached Portland has ever tasted like that." So she used the canned variety, and so do I, although I also find frozen pineapple acceptable. One cannot find fresh pineapples in this country that taste as they do when dead ripe and freshly picked.

At any rate, the pineapple was cut up and the apricots seeded. A great many of the seeds were cracked, because the kernels also went into this jam, at least into the portion of jam that was not to be used for cakes and desserts. Both the seeded and unseeded jams were rich and full-flavored, and there were a hundred jars or more of them on the shelf when the canning season was through.

Fabulous Apricot and Pineapple Jam

Wash 6 pounds ripe apricots well. Halve them and remove the pits. Cover the halved apricots with 6 pounds sugar and let them stand for 2 to 3 hours. Crack the pits and remove kernels from enough to make 1 cup. Drain 2 large cans sliced pineapple and cut the slices in small sections. Add 2 cups juice to the sugar and apricots. Bring the apricots to a boil very slowly, stirring so they will not burn. Add the pineapple and pits and cook the mixture very slowly, watching it constantly, until the fruit is transparent and the syrup quite thick. You may test a bit of it on a cold saucer to see if it has set.

Fill sterilized jars with the jam and seal them at once.

A tiny bit of gooseberry jam and a few canned gooseberries for tarts were always added to the stores, and sometimes currant jelly, although the general opinion was that the currant jelly made by Dickinson's, then in its infancy, was probably just as good.

At the beach we turned to the wild rather than to the farmer. Wild blue huckleberries were canned for use in pies and tarts. Many people used the wild salal berries for jelly, but my mother felt they required so much sugar that the taste of the berry was obscured. But the wild blackberries or brambles were another story. For weeks before they were ripe we reconnoitered for the best patches, and as soon as they were ready, the raid began. Family, guests and all were set to work gathering berries (and some brutal scratches). The jam was made on the beach stove and bottled and stored, to be carried home in September. And it was well worth the trouble. Sometimes there were enough wild strawberries to provide a few jars of elegantly flavored jam, and this treasure was carried to Portland by my father when he went home after a weekend and put into the cellar vaults.

When we returned from the beach at the summer's end, work began in earnest. Our farmer in the country was visited and asked to slaughter two hogs for us, always two. He made sausage and bacon and smoked the hams, while we made head cheese, chitterlings, scrapple and all the other delicacies one makes from the pig. We ate copious quantities of spareribs and knuckles, as well as some smoked loin. Our farmer also made us a barrel of sauerkraut and a barrel of pickles. Sacks and sacks of potatoes were ordered—several different varieties.

And the canning went on: early apples from our trees—magnificent Gravensteins—for jelly and applesauce; corn on and off the cob; prunes, petite prunes and red plums, whole and in conserve; damsons for jam and damson cheese; oil pickles, sweet pickles, tomato pickles, hot apple chutney, piccalilli.

Pickled Prunes

Make a syrup with 3 pounds sugar and 2 cups cider vinegar. Add 6 to 8 cloves and a slice of fresh ginger. Cook whole Italian prunes or damsons, about 2 to 3 pounds, in this syrup until prunes are tender but not mushy. Fill sterilized jars and seal them at once.

Damson Cheese

Wash 3 pounds damsons, cover them with cold water, bring the water to a boil and cook the fruit until it is tender. Put the cooked damsons through a food mill. Add 3 pounds sugar, grated rind of 1 orange and 2 teaspoons cinnamon, bring the mixture slowly to a boil, and cook until it is quite thick.

Pour the "cheese" into sterilized jars and seal them at once.

Our Favorite Oil Pickles

You need small pickling cucumbers for this pickle. Cut 36 to 40 cucumbers into thick slices on a wooden cutter with a steel blade, sometimes called a mandolin, or on a pickle cutter. Add 6 to 8 onions. Cover these with ½ cup salt and soak them for 2 hours. Drain them. Fill pint or half-pint sterilized jars with the cucumber and onion mixture and add a small piece of rock alum to each jar. Combine 2 quarts vinegar with 1 teaspoon salt. Bring this to a boil and cool it. Add ½ cup sugar, ¾ cup mustard seed, 2 teaspoons celery seed and 1½ cups olive oil. Pour this mixture over the pickles and seal the jars.

Another farmer supplied Hubbard squash, banana squash and pumpkins, winter apples were ordered from Hood River—many varieties—and pears began to arrive. Bartletts were canned in halves and made into pear butter. The harder pears were used in a sliced pear preserves which was stringy, syrupy and utterly wonderful. Then came the peaches. We usually waited for the late varieties, the Muirs and the Crawfords, and these were also canned whole and in halves, and made into peach butter. Some were brandied as well. Grapes followed and were used for juice, jelly and conserve. Then finally tomatoes were canned and chili sauce made.

My Father's Favorite Pear Preserves

We used Winter Nelis or other firm pears for these preserves. The syrup would turn rather delicate pink and the pear slices remained firm and rather translucent, excellent with hot breads.

Prepare a syrup with 4 cups water and 4 pounds sugar, and boil it for 10 minutes. Add 4 pounds peeled, sliced, firm pears and cook them until they are translucent and the syrup has cooked down. Fill sterilized jars with the mixture and add to each jar 1 or 2 cloves, a bit of cinnamon bark and a small piece of fresh ginger.

Seal the jars at once.

Peach Preserves

Cook enough—18 to 20—ripe unpeeled peaches in boiling water for 10 minutes to make 1 quart of pulp when the peaches are peeled and seeded. Put the pulp through a food mill and add an equal quantity of sugar, ½ cup cognac and a touch of vanilla. Bring the mixture to a boil slowly and cook it until it is thick. Pour the preserves into sterilized jars and seal them at once.

Green Tomato Slices

Wash 4 pounds green tomatoes and cut them in uniform slices. Arrange them in a deep bowl. Add 1 package Lilly's lime which has been mixed with enough water to cover. Let this stand for 12 hours. Drain the tomatoes and wash them with ice water. Combine 2 quarts vinegar and 3 pounds sugar in a

fairly flat container. Bring this to a boil and boil
5 minutes. Add 1 tablespoon whole cloves, several
pieces of cinnamon bark, several slices of fresh
ginger and 1 teaspoon allspice berries, and cook
tomato slices, a few at a time, until they are just
transparent. Arrange them in jars. Lastly, add 1
pound sultana raisins to the syrup and spoon the
syrup over the tomatoes, sealing the jars at once.

If you wish to vary these pickles, you may add
large onion slices, which should also be soaked in
lime water and cooked in the syrup with the tomatoes.

By this time everyone in the family needed a long
rest, but the larder was a beautiful sight and a challenge
for anyone to equal. With the addition of wines, flour
and sugar, and such canned luxuries as good sardines,
specially packed salmon, anchovies, olives, French peas
and mushrooms, imported chutney and Cross and
Blackwell's chowchow, we were ready to face the
winter! But first came the game season.

Father was not a hunter, but Mother's friends, knowing her penchant for game, were more than generous
with their kill. At the beginning of the season it was
unusual to go to our cellar and not find several ducks,
both large and squab-sized, and pheasants hanging in
feather.

Both Mother and Let could tell by touch whether a
duck was tender and young or more mature and best
cooked in a salmi. With her English background,
Mother felt that ducks and pheasants should hang before they were eaten, and I think she was right. Certainly I have never had better ones, except for those
specially prepared by a chef in France or those done
myself in the last ten or twelve years.

There was always a tremendous show of tempers in
the house when we had duck. I liked mine cooked rare
with a little onion and parsley inside. Mother liked hers
not so rare with the simplest seasoning of parsley, salt
and pepper. My father said that rare duck was for

savages and insisted on having his stuffed and braised till it was thoroughly cooked. Naturally, out of sheer spite, Mother always gave him the oldest birds and refused to taste one of them. But Father was happy: the ducks were tender and deliciously savory, for the stuffing contained duck liver, onion or shallots, crumbs and either sage or thyme, my father's two favorite seasonings. Since those days I have learned several other ways of doing older duck, aside from a braised dish and a salmi, and I find their flavor totally captivating.

Let's Braised Ducks

Wild ducks were always used for this recipe. They were stuffed with a mixture of sautéed onion, apple, chestnuts and a few bread crumbs, with a seasoning of thyme, salt and freshly ground black pepper. For 3 ducks you will need ¼ pound butter and either 10 shallots or 12 to 14 scallions cut fine. Sauté these until they are just soft, add 1½ cups diced tart apples and blend well with the onion. Add 1 cup crumbs, 2 cups broken cooked chestnuts and 1 generous teaspoon thyme. I like to add ½ cup Madeira to this mixture and usually more melted butter to give it a rich butter flavor. Season it to taste with salt and pepper, and stuff the 3 ducks, securing the vents.

Brown the ducks quickly in half oil, half butter or half lard, half butter. When they are nicely browned on all sides, salt them, place them in a braising pan or large Dutch oven and add the fat in which they were browned, a sprig of parsley, 1 whole onion and 1 cup red wine or Madeira. Cook ducks covered at 400° for 20 to 25 minutes or until they are tender and not overdone. It may be necessary to cook them longer—I have known some large ducks to take as long as 40 minutes. The ducks should be moist but not bloody for this dish. Remove them to a hot platter and skim excess fat from the pan. Add 1 shallot or 2 green onions chopped fine, and cook them for 2 minutes. Add ½ cup Madeira, 2 tablespoons chopped truffles and 1½ cups brown sauce or canned beef gravy. Cook the sauce until it is blended and reduced

slightly. Add a pat of butter and correct the seasoning.

Serve this duck with barley or with a rice pilaf and
small buttered turnips.

Another variation is to add 1 cup small green
olives to the sauce just before serving.

We always had one or two duck dinner parties a
year, and then my father and all of us had to eat it the
same way—cooked to my mother's taste. The menu
would usually start with an old favorite of hers, turtle
soup, which was followed by the ducks and her own
version of polenta, cut into squares and browned in
butter. There was never wild rice. For some reason we
all hated it, and the bias remains with me still. I feel it is
far overrated and appeals to people largely because it's
expensive. It has no delicacy but rather a crude and
overpoweringly strong flavor, and the more I think
about it, the more I believe it is fit only for the birds, for
whom it was probably meant anyway in the overall plan
of the universe!

The crispness of the polenta squares made a superbly
good contrast with the duck, and also we often had tiny
onions—or good turnips, when they were in season—steamed in butter. Apple compote, not sauce—a
bow to England again—was often passed with the
duck, or sometimes currant jelly. Mother never realized
how the flavor of currant ruined the palate for the accompanying wine. She was not, I'm afraid, as sensitive
to wines as she was to food. She served wine with some
dinners and no wine with others, as the mood struck
her. Father, on the other hand, had more flair for wine
and enjoyed a good one.

The dessert with duck was either an orange soufflé,
made in the double boiler, or a Spanish cream. Often
there would be a cheese course and coffee.

Dessert was never a forte of Mother's. It was seldom
served when we were alone, except for fresh fruit in

season and preserved and cooked fruit. For guests there might be a Bavarian cream, a soufflé, sometimes apple charlotte, as often as possible Let's fabulous charlotte russe, and during the holiday season simple tarts and pies.

Orange Soufflé

We often did this one, which was simple and good. Beat 4 egg whites till they are stiff and add gradually 4 tablespoons sugar. Fold this into 1 cup orange marmalade to which you have added 1 tablespoon cognac, and steam the mixture in the upper part of a double boiler for about 35 minutes or until it stands firm. This may be unmolded and served with an orange sauce or with whipped cream.

We often had another orange soufflé, which was baked. Beat the yolks of 6 eggs till they are extremely light and lemon-colored. Beat in ½ cup sugar, the grated rind of a large orange and ¼ cup Grand Marnier or Cointreau. Beat the whites of 8 or 9 eggs till they are stiff, and fold them into the yolk mixture: fold in one-third of the mixture very thoroughly and the remaining two-thirds lightly. Pour the soufflé into a well-buttered and heavily sugared soufflé dish and bake it at 400° for 20 to 25 minutes or until it is puffy and brown. Serve it at once.

This is definitely still my favorite soufflé.

Serve it with an orange sauce or with whipped cream flavored with sugar and a little Grand Marnier.

Let's Apple Charlotte

For 6 persons peel and cut into sixths 8 greenings or crisp Gravenstein apples. Cover them and steam them in 6 tablespoons butter to which you have added 2 teaspoons vanilla, stirring occasionally till the apples are soft but not mushy. Taste them for sweetness and add sugar accordingly. I seldom find it necessary.

Fry 12 to 18 thin slices white bread, from which the crusts have been removed, in butter till they are brown and crispy. Line the bottom and sides of a mold with the toast, overlapping the slices to make a practically leakproof lining. Fill it with the apple mixture and top the apples with more fried toast. Bake the charlotte at 350° for 20 to 25 minutes. Unmold it and serve it while it is warm with heavy cream or with whipped cream.

Sometimes Let would add some grated orange or lemon rind and a touch of cognac for a change. I have also done it successfully with the addition of sultana raisins and some good Calvados.

Let's Charlotte Russe

Let used a large bowl or individual molds for charlotte russe. He lined the bottom and sides with ladyfingers and filled it with flavored whipped cream.

For his whipped cream he would use a pint or quart of whipping cream according to the size of charlotte he wished to make. He whipped the cream fairly stiff and added sugar, vanilla and a dash of cognac or rum. If it was to stand, he added melted gelatin to the cream when he added the sugar—before the cream became stiff.

To add gelatin to whipped cream, dissolve 1 teaspoon unflavored gelatin in 1 tablespoon water for each cup of cream used. Melt it over low heat till the mixture is clear.

Garnish the charlotte with cherries or with currant jelly or with candied violets.

Ladyfingers

Beat the yolks of 2 eggs until they are really light and lemon-colored. Beat the whites of 3 eggs until they are stiff and hold peaks, and beat in 6 tablespoons powdered sugar, 1 tablespoon at a time. Add a dash of cognac to the yolks and blend them with the stiffly beaten meringue. Fold in ½ cup sifted flour to which you have added a good ¼ teaspoon salt. Fill a pastry bag with a plain tube with the mixture and form 4-inch fingers on silicon paper or brown paper. Dust the fingers with powdered sugar and bake at 350° for about 8 minutes or until they are delicately brown at the edges. Remove them from the paper while they are still hot.

When there was good pheasant, special friends were invited to a rather informal gathering. We had a way with pheasant—sautéed in butter, *flambé* with cognac, and served with a sauce made with cream, the pan juices and the giblets chopped fine. This was the most delicious pheasant I have ever eaten. It was moist, tender and sensationally good. Pheasant always called for perfectly mashed potatoes, a garnish of watercress, if possible, and braised celery or some of Mother's special asparagus, served separately. To start the menu there was usually a clear soup, and to finish, for some reason, we invariably had pears baked in brown sugar with cloves and a little rum added to them. They were winter pears, full-flavored and exquisitely rich with syrup. Sometimes this dessert was varied with a little ginger or ginger syrup from the large crocks of preserved ginger we kept on hand. With the pears went small sugar cookies or shortbread cookies, which Let made and which later on became a specialty of my mother's.

Let's Sugar Cookies

Cream 1 cup butter with 1 cup sugar, ½ teaspoon salt, and ¼ teaspoon mace. Add 1 egg lightly beaten with 3 tablespoons heavy cream and 1 teaspoon vanilla. Gradually beat in 3 cups sifted flour, sifted with 1½ teaspoons baking powder. Chill the dough for 15 minutes, divide into thirds and let the remainder chill while you roll the first and second thirds. Roll to ⅛- to ¼-inch thickness and cut with any desired cutter. Brush the cookies with slightly beaten white of egg and sprinkle them with sugar. Bake at 350° for about 8 minutes, or until delicately brown.

Ice cookies and add any type of decoration. They have a delicious crispness. If you wish to vary them, you may sprinkle them with sugar and cinnamon and place an almond half on each one before baking. Then they are called sand tarts.

Older pheasants were done for the family alone, and perhaps one close friend. These were braised with our farmer's homemade sauerkraut and either apple cider or white wine and with bits of garlic sausage scattered through the sauerkraut, all somewhat in the Alsatian fashion. This was a superlative dish when eaten with boiled potatoes and pickled prunes, canned during the harvest season.

Our Wonderful Pheasant with Sauerkraut

This is best made with slightly older pheasant. Quarter two pheasants and brown them lightly in 4 ounces (1 stick) butter, turning them several times to color them evenly. Salt and pepper them to taste.

Wash 3 pounds sauerkraut well and put it on to cook with 2 cups white wine and several generous grindings of the pepper mill. When it boils, turn the heat down and simmer it for 1 hour.

Poach 1 large garlic sausage or several well-seasoned Italian sausages in water for 2 minutes. Cool the sausage and, if you are using the large one, skin it.

Remove the pheasant pieces from the browning pan. Line a large baking dish with salt pork slices and make a bed of sauerkraut. On it arrange the pieces of pheasant and some slices of garlic sausage. Cover them well with wine. Cover the casserole and bake it at 350° 30 to 45 minutes or until the pheasant is tender.

Serve the pheasant with mashed potatoes or with a chestnut purée, or even with squares of fried hominy.

A light Alsatian Riesling is delightful for making this dish and for drinking with it.

Venison was not a great favorite with us, although I was very happy when we had the luck to receive some jerked venison. If properly prepared and sliced, it has a texture and flavor not unlike the famous *viande sèche* of the Swiss. Mother felt that vension which had to be marinated and cooked a long time in wine and spices wasn't worth the trouble, and I am inclined to agree. If, on the other hand, we had fresh chops or filets or an occasional saddle, that was another matter. These cuts were prepared with herbs and spices and some red wine and roasted rare or sautéed rare. A fine dish it was, which we enjoyed thoroughly but never offered to guests.

When we had teal, this also was reserved for the household. These tiny members of the duck family are devastatingly good when roasted simply and quickly—basted with butter and seasoned only with salt and pepper—and, like squab, eaten with the fingers. As an accompaniment we often ate braised celery or tender, raw celery, and potatoes cooked in the oven with broth. Years later I learned about a celery salad from a very great cook, which is perfection with this type of meal. Several years ago when I was staying in Yucatán I had teal served to me; it migrates there from the Northwest. It was the most sentimental meal I ever had eaten, and I relished each bite. In France one occasionally finds teal. It is called the *sarcelle*, and is as good there as it was in Oregon in my youth.

Mother's salmi was famous with the women friends whom she entertained from time to time. During the holiday season she would invite some of these friends over to "spend the day," as she put it, and when they arrived, she would arrange to be busy working on candied fruits for a cake or for mincemeat. Naturally they would fall to and assist her, and when enough work had been accomplished she would whip together the salmi and other goodies and feed them lunch. Often after lunch she'd manage to get another couple of hours' work out of them, charming them all the while with her witty talk. They spent the day, indeed! But the bait of Mother's food and company always caught.

Salmi of Duck

Prepare a mirepoix: cut 2 leeks, 2 or 3 stalks celery, and 2 carrots in matchlike pieces and place them on the bottom of a heavy saucepan or kettle. Add 2 table-spoons oil, 1 teaspoon salt and the bones and giblets of 4 ducks that have been previously roasted. The breasts are reserved for service with the sauce. Add 2 cups broth, ¼ cup Madeira or rich sherry, and a sprig or two of parsley. Cover the sauce and simmer it for 2 hours. If you have a blender, remove the bones and giblets and put the vegetables and liquid through the blender. If not, use a strainer. In either case re-duce the liquid to 1½ cups over a brisk flame. Com-bine it with 1½ cups brown sauce or beef gravy and bring it to a boil. Reduce the heat and simmer the sauce for 5 minutes. Correct the seasoning and add ⅓ cup cognac and the breasts of the ducks. Simmer till the breasts are heated through. Remove the breasts to slices of fried toast and cover them with the rich sauce. Garnish them with sliced truffles and serve them with rice and sautéed mushrooms. Mother often added mushrooms to the sauce.

Aside from the game dinners, the usual winter dinner for company was roast beef. Beef had to have a good green mold covering the outer surface before it was worthy of Mother's table. So she would order a roast to be hung an extra ten days to two weeks before she used it, a longer time than was standard procedure in the market. Her butchers knew better than to cross her, and she always got the best.

The roast beef dinner generally began with a cream of tomato soup, for which Mother was justifiably fa-mous. It had been Let's recipe before her, but she took the bows anyway. The soup was rich and pungent and its glory was her home-canned tomatoes, which really tasted like tomatoes. This was before the thick-skinned pellets now marketed as tomatoes came into being! Following the soup there was the roast beef, with mustard pickles—don't ask why—potatoes browned in the beef fat and beautifully crunchy, and an enormous Yorkshire pudding made right in the roasting pan. The beef, usually four or five ribs, was roasted on a rack in a great black pan, seared at a high temperature and then cooked at a reduced temperature, with frequent bastings from extra suet in the pan until it was handsomely crisped. Then it was removed to a carving board and allowed to stand while the pudding was cooked.

Mother's (Originally Let's) Cream of Tomato Soup
We always used home-canned tomatoes. In this day and age I find that I get a better soup by using the canned Italian tomatoes. Combine 1 large can Italian tomatoes with 1 cup beef broth, 1 onion stuck with cloves, 1 teaspoon salt and a pinch of basil, and cook, covered, for 30 minutes over low heat. Remove the cover, add 2 teaspoons sugar and additional salt if needed, and cook briskly for 10 minutes. Strain tomatoes through a fine sieve. Add a pinch of soda to the mixture and correct the seasoning. Heat 2 cups heavy cream to a boil, combine it with the tomato mixture very slowly, to prevent curdling, and bring the soup again to a boil. When it is available fresh basil or fresh thyme is perfect, chopped and served with the soup. And if you have fresh ripe tomatoes, they make a remarkably good soup the same way. If you feel that you need a thicker soup than this offers, you can thicken it with just a trace of arrowroot —about 2 teaspoons mixed with a little water. We always liked it much better with the heavy cream without thickening.

As a variation, if the fresh tomatoes were exceptionally good, the seeds were squeezed out, the tomatoes heated and cooked whole, the soda added along with the other seasonings, and the cream added to the unsieved mixture. This gave a flavorful and rather different soup.

For the Yorkshire pudding Mother used twelve eggs, twelve tablespoons of flour and something over a quart of milk, and it rose to unprecedented heights just before it was removed from the oven. It was deliciously crisp and tender—not the soggy mess that usually crowns a roast beef platter.

With roast beef Mother would sometimes offer a dish of puréed parsnips with buttered crumbs, another bow to her homeland, and again she could offer a salad of her home-canned white asparagus. Once, at a dinner of this description, my half sister, who would not take my mother's counsel on food, introduced a salad which she had learned to make at a YWCA cooking class. Her teacher, Miss Hannah, was of the fussy school of cookery, and the salad which she had taught my half sister to make was composed of pineapple and grated cheese. My mother's response to the innovation was violent, and her subsequent description of this rather sordid tearoom specialty would not bear printing. At any rate, my sister's independent cooking adventures came to a halt, and she later became a pretty good cook by tasting and using good sense.

Puréed Parsnips

For six persons 2 to 2½ pounds of parsnips are ample. People used to say they were not edible till after the first frost—but like many other superstitions this has been found to be false.

Boil the parsnips in their skins till they are pierceable. Drain them and let them cool. Peel them and either put them through a food mill or mash them and push them through a sieve or ricer. To each cup of purée add 3 tablespoons butter, salt to taste, and a few grains of nutmeg or Spice Parisienne (Spice Islands); whip or beat the purée well. Arrange it in a buttered baking dish, dot it with butter and top it with buttered crumbs or toasted sesame seeds. Bake at 375° till the purée is heated through and delicately brown on top.

When there were no dinners on the schedule, there were still numerous luncheons—the small luncheons Mother loved to have with her intimate friends, and sometimes a superb impromptu luncheon, because our larder was always overflowing. Mrs. Harris usually stayed for potluck once a week when she came in from the country to sell her butter and eggs. She was a woman with great charm, a disgustingly difficult husband and a rich mother, who would come and tempt her away to Florida from time to time. But Mrs. Harris always returned. The butter and egg business kept her supplied with modest comforts, and at the same time kept us supplied with fresh, wonderful food. Her butter was made from Jersey cream and was delicate and sweet—and unsalted, naturally. This was table butter. Cooking butter could be salted, but that was a different matter. The eggs were fresh and delicious and made some of the best omelets and scrambled eggs imaginable, to say nothing of soufflés.

If Mrs. Harris decided to stay and gossip and have some food, Mother might use the leftovers from a *pot-au-feu*. There was always enough beef bought for this dish so that some could be placed in a bowl with its broth, weighted down, chilled and then unmolded. Encased in its rich, lovely jelly, it was sliced thin and served with a salad or, occasionally, crisp, sautéed potatoes and relishes or pickles from the cellar. Together with homemade bread and tea and perhaps a slice of seedcake or cookies, this made a delightful luncheon. The same impromptu meal was often built around chicken or, in season, salmon. We always kept a large bowl of pickled salmon on hand, flavored with onions, bay leaves, peppercorns and parsley. It made an enchanting dish for lunch when served with homemade mayonnaise, toasted bread and perhaps a salad. Or again there might be bowls of Mother's best canned tomatoes served with a topping of poached eggs, butter, chopped parsley and salt and pepper. This dish was excellent with bread and butter and sometimes a rasher of good smoked ham.

Pickled Salmon

Wrap a 4- to 5-pound piece of salmon in cheesecloth. Poach it in boiling salted water for 25 to 30 minutes or until the fish flakes easily when tested with a fork. Remove it from the bouillon and cool it. When it is cool, carefully remove the skin and bones, and place it in a deep bowl. Add 1 large or 2 medium-sized onions, peeled and sliced thin, ½ cup olive oil, ½ cup red wine, 1 teaspoon freshly ground black pepper and enough wine vinegar to cover the fish. Let it stand for several hours. Remove the fish to a chilled platter. Serve it with a bland mayonnaise or rémoulade sauce, cucumber salad and crisp toast.
Note: The fish will keep several days this way and may be used in salads or as a sandwich filling.

By now we were getting close to the holidays, and preparations began for Mother's cakes and puddings. It was her custom to make fruitcakes—a black one, a white one and an English currant cake—the year before they were used. The same was true of the plum puddings and the mincemeat. (Mother kept some of her wedding cake for twenty-five years by covering it with cloths bathed in cognac and keeping the container tightly sealed.)

The making of these holiday specialties seemed to go on and on and on, and assembling the ingredients was a colossal undertaking in itself. Mother went to all the best stores—Sealy-Dresser and L. Mayer and Meier & Frank—to compare prices and order. Currants, seeded raisins, sultana raisins, citron, lemon peel, candied pineapple and cherries, angelica, almonds, walnuts, hazelnuts, spices—all were bought in tremendous amounts, together with a store of the proper apples for the pudding and mincemeat. Orange and grapefruit peel were candied at home, cider was boiled, and frequent visits were made to Mr. Waddle and other wine and spirit dealers to obtain cognac, rum and sherry.

The plum puddings, which were made in large quantities and used as gifts, were first on the schedule. Bread crumbs were made, suet was chopped till it was almost a powder, and an order for the freshest eggs was placed. Then all the fruits and flavorings were combined. When the entire mixture was finally put together, everyone in the house, as well as the closest neighbors, came to give it a stir for luck, inhaling at the same time a smell that was overpoweringly pungent. The vast collection of one- and two-pound coffee and baking powder cans came out of storage to be filled, sealed, placed in their water baths, and allowed to steam for hours and then dry out. At this point each pudding was given a drink of cognac and put away with the promise of another nip every few months. These puddings were light and mellow and filled with a lasting and deliciously intoxicating flavor. Served with either a hard sauce laced with rum or a cognac sauce, they were as good a dessert for the holiday as could be imagined. Indeed, those who received them as gifts felt incredibly lucky.

Five-day Plum Pudding

(an adaptation)

Chop ½ pound beef suet very fine and sprinkle it with ½ cup flour. Clean ¾ cup seeded raisins, 1 cup sultana raisins, and ½ cup currants, and dust them lightly with flour. Make 3 cups fresh bread crumbs. Chop ½ pound mixed peel (orange, lemon and citron) very fine and dust it with flour. Grate the rinds of 1 orange and 1 lemon, add the juice of each, and combine in a large bowl with the suet, raisins, currants, bread crumbs, mixed peel, 1 cup flour, 6 to 7 tart apples peeled and chopped, ½ cup ground filberts, 1 cup brown sugar, ½ teaspoon cloves, 2 teaspoons cinnamon, 1 teaspoon ginger, 1 teaspoon mace and 1 teaspoon salt. Add ½ cup cognac, rum or brandy, and place the mixture in a cold spot or in the refrigerator for 5 days. Add ¼ cup more spirits each day and stir mixture well each time. On the last day,

stir it well again. Beat 6 eggs slightly and stir them
in thoroughly. If the batter is too thick, thin it with a
little beer. Pour the well-mixed pudding into a mold
and cover it with a floured, buttered, damp cloth or
seal it with aluminum foil. Cook it in a boiling water
bath 6 hours. Unmold the pudding and serve it with
a cognac sauce.

Cognac Sauce

Combine 1 cup heavy cream, 3 egg yolks, 2 tablespoons sugar, a pinch of salt and ⅓ cup cognac in the
upper part of a double boiler, and stir the sauce over
hot water until it thickens slightly.

Mincemeat was the next enterprise. This too was prepared a year in advance. Great crocks were brought up
from the cellar, washed out and prepared for the day of
work. Meat—good beef chuck and tongue—was boiled
and allowed to cool in the broth. The fat was skimmed
off and the beef taken out, relieved of all fatty particles
and chopped till very fine. Chopped suet, chopped fruit,
raisins and currants were put to soak in boiled cider,
cognac and sherry. Then all the ingredients were combined and put in crocks to mellow for weeks before
being transferred to jars, usually preceded by several
baths of wines and spirits. When the mincemeat was
ready for use, chopped apple and sometimes nuts were
added to it to give it firmer texture. This mincemeat
made superb tarts and pies and was used throughout
the winter months for baking and for varied desserts,
such as a mincemeat pudding and even a flan with
whipped cream, so help me.

Our Fabulously Good Mincemeat

We used great crocks for mincemeat, and each year
twice this amount was made for use the next year.
It was not put in jars until it had aged and been
treated to additional cognac for about four months.
However, the mincemeat is so good you don't have to
wait a year to enjoy it.

154

Boil 3 pounds lean brisket or rump of beef and 1 fresh tongue of about 3 pounds in water until tender. Cool the meat and put it through a coarse grinder, or chop it by hand if you wish. Combine it with 1½ pounds fine-chopped beef suet, 2 pounds seeded raisins, 2 pounds sultana raisins, 2 pounds currants, ½ pound diced shredded citron, ½ pound chopped shredded orange peel and ¼ pound diced shredded lemon peel. Chopped dried figs or dates may be added to the mincemeat if you wish. Place all this in a deep crock and add 2 cups sugar, 1 pint strawberry preserves, 1 tablespoon salt, 2 teaspoons nutmeg, 2½ teaspoons cinnamon, 1 teaspoon allspice, 1 teaspoon mace and a little ground cloves. Add one fifth good sherry and enough cognac to make a rather loose mixture of the fruits and meats—it will take about 2 bottles. Mix ingredients thoroughly, cover the crock, and let the mincemeat stand for a month or so before using it.

It should be checked each week to see if the absorption necessitates adding additional sherry or cognac or both.

To Make a Mince Pie

Line a 9-inch pie tin with rich pastry. Combine 2½ cups mincemeat with 1 cup fine-chopped apples and put this filling in the shell. Top it with a rich crust or with puff paste or with a lattice crust and bake at 450° for 10 minutes. Then reduce heat to 350° and bake till the crust is brown and rich-looking. You may brush the crust with egg wash (1 egg yolk blended with 2 tablespoons water) before baking if you wish. Serve the pie warm.

Our Favorite Mincemeat and Apple Flan

Prepare a rich pastry and line a flan ring, either a square or an oblong one.

Peel and cut 6 apples into sixths. Steam them in 4 tablespoons butter with 1 teaspoon vanilla in a heavy skillet over medium heat. Cover the pan and do not let the apples get mushy. Cool them slightly and place them in the flan ring. Cover them with a layer of mincemeat and bake at 375° till the crust is baked and well browned. Cool the flan and glaze it with apricot glaze.

My mother adored mince pie. In fact, we all did, and it is still a favorite of mine. My father, always the individualist, loved his pie piping hot. He would lift the top crust, insert a generous square of butter and a thin slice of Roquefort cheese and let it settle a minute or two before attacking it. As for Mother, she once had a long convalescence from typhoid fever and was sent to Astoria, Oregon, where the air was thought to be more beneficial for her recovery. Christmas came and went, and no mince pie. She could hardly bear it. Just before New Year's she was allowed to go for a walk. Covering herself with a great traveling cape, she went past every bakeshop till she found mince pie. She bought two pies, smuggled them into her room under the cape and ate one whole one before dinner and the other the next morning before lunch. There were no evil effects except an increasing hunger for more mince pie!

The making of the holiday fruitcakes was another ritual. Usually one or two of the regular "spend the day" friends would come along to help for the reward of a good lunch. The first of these cakes—the black one—contained fruits, spices, eggs and a little flour and chocolate. The English currant cake called for more flour and less fruit and nuts. It was lighter in texture and much enjoyed by all because it was not so overpoweringly rich. A great array of these two varieties were baked in round bread tins and one-pound coffee tins. Upon cooling, they were treated to a drink of cognac or rum and then stored with apples and cloths damp with cognac or rum for a year or more.

My Mother's Black Fruitcake

(*also used for wedding cakes*)

First preparation: Cut into thin shreds ½ pound citron, ¼ pound orange peel and 1 pound candied pineapple, and halve ½ pound cherries. Combine these with 1 pound seeded raisins, ½ pound sultanas, and ½ pound currants. Add to this mixture 1 cup cognac and let it sit, covered, in the refrigerator for two days. Toast ½ pound filberts in a 350° oven for 30 minutes. Chop them coarsely or leave them whole as you wish.

On the day you bake the cake, remove the fruit from the refrigerator, sprinkle ½ cup sifted flour over it and blend the mixture well. Add the nuts and mix again.

Sift 1½ cups flour and then measure to exactly 1½ cups. Combine the flour with 1 teaspoon cinnamon, a pinch of ground cloves, ½ teaspoon mace and a touch of nutmeg. Add ½ teaspoon baking soda.

Cream together ½ cup butter and 2 cups sugar —you may use part brown sugar if you wish. Add 6 lightly beaten eggs, 3 ounces unsweetened grated chocolate, another ¼ cup cognac. Blend all this very firmly with the flour, which you should add a little at a time. When it is perfectly blended, pour over the fruit and nut mixture and mix well with your hands.

Line a pan or pans with silicon paper or brown paper. If you use brown paper you will need to butter the pans first. For fruitcake I like to use 9-inch bread pans or one large square pan or two 9-inch spring molds. The cakes should be baked at 275°. If bread pans are used, only 1½ hours' baking time is required. Cakes baked in the square pan or spring molds take about 2½ to 3½ hours. If you use a very large spring mold, the cake should bake about an hour longer.

Let the fruitcake stand for an hour or more after it comes from the oven.

When it was just warm Mother used to add a bath of cognac and put the cakes in tins to rest till they were to be used. She would make five times this recipe every year and often keep the cakes through the year with towels dampened in cognac wrapped around them, and in airtight containers, of course.

As soon as the next year's supply of cakes and puddings was done, cookies and shortbreads were baked in quantity. Mother never made as good shortbread as dear Mrs. Stewart, and there was an undeclared understanding about this, for every year Mrs. Stewart would spend a whole day in our kitchen making her superb shortbread and sometimes a currant loaf or Scotch bun, a deliciously fruity fruitcake baked in a shell of bread dough, which I loved.

The shortbread was cut into all sorts of delightful shapes, and some of the round, traditional cakes were decorated with cherries and peel. They made quite striking gifts. I still relish shortbread, and the smell of its buttery dough coming from the oven is too tantalizing for even the most disciplined dieter. Sometimes there was ginger shortbread—a far cry from the purists' version, but nevertheless a delectable morsel.

Shortbread

Sift 1½ cups cake flour, ½ cup potato flour and 1 cup sugar together and blend thoroughly. Work in 1 cup butter and ¼ teaspoon salt until the mixture is crumbly. Pack this into 8-inch buttered tins and bake in a 350° oven for about 25 to 30 minutes or until the shortbread is lightly browned. If you like, you may bake the shortbread in small rounds or in fancy shapes. Decorate the tops of these tiny shortbreads before baking with bits of candied fruits arranged in designs. Small shortbreads take only half as long, or even less time than that, to cook. They are done when lightly browned.

Shortbread will keep rather well in an airtight tin box.

Ginger Cakes

Mix 2 cups sifted flour, 1 firmly packed cup brown sugar, 1 tablespoon ginger and 1 teaspoon soda thoroughly, and then combine them with 1 cup butter until the ingredients are well blended and crumbly. In 6- to 8-inch layer cake pans, put ½-inch thickness of the mixture and bake in a 325° oven for 45 minutes to 1 hour. Cut the ginger cake into finger-shaped pieces while it is still warm. Remove the pieces carefully with a spatula and store them in covered tins.

The white fruitcake had been created by Let, and it was the only fruitcake too delicate to last through the year. Mother kept the recipe a secret, or thought she was keeping it, and wouldn't permit any of her friends to help prepare it. But this was it: The fruits—white raisins, citron, cherries, angelica and pineapple—were cut fine and mixed with a little preserved Chinese ginger. Then a batter of eggs and flour and butter was beaten till light and added alternately with the fruits and blanched almonds to an old wash boiler, in which the mixture was beaten by hand. This was scooped into pans, baked, cooled, anointed with a draught of white rum and then allowed to mellow for several days before being cut in delicate slices with the sharpest of knives. No wonder we didn't eat many desserts the rest of the year!

White Fruitcake

Our white fruitcake was delicate and difficult to slice but rewarding as to flavor. Sometimes we used almonds in it and sometimes pecans. And one year Mother added slivered candied ginger to the fruit with startling success. The ginger tends to overshadow the other flavors, but I think you would find this variation worth trying.

For the Fruit: Combine ¾ pound candied citron cut in paper-thin slices, ¼ pound candied pineapple cut in shreds, ¼ pound candied cherries—sometimes

160

you can get the white ones, which make the cake more attractive for me—and ½ pound bleached sultana raisins. Mix with the nuts—1 pound sliced almonds available in tins or at bakery supply shops—and ½ pound blanched almonds or ½ pound pecans. Sift ½ cup flour over the fruits and nuts, and blend.

For the Cake: Cream ¾ pound butter well and gradually add 2 cups sugar. Separate 6 eggs. Beat the yolks rather well and add them to the sugar and butter mixture. Add ¼ cup sherry and ½ cup cognac alternately with 3½ cups sifted flour. When the batter is well blended, fold in the fruit. Beat the 6 egg whites till they are stiff and glossy but not dry, and just before they are ready to be added, beat in 1 teaspoon cream of tartar. Fold this into the fruit and batter mixture lightly but firmly.

Have four small pans—if you can get the small 6-inch bread pans, they are ideal—or small molds. Line them with buttered paper or with silicon paper and fill them with the mixture. I usually arrange some whole blanched almonds and a few cherries on the top. Bake at 275° for about 2 hours.

The pride of Mother's kitchen, it seems to me, was these holiday cakes, cookies and other Christmas specialties. Few people have loved Christmas as she did. Her great joy in the holiday season was infectious, and for once in the year we were a united family.

I am happy to say that we never got involved in the making of homemade candy. We received several large boxes each Christmas, and after we had tasted one or two of the candies, they were consigned to the cellar. Mother thought, and rightly, that most of this candy was fit only for the pigs. How tired and really unsavory homemade candy generally is! Marshmallows and bonbons and taffy and brittles—all of them should be dispensed with.

I hold similar views about Christmas cookies. I know they are fun to make, but—I don't care who the baker is—cookies are not going to survive packing, traveling through the mail, and unpacking without losing their pristine charm. They are fine for the household if served fresh. But have pity on us, all you bakers—the spirit of Christmas notwithstanding—and deliver us from cookies that have crumbled or gone stale.

Preparation for Christmas didn't dim the intervening celebration of Thanksgiving. This was not a special family event for us. Let didn't appear for this all-American day. There was no going over the hill to Grandmamma's or to Uncle Ned's. Mother's relatives were thousands of miles away, and between her family and my father's there was an armed truce. However, Mother loved to bring together those who were alone in the city, and somehow she always managed to have a group that was amusing and gay. The dinner was a simple, good meal, usually served in late afternoon, which gave time to sit around the table afterwards for long discussions, a custom dear to my mother's heart. I seem to have inherited it and love to sit at the table and talk long after dinner is over, sipping coffee and a liqueur. An attractive table is somehow the appropriate place for mellowed thought and sparkling conversation.

Mother would have beaten the poulterer who offered her the poor excuse for turkey we have nowadays. Scientifically plucked, which removes part of the skin and practically all the oil sacs, and frozen in a plastic case, today's bird has about as much flavor and texture as a piece of asbestos. To market these turkeys is a crime against good food and an insult to the consumer. No, I will not eat such a fowl, nor would any of our family have done so! We had hand-plucked turkeys, and if there was an occasional pinfeather left, who cared? The flavor was superb, and the skin was deliciously crisp. At our house there were always two turkeys roasted—one for dinner and the other to assure us of plenty of leftovers, for we were a family passionately devoted to cold turkey. To my mind, bits of cold turkey on toast for breakfast, and cold turkey served with salad, reheated stuffing and potato cakes are even more tasty than the roast turkey served at a formal dinner.

Our Thanksgiving menu took little notice of tradition. We started with something simple—sometimes *foie gras*, sometimes smoked salmon, occasionally caviar if a friend had been generous. Then came the turkey with a magnificent stuffing—good bread crumbs, plenty of butter and excellent seasonings, enhanced at times by nuts or ham or sausages. Served with this were whipped potatoes (never sweet potatoes), onions and dried corn, or sometimes string beans or petits pois, homemade rolls, and, for those who had to have them, cranberries. We were never a cranberry family, thank heavens. To me, the berry's rather bitter tang is an offense to the palate, an abomination in any menu. And why the cranberry has become so generally accepted with turkey as to become a gastronomic cliché I will never be able to understand.

Thanksgiving dessert was uniformly traditional with pumpkin pie and mince pie. Our mince pie was a tribute Mother made to herself, for, as I have said, she had a passion for it. I have followed in her footsteps for years and feel that a good mince pie belongs with Thanksgiving. The pumpkin pie varied from tradition in that it was done with a rich custard and fine-cut ginger, and was laced with sherry, cognac or rum to make it more pungent. These touches gave it the taste of true greatness, and it was a far cry from the usual mealy and sticky pumpkin pie.

Pumpkin Pie

Mother's pumpkin mixture was delicious. She usually did not use pumpkin but Hubbard squash which was steamed and put through a fine sieve. 2 cups of the purée were combined with 8 eggs, 1½ cups heavy cream, ½ teaspoon cinnamon, a pinch of cloves, a pinch of mace and ⅓ cup cognac. To this was added

⅓ to ½ cup fine-cut candied ginger, and the whole
was poured into 2 small pie shells which had been
baked at 400° for 10 minutes. The pies were returned
to the oven and baked at 375° for 25 to 30 minutes
or until they were just set. These were served warm—
never chilled.

Following dessert there were the usual relishes, nuts,
and wine or champagne. (We had the latter even for a
few years after Prohibition, which completely changed
the palate of American eaters till long after its repeal.)
Thanksgiving was a happy meal and in every sense a
harvest feast. The best of our larder was brought forth,
the table was handsomely decorated with fruits and
vegetables, and the nice old silver and my mother's best
gold-and-white china made their appearance. It was a
leisurely dinner; no one felt pressed to hurry away from
the table except my father, who wanted to get to his
cigar and his chair away from the gathering. I look
back on these Thanksgivings as memorable eating adventures, with good company all around. In her role of
Lady Bountiful, Mother now and then found a kill-
joy among her guests, but on the whole the people she
invited to the feast were worthy of it.

Christmas was celebrated in an entirely different
style. Never did a family have such a jumble of traditions, and it was a joy from beginning to end. First of
all, Santa Claus entered my life—in the person of my
godfather, General Summers, who was one of the great
bons vivants of his time. A good military man and a
perfectly delightful host to his friends, he was unfortunately married to a charming woman who, with her
strict Southern upbringing, never quite understood him.
He should have married my mother. He had a twinkle in
his eyes and a jovial laugh, and he was rather like Santa
Claus any time of year. Our wonderful Let worshiped
him and often stroked his tummy as if he were a giant

164

dog, saying, "Nice General, nice General," much to the General's delight and the bewilderment of his wife.

Another feature of Christmas was Let himself, who took to the Western custom in a big way, spending too much on everyone's gifts and participating in the festivities with an excess of vigor.

Our main celebration was a big party on Christmas Eve, and I was permitted to stay up for Santa Claus—who I knew was my godfather, but I went along with the trick being played on me. The tree was decked, and piles of packages were arranged around the room. Such a quantity of them! There were never fewer than twenty guests and sometimes up to thirty or forty. We exchanged gifts with all these friends and with friends out of town as well. Then there were the gifts that poured in from members of the Chinese colony, who idolized my mother and respected my father. This display of their affection was staggering.

A wassail drink was served—eggnog or Tom and Jerry, and, during the era when it was available, champagne. Then around eleven o'clock Santa Claus arrived to the tinkling of a small bell on the tree, and all became engaged in present opening till they were exhausted. In the midst of it, Let would climb to the upstairs porch, attach a large string of firecrackers to a post and light it—a sure Oriental touch. Everyone knew it would happen, but every year it took us by surprise and added to the hurly-burly of the evening.

At midnight there was a huge buffet of turkey and chicken salad, a vegetable salad, a variety of tiny sandwiches, usually a hot Olympia oyster stew and then a variety of sweets. The late buffet made it certain that guests would linger for hours. Occasionally they were joined by people dropping by after midnight Mass, and the talk and the sipping of holiday potables—including tea—continued till early morning. I often crept away upstairs without anyone's noticing and fell into my bed. Despite my fatigue, I can think of no better way to have been initiated into the world of Christmas than this one.

Olympia Oyster Stew

It seems to me that the milk we had with cream at the top was richer and more satisfying for cooking than much we have now. I know that if I do an oyster stew today, I use light cream or half-and-half plus heavy cream. So I advise you to do the same with this delectable stew. Naturally if you don't live where the delicious little Olympia oysters are available, use others or use clams or even scallops.

For each person heat 1 cup half-and-half and heavy cream mixed according to your taste. Add the oyster liquor and for each person use about ½ cup or a few more oysters. It is plainly and simply a matter of your own taste. Heat the milk and oyster liquor and put a good dollop of butter in the dishes in which your stew is to be served. Add to the stew a dash of Tabasco, salt to taste, and lastly the oysters. Let them cook just long enough to give them a chance to heat through and curl slightly at the edges. Serve the stew very hot with paprika and plenty of buttered toast.

The utter simplicity of these flavors makes it a classic dish. If you are on the Pacific Coast in the Northwest or the part of California where the Olympias are available, do make a stew for yourself or find a good restaurant where it is carefully and lovingly made.

No one slept very late the next morning, astonishingly enough. Everyone was up and ready for more celebration. Our traditional Christmas breakfast was a good porterhouse steak done to rare perfection atop the stove—Mother always had steak cooked in the French way until a much later period in her life—and served with merely a bit of butter on it. With this went sautéed or home-fried potatoes, coffee and probably grapefruit or oranges. Mother carved the steak herself, since she held no great opinion of my father's skill, but it is my opinion that she thus did him an injustice. Using a sharp knife, which resembled a scimitar with an ivory handle, she deftly ran the blade around the bone and removed it in one swift gesture, leaving the filet and the sirloin sides ready to be carved into diagonal slices about one inch in thickness.

Later in the morning it was my father's turn to play host, and he invited friends for Tom and Jerries. Incidentally, this concoction and eggnog are two of the most disappointing celebration drinks I can think of. As a matter of fact, I take a very dim view of all punches. I know they are a necessary evil, but I myself don't wish to absorb any more of the evil than is required to be polite. I may have had to dispense a thousand different punch recipes in my day, but I haven't had to drink them, by God! Anyway, Father loved his Tom and Jerry, and his friends seemed to share his taste. Mother would set out a selection of sweets for the group, and the gaiety went on for hours, while the rest of the household made Christmas calls or prepared dinner.

Dinner was seldom more than a family affair and not a tremendous effort. It might consist of cold turkey or hot turkey or, a great favorite in the house, goose, although this was usually reserved for the New Year's menu. Like as not, it was a small turkey done with a sausage stuffing and giblet sauce. No potatoes were served because of other heavy foods on the menu. There were hot rolls, a tasty vegetable, a salad and then a pudding surrounded by holly and burning with cognac. It was delectable, this year-old plum pudding—soft and ripe and blended to a glorious fruity flavor. A sauce went with it, and after that came cheese and crackers and fruit and nuts, in the English manner, and coffee.

This was an appropriately intimate close to a tumultuous two days and somehow was especially precious to all of us. For the next week festivities would continue on a smaller scale with teas and lunches. Then one afternoon my father and mother would gather up their Christmas presents, my father counting up his cigars and Mother her teas, signaling the completion of the holidays.

Early in the New Year Mother would blend these teas into her own inimitable mixture, which everyone praised and which, I imagine, was responsible for my present love of tea. I prefer it to coffee no matter how well coffee is made, although I am capable of enjoying good coffee. Mother's famous tea was a compound of fine China and a little India tea, which was transformed into a flowery, full-bodied tea with superb flavor and a lovely, exhilarating bouquet.

When this ritual was over, there was enough tea for another year.

CHAPTER

6

On working days my father loved to rise early and get breakfast for himself, usually preparing a tray for me also and sometimes one for Mother, before putting the final flourishes on his toilette. He was a very vain man and was always well groomed. His wardrobe, while not enormous, was very handsome, and he never set out on his morning walk to the office without a red carnation in his lapel.

Occasionally, instead of coming home for dinner, he would arrange to meet Mother and me in town, and we dined together in one of our favorite restaurants. At the age of four or five I had already begun to learn the art of restaurant dining: recognizing what was good and rejecting what was inferior. I soon grew very particular about where I ate. Going to a restaurant became an event for me, and I still feel that a good restaurant meal can be stimulating. Naturally if one dines in restaurants constantly, each meal cannot be a triumph. But if one is able to choose *when* he will dine out, it is possible to make eating away from home a special pleasure.

In addition to the odd weekday trip to a restaurant, we nearly always had dinner in town on Saturday nights, either the three of us or Mother and I alone. Very often Mother had taken me to the theater in the afternoon. (She believed in sharing her love of the theater with me while I was practically an infant. As I grew up, we remained at one on the theater and on music and food, but disagreed about almost everything else!) If we dined with my father, it was always at House's Restaurant—in the early years—with a sally to Huber's now and then. Father lunched at House's nearly every day, so we were closely acquainted with the entire family of Houses and with their niece and nephew, the Feldmans.

This old, sprawling restaurant was primarily German in conception, but Mr. House had apprenticed in France and other countries and had a fine, general European approach to food. There was, of course, run-of-the-mill food on the menu, because this was a popular spot. But if you sat in the back room, delicious specialties came your way. We often took game to House's to be prepared, especially venison, and they would do it with a rich red wine sauce and serve along with it tiny turnips and *preisselbeeren*. House's didn't have a bar, so one brought his own bottle of wine to accompany the meal —that is, until Prohibition hit Oregon, which was two

170

or three years before it was felt in the rest of the country.

We often had duck or chicken at House's or wonderful large porterhouse steaks, served with broiled or sautéed tomatoes and true country fried potatoes and beef fat. The chef, Billy, was Chinese and a good friend of Let, so we had the best the house afforded. I shall never forget the other marvelous dishes that issued from Billy's kitchen, and I recall especially his cole slaw. We used the recipe for years. It was different from the one Mother usually did in that it was marinated for several hours in a rather bland but herby oil dressing.

Billy's Cole Slaw

Heat ½ cup olive oil in a sauté pan or skillet. Add 2 tablespoons flour and blend well. Add ½ teaspoon salt, 2 teaspoons dry mustard, a dash of Tabasco and 6 tablespoons sugar. Blend these thoroughly and stir in ½ cup wine vinegar. Continue stirring till the mixture thickens. Add 1 cup heavy cream mixed with 2 egg yolks and stir until ingredients are well blended and sauce is smooth. Correct the seasoning and cool the sauce slightly.

For 6 people shred 1 large cabbage or 2 smallish ones and blend this with the sauce. Let the slaw cool. Chill it for several hours and toss it thoroughly, thinning it with a little more cream if necessary or adding ½ cup mayonnaise if you wish. Drain it well before serving.

There are many additives for this cole slaw. You may use any of the following: 1 cup shredded green and red pepper; 1 cup shredded pineapple; 1 cup fine-cut green onions; 2 cups shrimp; 2 cups crabmeat; 2 cups lobster meat; 2 cups cold salmon or canned salmon; two 7-ounce cans tuna.

When this cole slaw is prepared for a smaller group, the portion of sauce not needed may be stored in the refrigerator for several days. Use smaller proportions of cabbage and additives, naturally.

During the smelt run in the Columbia, we frequently went with the Hamblets to a restaurant called Richards'. Mr. Hamblet thought they did the finest job on these small fish, and the fish *were* exceedingly good, with a crisp skin and unctuous and flavorful flesh. They differed from the Eastern smelts in being much more oily. The Indians called them candlefish, for they dried them and used them as candles.

A few days after such a dinner at Richards', Mother would go to House's, for she secretly felt that Billy did better smelts, and I'm sure I agreed with her. Years later I discovered his trick. First he boned them, then he dipped them in flour and sautéed them in butter until they were crisp on either side. Billy's cole slaw went with this and often a good tartar sauce.

This is a sauce that has suffered terrible transformations over the years, even though it is not difficult to make properly. Basically there are two versions, both with a mayonnaise base: one has chopped pickles, onion and capers in it; and the other, fresh dill, fresh chives, fresh parsley and a touch of garlic. Sometimes dill is not available, and dill pickle is substituted. This is fine if the pickles are good, but if they are the monstrous things made with dill oil one gets nowadays, they will be certain to ruin the sauce.

We used to be invited to a New Year's Day dinner at the Houses', and it was a feast indeed—*foie gras* sent to the Houses from Europe; roast goose with an apple and chestnut stuffing, which Billy did magnificently; and endless holiday specialties made by the Houses and Feldmans combined, including a huge box of springerle and anise cookies done especially for me. At that point in my life I loved them. It was a family party of about twenty, and I was usually the only child. I enjoyed the limelight, shone brilliantly and ordinarily ate myself into a state of enormous discomfort. I must say, my gourmand tendencies began early.

172

If Father was away, my mother many times took me to Falt's Quelle Restaurant. Mr. and Mrs. Falt were good friends of hers, and their restaurant was considered very gay and slightly "fast." There was music and a bar, and it was patronized by traveling men and their ladies and by certain ladies also considered "fast." Mother was much criticized for taking me there, but I was enchanted by the beautifully dressed women, the clinking of glasses and the general gaiety. This was the first place, outside of our home, I ever saw food served with drinks. Plates of tiny round rolls filled with ham, smoked fish and meat pastes were passed among the drinkers. The glamour of Falt's quickly made its impression, and after the first visit I knew that the gay life was for me. For our dinner there, we often had crawfish as a first course or Olympia oysters, followed by salmon, if it was in season, some other good native fish, or a delicate little filet, which was a specialty.

Mrs. Falt was French and devoted to good food. She had taste in clothes and jewels, too. Part of the year she spent in her house in The Dalles up the Columbia River with her maid, Mima, whom I doted on, and Mother and I often went to visit. This entailed an adventurous voyage on—before it was dismantled and sent to California—the old *Bailey Gatzert*, the fastest riverboat on the Columbia. We had breakfast or lunch aboard, and while the food was pretty bad, it was still exhilarating to tear up the river and pass through the Cascade Locks before continuing to The Dalles. We'd always have cooling drinks at Mrs. Falt's, then for dinner she might serve tiny chickens cooked with cream and tarragon, or if she found good veal, she would have thin, thin scallops with lemon and salt and pepper. With either of these went tiny peas and new potatoes and a delicious salad. We might have a berry tart for dessert, flaky and buttery.

I feel that this enchanting woman found solace in her exquisite food and wines. For Mr. Falt, handsome and debonair, had a weakness for the women who frequented his tavern. Mrs. Falt died rather young, Prohibition came, Mr. Falt disappeared, and the restaurant—one of Portland's most delightful landmarks—gave way to mediocrity.

Another restaurant we went to occasionally, as I have said, was Huber's. This was a saloon and restaurant until Prohibition, when it was turned into a dining room. The décor was left intact—mahogany paneling, and *art nouveau* drawings, paintings and stained glass, and it's a pity it hasn't been preserved to this day as a perfect example of the period. Here, too, the chef was Chinese, and he wore four remarkable jade bracelets, one above each wrist and one above each elbow. He had supervised both the free lunch and the regular lunch in the days of the saloon and afterwards kept the restaurant running for many years with a small menu and an enormous patronage. Like Billy, he made wonderful cole slaw—creamy, sour and delicious. This and freshly cooked and cooled giant turkeys, ham, shrimp, oysters, chops and steak were all that he served. Most customers were content with the turkey, which I must say was as good as any I have eaten. But if you wanted a great treat, you combined shrimp or crab with the cole slaw and had one of the best versions of seafood salad imaginable. I think I have recaptured the flavors of the superlative cole slaw, and I sometimes do the seafood salad with much success.

Just once, when I was five years old, I was taken to the most famous—and in a way, the most notorious—place in Portland. Some friends of Mother were in town and gave a dinner there, and for some capricious reason she took me along. This was the Louvre, a palace of high living. There was dancing, and cuisine, naturally, was French. Upstairs there were private rooms for dinner *à deux*, just like those in France—the type with a slit in the door through which the waiter peeked before knocking to announce the next course. That evening there were champagne and oysters and all sorts of wonderful things which contributed to elegant dining and great gaiety. If I was exhausted before the evening was over, it wasn't my fault. Mother was out of her mind to take me there in the first place. But I was fascinated by the Louvre and can proudly say I knew the place which was, without question, the liveliest that Portland ever sported.

We were sometimes invited by friends or by my Chinese godfather to dinner or a late supper in Chinatown. This was given in a private room in one of the restaurants on Second Street, usually on the top floor where there were balconies. Beautiful hangings were used to screen off the room from the street. I was never permitted to stay for the entire party and was taken home after introductions and one or two courses. I have always regretted this, for superb food was served at those dinners that would have been of interest to me professionally in later years. I have talked about this with John Kan, the San Francisco restaurateur, whose uncle was an important figure among Portland's Chinese population, and we attempted to reconstruct the menus that might have been served on those occasions. But I'm afraid that the recipes for some great specialties have disappeared for all time, along with the chefs.

The old Portland Hotel was a stately building designed by Stanford White and decorated in a most enchanting style. Beautifully arched windows embellished the main floor, the rooms and corridors were generously proportioned, and there was an enormous porch where one could sit and see Portland stroll by. The dining room was very long, as I remember, with windows on three sides, and there was also a lively grill. We often had tea with a friend of Mother's, Mrs.

Frohman, who had a shop in the hotel that offered lovely Oriental things and assorted gifts, and she also had two parlors in the hotel. We had our cup of tea with scones, rolls or toast from the hotel kitchen, and it was a delight to use the glittering silver service and be attended by the Negro waiters, who seemed to have been around from the day the hotel opened.

On state occasions we had dinner at the Portland, but Mother felt the food was rather bad, and perhaps it was. At any rate, she never did anything but criticize it, and I recall an evening when she sent some capon back to the kitchen, made the maître d'hôtel very uncomfortable and finally ate nothing at all. She said afterwards it was silly to order capon in a place like that, because you knew it was cold-storage and not any good; she should have had better sense, etc. Mother wouldn't order roast beef in restaurants either, because she claimed it was always kept steamed and had that awful juice on it and wasn't fit for eating. Consequently, she usually ate fish or a chop.

I always looked forward to Saturday lunches before the theater. They would be quick but exciting, because they were the prelude to a day of gadding about, to the theater (later, to the movies, as they became popular) and to dinner. We often went to the Royal Bakery near the theaters and ate one of their remarkably good club-house sandwiches, or chicken sandwiches, salad and tea and some of their extraordinary charlotte russe or marzipan cake. Or we went to Swetlands, where I especially liked the dessert, hot butterscotch on ice cream with toasted almonds. No matter what went before, if I had this dessert I was content with the world. Also, at Swetlands I could stock up on stick candy. And if I was around at the right moment, I would be given a few candied violets. I prized them and picked them out of every box of chocolates that ever came into the house. And I still love their flavor and crystalline texture. I had no taste for chocolate until I grew older.

Two restaurants in Portland, more than any others, advanced my life of good eating. Both had character and offered food which one cannot find any more in cities such as Portland was before the twenties.

One of these restaurants came into my life through a classmate of mine in high school, whose name was Chester Benson. Chester's parents were divorced—his father was tremendously wealthy and a great figure in the development of Oregon—and he lived with his mother and brother not too far from us. Chester and I became good friends—we liked music and theater, and we liked to eat—and our mothers found a common ground of interest as well.

Mrs. Benson was a very good cook, and she made marvelous cakes and pastries for the pleasure of her two sons, and I was often given delicious snacks there and was sometimes invited for lunch. The boys' birthday parties were famous. Mrs. Benson made elaborate preparations for them and would do huge poundcakes, ribboned inside with every imaginable color, heavily iced with royal icing and decorated with silver balls, ornate inscriptions and all sorts of furbelows. They were masterpieces of late Edwardian birthday cake art, and could someone re-create their charm today, he would make a fortune.

At Christmas Mrs. Benson made sugar cookies by the gross. They were crisp, buttery, thoroughly delicious and cut in every imaginable shape with an assortment of cookie cutters I wish I had now. On a certain Saturday before Christmas about twelve or fourteen children and several mothers were invited to the Bensons' for an afternoon of cookie art. Icing of every shade was provided, together with brushes, and the children were given free choice of design. I remember that, between eating and painting, the afternoon was a great success. However, the decorated cookies made a somewhat startling exhibition. Some should have been preserved for the currently popular shows of children's art, although others were better eaten on the spot.

Several years after we became acquainted with the Bensons, Chester's father took over a hotel that had originally been built for someone else. It was named The Benson and was the first great luxury hotel in Portland, more up-to-date than the Edwardian *luxe* of the charming old Portland, with beautifully decorated suites, fine bathrooms and exquisitely appointed dining rooms. And it also provided Portland with its first famous chef, Henri Thiele, a Swiss who had trained in France. This man had a fawning manner and great ambition, but he was a great, creative chef.

Though Mr. and Mrs. Benson were divorced, the boys had charge accounts at their father's hotel, and we were often their guests for dinner or lunch. So it happened that I became a frequent visitor to the hotel, learned to know and admire Thiele and experienced some new and utterly delicious dishes. For example, Thiele did beautiful *paupiettes* of sole, sauced and then garnished with our tiny Olympia oysters, and he did a marvelous crabmeat Newburg, which he served on toasted muffins or toasted brioche, made by him in the hotel bakery. And he did a mutton chop, cut across the saddle in the correct way, served with a stuffed potato, done to order, and an incredible cole slaw shredded into a thin film and flavored with a very tart French dressing containing a little turmeric and hot pepper.

Thiele soon discovered that the Beards loved food, and on occasions when Mother was invited to dine with the Bensons he offered the best of his creative skill. I will never forget the béarnaise sauce he made one evening—as tarragoned as possible and light and fluffy withal—which was served with a roast filet of beef, crusty and rare. The combination was perfection. But Thiele's salmon dishes were his true forte and became the feature of the Columbia Gorge Hotel, which **Mr.** Benson later built for him. I can remember a whole baked salmon done with cream, and fillets of salmon stuffed with a salmon mousse and then poached in a court bouillon.

And Thiele's Princess Charlotte pudding! I have tried for years and years to duplicate it, from the first days of The Benson, but have never achieved the same quality. It was rather like a fine *bavaroise*, but creamier, with praline in it and a supremely good cassis sauce over it.

I recall visiting Thiele's pastry kitchens, where I saw *petits fours* turned out by a good *pâtissier*, ate some of the creams from the pot and learned a great deal about assembling these little cakes. And I shall never forget a puff paste tart Thiele made with coarsely chopped toasted hazelnuts, a rich pastry cream and a melted sugar and nut topping.

Nor shall I forget his simple dishes, such as grilled liver with a sour cream sauce, very much like the Swiss *suri leberli* but more delicate. And he had a way with the tiny crawfish of the Coast that was sensational, for he combined its meat with avocado and a special sauce of highly seasoned mayonnaise and cream. Then there was the magnificent simplicity of Thiele's steak, done with butter, shallots and pepper and served with his version of roesti.

I shall be forever grateful to the Benson family. Alas, the hotel is no longer owned by the family. It now sports a Trader Vic's, instead of the subtle cookery of Thiele. But Thiele made its name. He reached his high point when he was under the direction of the Bensons. Later, he went into business for himself and became a mass producer without any of the finesse he had brought to his original kitchens. In my files I have a small announcement of the opening of his new business, when he pioneered the practice of sending out lunches to

businessmen and office workers. For fifty cents one got
three sandwiches, salad, hard-boiled eggs, fruit and pie
or cake, and for fifty cents more one could have the
addition of two salads, and half a cold chicken. No
charge for delivery either. And that was as late as
1924.

The second great Portland restaurant, which still
exists in different and more elaborate form, is located in
Meier & Frank's department store, run by the two
families since the early 1850s. It is a landmark and has
a personality unlike that of any other store in America.
My father's family traded there in bartering days.
Mother had one of the lowest account numbers on the
books and felt as much at home there as she did in her
own house.

The restaurant began as a novelty and became for a
long time the best eating place in all of Portland. It was
as hard to get a table there as it is now at "21" in New
York. The men's grill has some regulars who have been
going there for thirty and forty years or more—every
day! This year Meier & Frank opened another fine
restaurant in their new shopping-center store, which
serves dinner and has a bar, grill and dining room.

One of the best chefs I ever knew was the chef at
Meier & Frank's for a number of years, Don Daniels.
He was paid extremely well for a chef by those days'
standards and was worth it, for he produced food of rare
quality—veal birds with a rich, creamy sauce, flavored
with dill or tarragon; a beautiful salmi of duckling; and
a remarkably good salmon soufflé with a hollandaise
sauce. And he did superb clams, shipped from Seaside
and Gearhart as fast as possible, which were sautéed
meunière or with parsley butter and served with an
excellent tartar sauce.

ı also served good caviar and wonderful salads,
ς them one which included chicken, walnuts and
ιn mayonnaise. His curry of crab was unforget-

table, as was his little boned squab with a rice stuffing. Desserts were beyond belief. His Frankco is still one of the greatest frozen desserts ever created. It is made with the heaviest cream possible, whipped and then frozen at a very low temperature. Then it is scooped out in jagged crystalline portions. In my day, this came in maple, cognac, lemon and strawberry, according to the season, and it is still a major attraction at Meier & Frank's. Don also made rich home-style coffeecakes with almond toppings and *streusel*, using butter by the ton. And there was a remarkable black bottom pie. It had a crumb crust and was really two different types of Bavarian cream on a chocolate base. If you cared for that sort of dessert, then it was your dish and a sublime one.

This man was unique, and fortunately the Meiers and Franks understood his genius. He had a true sense of the seasonal aspect of menu building and was one of the first restaurant men to feature seasonal foods when they were at their height. He had an established clientele who wanted the best and paid for it, and he ran the restaurant according to his own gastronomic pleasure. (They are the same ideas, on a smaller scale, which Joseph Baum applied so successfully to the Four Seasons.) I am glad I knew this man and grateful that, for a period of time, I could eat in his restaurant four or five times a week.

San Francisco, during my childhood and early teens, was my dream city. We spent a week or two, sometimes a month, there each year, making the trip usually on the Shasta Limited of the Southern Pacific. This train was my idea of true luxury, and two meals in the diner were heaven (and in those days my family considered Southern Pacific food well below the standards of the great cross-country lines). It was a treat to rise with the Siskiyous and the Coast Ranges rolling by and to breakfast on ham and eggs, sausage and eggs, or occasionally fresh mountain trout which had been taken on during one of the stops—all rather well prepared.

Sometimes we had the thrill of taking a boat trip from Portland aboard *The Beaver*, *The Bear* or *The Rose City*, which plied their way between Portland, San Francisco and Los Angeles. It was a two-day trip to San Francisco, and the excitement of a short sea voyage made up for the food. At best it was ordinary, but that only gave one greater appetite for the restaurants of San Francisco.

For two wonderful years, during the 1915 fair (the Panama-Pacific International Exposition) and part of the following year, the two great liners *Northern Pacific* and *Great Northern* sailed from Flavel below Astoria to San Francisco and back; and this really was luxury travel. A boat train left from Portland, raced to Flavel at great speed, and soon one was aboard. One of these liners, renamed the *H. F. Alexander*, became one of the

fastest ships on the Atlantic during World War I. There wasn't time for much eating aboard either ship—one had dinner and breakfast, and he was ready to dock. But the food was memorable. Dungeness crab and razor clams and Columbia River salmon starred, along with the best of California fruits and vegetables and a great profusion of imported delicacies, such as *foie gras* and occasionally good caviar. I still remember the whole Chinook salmon of enormous proportions in a wine aspic, served with an anchovy mayonnaise remotely related to some of the Provencal sauces. My father loved it, got the recipe, and it became an occasional treat, especially at the beach, where salmon flowed into our house as if it were a tributary of the Columbia.

I can also remember my first *salade russe* aboard one of these ships, and wonderful smallish cantaloupes, somewhat like the Charentais melons, served with delicious ice cream or with fresh raspberries and port.

I cannot describe the excitement of pushing through the Golden Gate in even such a small tub as *The Beaver*

or *The Bear*. One had the feeling of having arrived in the Promised Land from afar. (I still succumb to the enchantment of San Francisco each time I go there.) We'd be off to the Palace or the St. Francis, and in later years the Clift. Then without stop there would be theater, music, shopping, visits and eating.

There were great restaurants in those days—Fred Solari's on Maiden Lane, Solari's on Geary Street behind the St. Francis, Marquard's, Tait's at the Beach and Techau Tavern, all of which have disappeared, victims of Prohibition or just tired and gone. But there is still Jack's, a restaurant that has changed comparatively little in all the years I have been going there. It has kept its *fin de siècle* décor and, it would· appear, some of its *fin de siècle* personnel. They still serve the same delicious crab, oysters, abalone and fine fish and such specialities as calf's head vinaigrette—and superb sand dabs. Mother once said, "If I'd been able to get fresh sand dabs every day and the best white asparagus from California throughout the season, I would never have sold the business." This is one of the great fishes of the world and is usually prepared so badly it loses its essential character. This delicate member of the flounder family should be either filleted or cooked whole, and the cooking should be nothing more than the lightest sauté *meunière.* It should be rushed to your table from the pan without further embellishment. This is as tender and as delicious a fish as I have ever eaten anywhere, and if you have never tasted it, make a trip to Jack's one day when you are in San Francisco.

Jack's also produced some excellent squab and chicken, including a wonderful *sauté sec,* which still appears on their menu and is unbelievably simple.

Chicken Sauté Sec

Disjoint a 2- to 2½-pound broiler. Melt 6 tablespoons butter in a skillet, and when it is bubbling, brown the chicken pieces lightly on both sides over a brisk flame. Add salt and pepper to taste. When the chicken is browned to the state you desire, reduce the heat and add ⅓ cup white wine or very dry sherry. Allow the chicken to simmer until it is tender, turning it once or twice during the cooking. Serve it with sautéed potatoes or rice pilaf and a salad.

For some reason San Francisco has always meant squab to me. Once when the family had an apartment there, we used to shop in the markets a great deal and bought squab at two and three for a dollar, and exceedingly good ones at that. Often they were just flattened and broiled *à la crapaudine*, and sometimes they were stuffed with a savory mixture, roasted and basted with white wine and butter—delicious food to be eaten with the fingers, else one would miss some of its goodness. How many times have I watched diners in restaurants too proud to lift bones to mouth. How they massacred the tiny bird! And what miserable return they got. I must say, I have never seen anyone who truly enjoys food who didn't use his fingers when necessary.

Down the alley off Union Square were two famous spots—Fred Solari's and a small French *bistro*, which I found enchanting when I was young. It was of the meal-plus-wine *prix fixe* type of restaurant. The dishes were piled at the table in readiness for customers, and silver, glasses, and linen were also close at hand so that the waiters had a minimum of work before a meal. One was served a huge ironstone tureen of soup, good sourdough bread, an excellent bourgeois dish, a fairly palatable California wine, and cheese and fruit, or sometimes dessert, for about seventy-five cents at lunch and slightly more at dinner. The main dish would be a good *pot-au-feu*, a *boeuf à la mode*, a *daube*, or a *poule-au-pot*. Such hearty, inexpensive dishes would not be ruined if they continued to cook an extra hour while a meal was being served.

We also used to lunch often in the recently demolished Fly Trap. This was as plain as any restaurant could be, but the cooking always remained honest and flavorful. If you wanted good fish or crab, or good chops and steak, you found the Fly Trap had a special quality about it, and this was proven by the loyal patronage of some of the old-timers.

185

For elegant dining, I think that Marquard's and Tait's at the Beach impressed me more than any other place in San Francisco, with the exception of the Palace Court. Marquard's had a buffet luncheon or hors d'oeuvre luncheon, which used to fascinate me as a child, for I loved the looks of the laden table and the idea of tasting a great many things. And Tait's at the Beach embodied such glamour that I have never forgotten it. But the cuisine at these two places, alas, declined during Prohibition, and I am left only with the recollection of their luxurious air, which, after all, is not the test of a good restaurant.

The Palace Court was another restaurant that prided itself on great food in those days. And with its palms, rich draperies and carpeting and smooth, luxurious service, the hotel was comparable to the best European hostelry. Dishes emanating from its kitchens became classics, for the food, as old San Franciscans know, was impeccable. Game, fine fish and seafood—all the glories of the region—were featured. It was here I learned the joys of the alligator pear, the versatility of the artichoke, the pleasures of ripe citrus fruit. And two famous dishes served there have stayed in my memory.

Crab Legs Palace Court

This dish is still available at the Palace Hotel, though I'm sure not done as well as formerly. Serve as an hors d'oeuvre or as a luncheon dish.

For each serving make a bed of crisp greens. On it place a large slice of tomato. On this place a good-sized artichoke bottom with the inner choke removed and a few leaves left to form a cup. Fill this with *salade russe* (a salad of diced cooked vegetables blended with mayonnaise), top with large Dungeness crab legs, and decorate with thin slices of pimiento. Around the artichoke and the tomato press fine-chopped hard-boiled egg yolk, and serve with a well-flavored Thousand Island dressing. The same dish may be prepared with large lump Atlantic crabmeat

or with lobster meat, but the Dungeness crab has a certain delicacy which seems to make the dish more delicious.

The other dish—another Palace original which restaurants elsewhere have copied—is oysters Kirkpatrick. The legend is that they were created for one of the staff at the old Palace. When Helen Brown did her *West Coast Cook Book*, the Palace sent her a recipe which she and I both think is not the original. Nor do she and I agree entirely on the one we first knew. The first one I ever ate, and the one which I had repeatedly, was this:

Oysters Kirkpatrick

For each person arrange 6 oysters in their shells on a bed of coarse salt. Loosen each oyster from its shell, dip it in catchup and return it to shell. Top it with fine-chopped scallions and a strip of partially cooked bacon. Bake at 400° just long enough to heat the oysters and crisp the bacon. Serve at once.

Sometimes a spoonful of grated Parmesan cheese was sprinkled over the bacon before it went to the oven.

Another famous recipe from the Palace, which has been subject to a number of variations since it was first created, was Green Goddess dressing for salads. This was much later than the oysters Kirkpatrick period and it was presumably done for George Arliss when he toured in *The Green Goddess*.

Green Goddess Dressing

Combine 1 quart mayonnaise—and it must be good homemade mayonnaise done with olive oil—with 14 to 16 coarsely chopped anchovies, ½ cup chopped parsley and chives mixed, 3 tablespoons chopped fresh tarragon (or 2 teaspoons dried tarragon, or more to taste), ⅓ cup tarragon vinegar, and salt and freshly ground black pepper to taste. Beat ingredients together for a few minutes, correct the seasoning and allow the dressing to stand for several hours before serving.

After San Francisco, London was the next great city whose restaurants I knew. I made my first trip there on a small freighter, *The Highland Heather*, which sailed from the West Coast. The ship was British, and as I recorded earlier, the food was poor British. By the time four weeks had passed, my fairly well-trained palate rebelled. I bartered with the stewards to let me have all the cheese and English biscuits I wanted, and I tasted nothing else for the last ten days of the voyage except for a rather throat-searing curry the breakfast cook made with tinned fish. This was so highly spiced that it obscured the flavor of everything that accompanied it and so was rather good. I'm sure it was what the chef existed on.

If I were asked to name the greatest meal I ever had, I think I might answer the luncheon the day I disembarked at Southampton. After I had passed through customs and attended to my baggage, I made for the nearby railway station restaurant with an appetite unequaled in my life. I remember the meal in detail. It happened to consist of a thick pea soup with croutons, breaded lamb cutlets and the most tremendous bowl of cauliflower *polonaise* I had ever seen. Naturally, there were also those extraordinary British browned potatoes, with skin so tough they seemed safe forever from penetration by knife and fork. But everything tasted ambrosial, and I knew that never again in my life would I experience a more sensual enjoyment of food than at that moment. If the same meal were served to me now, I would probably hurl it through the window.

London in the early twenties was far different from today. Soho was really an international settlement, and few of its restaurants had succumbed to British influence. Some places, like the Rendezvous, had become frightfully posh with the West Enders and the theater crowd, but for the most part the small eating places remained unfashionable and delightful.

Among the great restaurants, one had Pagani's, Scott's, Oddenino's, the Ivy, the Savoy grill, the Ritz, the Carlton and Claridge's. The small, intimate, rather Bohemian-style tearooms, such as the Good Intent in Chelsea, were just beginning, and one ate well in some of the clubs.

I'll always remember a remark made to me at Pagani's. Helen Dircks, who was at that time publicist for the Palladium and afterwards one of the great advertising and publicity women in England, was my guest for dinner at the restaurant. At the end of the meal I hoped I wasn't embarrassing her when I took the trouble to add up the bill before paying it. Helen said, "If you had paid the bill without examining it, I would never have gone out with you again."

This woman was a great force in my London life. It was she who introduced me to the man who became my voice coach, and she who guided me to restaurants, theaters and interesting places. Her father had been one of the great drama critics—on a London daily—and Helen had had a remarkable childhood and youth among the literary and theatrical lights of the time. I had my first London dry martini with Helen at the Rendezvous, and with her and her husband, Ralph Goome, I was first introduced to Verreys, which at that time was an enchanting bar patronized by a cosmopolitan group of people.

I also became devoted to a small Belgian *bistro* near the Palladium where, when you were "accepted," you were given a pigeonhole for your napkin and a fresh napkin each Monday. Here one ate quite good bourgeois dishes and, surprisingly enough, from time to time a typical English specialty. Once every fortnight a beefsteak-and-kidney pudding appeared on the menu, and it was the best I ever ate, by far. The pudding was steamed in individual molds and was always in demand by the regular customers.

Beefsteak-and-Kidney Pudding

For the Crust: Blend 1½ cups fine-chopped suet (it must be almost powdery) with 3 cups flour and salt to taste—about 1 teaspoon. Add just enough ice water to make a stiff paste of about the same texture as pie-crust dough. Chill this for 30 minutes. Roll out enough dough to line 1 large bowl or several small ones, and reserve the rest to make a top crust.

For the Filling: Remove the core and fat from 3 veal kidneys and slice them thin. After dredging them in flour, combine 2 pounds chuck, cut in 1½-inch cubes, with the kidney slices. Add 1 clove garlic, 12 fine-chopped shallots, chopped parsley, thyme, and salt and pepper to taste. Place the filling in the dough-lined bowl and fill the bowl to 1 inch below the rim with beef bouillon. Roll out the remaining dough and place it over the pudding, allowing it to overlap the edge of the bowl enough to seal it. Wring out a cloth and place it over the bowl. Sprinkle this with flour and then cover all with aluminum foil, tied securely to make it leakproof. Place the bowl in a pan filled with hot water to within an inch of the top of the bowl. Bring the water to a boil. Boil a single, large pudding 3 to 4 hours and small puddings about 3 hours.

Boiled or mashed potatoes and brussels sprouts are excellent with this, and a good beer is a perfect accompaniment.

My coach, Tano, was a famous Italian authority on opera and song lore. He had been Caruso's secretary and assistant in New York and had coached practically every great singer of the age. He was short, round, jovial, loved good food and often entertained delightfully in his home. He frequented several Italian restaurants in London where he was always welcomed with much fanfare, and one of his favorite spots was Gennaro's in Soho. Gennaro, who had been a ballet dancer in Milan, was then enjoying his new role as restaurateur. He had lost his figure but not his grace, and I shall never forget the sight of him tossing his fourteen stone across the floor to present a long-stemmed rose to some glamorous lady client. The food at Gennaro's was sensational—a far cry from the restaurant of the same name in London today.

Gennaro served a cold hors d'oeuvre in summer which is worth repeating here. Mother, when she came over to visit me, declared it was the most delicious lobster dish she had ever tasted, and she couldn't eat enough of it. I have used the recipe all my life, simple though it is.

Eggs Gennaro

For each serving you must have a large thoroughly ripe tomato. It should be depipped and drained, and most of the pulp should be removed. Into each tomato put a touch of chopped basil, a bit of salt and then a large medallion of lobster, which has been perfectly cooked and cooled. Top this with a cold poached egg, well trimmed, garnish it with fine-chopped lobster and parsley, and serve with a Gennaro dressing.

For the dressing combine 1½ cups mayonnaise made with olive oil, a touch of garlic (enough to perfume the dressing but not overpower the delicate flavors), 1 anchovy fillet chopped fine, 1 tablespoon basil and 2 tablespoons parsley chopped fine, 1 tablespoon capers chopped fine, and a dash of lemon juice. Allow the ingredients to mellow 1 or 2 hours before serving.

Gennaro prepared other fascinating Italian specialties with a Milan-Parma overtone, for he hailed from that part of Italy. And he would do particular dishes to order for the kind of patron who had to have his favorite food or die. Great Italian singers, from Battistini to Gigli, came to Gennaro's, as well as singers from Covent

Garden; and the Guitrys came whenever they were in London. It was an exciting experience for me to dine there with Tano, for he knew everyone. Strange and wonderful meals came through the kitchen doors, and I grew to appreciate the delight of really good Italian food.

There was a *bistro*, or *albergo* rather, near Soho Square where Tano sent me one day for lunch. I immediately took a fancy to it and to the wonderful family who ran it. The daughter, Lisa, was stout, full of life, and she enjoyed looking after the American visitor. She loved food herself and was well versed in its lore. The Ristorante del Comercio was tiny and gay, with checked curtains, tables and chairs painted green, and many *bibelots* and canned and bottled foods decorating the room. There was no bar, but one of the family would willingly run out for a carafe of wine or a pitcher of beer for you. Everyone who came to the restaurant seemed to know everyone else.

I first learned to eat raw artichokes there. Lisa had brought me a plate of magnificent ones, and I asked how I should have them. "Raw," she said, "with a little dressing I make for you." So she took a touch of garlic, rubbed it into salt, added oil, vinegar, freshly ground pepper and a bit of crumbled red pepper and then stirred and tasted until she had achieved the balance she wanted. "Now try," she said. "Eat only the ends, and when you finish, I show you what to do with the *fondo*." Thus I discovered a new way with artichokes, which I had eaten all my life in the usual manner. The tiny tip of green was tender and crisp, and the dressing enhanced it beautifully.

Another time Lisa said, "You know dandelion?" I said I did, and then she proceeded to fix the greens for me, the first of many occasions. She sautéed cubes of the rather fat smoked pork from Italy, added garlic and then the dandelion, followed by fresh mint and wine vinegar. It was sent to table still crisp and underdone, flavored superbly with the mint-garlic-bacon combination.

Another dish at the Comercio I shall never forget was the simple delight of veal scallops with lemon.

Scallopini alla Limone

Pound 12 scallops of fine white veal very thin and sauté them quickly in a combination of 3 tablespoons olive oil and 3 tablespoons butter. When they are nicely browned on both sides, add 1 teaspoon grated lemon rind, add salt to taste and a grinding of fresh pepper. Just before removing them from the pan, add the juice of ½ lemon and turn the scallops once. Transfer them to a hot platter, and serve them with thin, thin slices of lemon and a few capers.

Each time I return to London I walk past the site of the Comercio and feel a deep sense of gratitude for the restaurant that once stood there. What happened to the family I will never know.

My favorite pastime for Sunday, or any other day, in London used to be tea at the Ritz. This charming experience cost only half a crown in the early twenties, which was within my budget for elegant diversions. But such a half crown's worth!—a posh atmosphere, great comfort and delicious little sandwiches, toast, pastries and tea. Besides, there was the passing parade of the most fashionable people. As recently as last year I had tea at the Ritz, and it is one of the few surviving examples of a bygone era. The service, the appointments and the tea are still admirable, and make one long to return to a more gracious age.

In 1922–23 I could have lunch or dinner at the Ritz only when someone invited me, and I lived on the memory of it for weeks afterwards. The food was magnificent and the service impeccable. I once heard my mother say, "A sandwich at the Ritz is worth three meals in any other restaurant, no matter how poor you may be and how hungry!" Alas, this is no longer true. The service is usually good, but except for tea and a few things on the luncheon menu, the Ritz is a pale image of its former days.

My first visit to Paris in 1923 was a tremendously exciting event, and one dream I had preserved for a number of years was to dine at Maxim's—no doubt because of the song from *The Merry Widow* and other alluring associations. This was to me the most glamorous place of all time, and I was prepared to spend my pittance for a good meal there. So one evening I reserved a table, put on my best suit, and went with a friend to the famed Maxim's. A couple of hours later I left, disillusioned and miserable. For the food was mediocre and the service indifferent. I was quite bewildered, and it was a long time before I tried Maxim's again. I have been there many times since, and only once have I felt that it measured up to its reputation. This was at a dinner in 1949 to honor a group on a wine tour of France, one of whom happened to be me. The food was superb, and Louis Vaudable did everything in his power to make the occasion memorable. The menu included pheasant Souvaroff, exquisite *rougets* and wonderful caviar, and the wines were chosen with great care.

The décor, the charm, and the ambiance of Maxim's still dominate the food, I'm afraid. It is not a great restaurant, nor will it ever be, since it can survive on its own legend.

I discovered many other delightful eating spots in those days. I lived in a remarkable pension on the rue Jacob where the food was good bourgeois fare and exceedingly cheap—so much so that one felt he could afford to wander to a more expensive restaurant now and then. We ate good *pot-au-feu*, calf's feet *poulette*, *blanquettes* and *boeuf à la bourguignonne*, with an occasional roast chicken or bit of game. With the francs saved here, I would often eat around the corner at another pension on the rue Bonaparte, where the food was excellent and they took transient guests for lunch. The hors d'oeuvre were delicious, the vegetables succulent, and I remember that in late summer we would sometimes have a marvelous cold *daube* or a jellied ham dish, which I have come to believe was a *jambon persillé*. Looking back, I am sure the chef was from Provence, because many of the dishes were typical of that region. They were consumed with gusto by a group of young Englishmen, Italians and Frenchmen who frequented the place. I seemed to be the sole American.

Paris, in the early twenties, was going through a Russian era, for White Russians were settling there by the thousands. It was natural that some of them should open restaurants. The Caneton in the rue de la Bourse was the one Russian-managed restaurant more talked about than any other and reputed to be elegant and blessed with a good chef. It happened that a friend from Portland arrived in Paris, someone I wished to impress, so I invited her to dine with me at the Caneton. I remember calling for her in a barouche, riding to the rue de la Bourse and being much struck by the décor and the maître d'hôtel's effusive welcome. We started the meal with caviar and blinis—my first public adventure with blinis—served with a great crock of cream. Champagne appeared to be *the* drink to have, and we had it—through shashlik and kasha, vegetables and an elaborate dessert. It was a dinner I have never forgotten, nor have I forgotten the bill. It was a hundred francs—the largest restaurant bill that ever was, I thought at the time. I paid it, hired a barouche to take my friend to her hotel, then went back to my pension, feeling that life in Paris was frightfully expensive.

But within the next week or two I was rewarded for my extravagance, for someone asked me to tea at Rumpelmayer's and someone else took me to the Boeuf à la

Mode, where I dined magnificently. Rumpelmayer's was so enchanting and offered such an array of pastries in those days—tiny éclairs, tiny *mille-feuilles*, beautiful frangipane tarts—I went on eating for hours, it seemed, and then I took a long walk through the Luxembourg Gardens to allow all the pastry to settle. The world took on new color each time I went to tea at Rumpelmayer's.

There were other places similar to Rumpelmayer's— Colombin and Louis Sherry at the Rond Point among them. But they have gone forever and with them the charm of small teashops and the art of producing great pastry. One had best learn the art of pastry-making for himself if he wants really good pastry. I often make little éclairs for a dinner party, or my favorite *pain de Gênes* or a fine poundcake. All these things are so delectable that I must refrain from making them too often.

One of the favorite tourist spots used to be Robinson, in the country outside Paris. While the food was never commendable, it was a stimulating experience to dine in the trees—for the restaurant was composed of little platforms built among the branches of a grove of chestnuts. One climbed to his perch, and his food was hoisted to him in a basket. There was music and a contagious air of high spirits. For impressionable young people who were in Paris for the first time, it meant really Living. I can remember going there with a group of friends on one occasion and getting separated from them during the course of a festive evening. I finally took the milk train back to Paris, and it was past dawn when I crawled into my pension on the rue Jacob. I recall sitting on the balcony outside my room and watching Paris wake up. The achievement of staying up all night seems to have eternal appeal for the young.

When Tano came to Paris, I was taken to the Tour d'Argent for dinner—this was before it moved up to the roof of the building it was in. I ate duck, and found the restaurant a supreme pleasure. I still think it is one of the greatest restaurants in Paris and one of the great restaurants in the world. Claude Terrail has kept the traditions intact and the food superb.

I only wish I had known in 1923 what I know now about Paris restaurants. I might have found many more interesting places, in vogue at the time, which have disappeared into history. I am unhappy every time I think that the great Montagne was cooking in Paris in that era, and I didn't know it. But I am grateful that I was enterprising enough to explore among the smaller restaurants and learn the basic dishes of French cuisine, when I might have been spending my money in the fleshpots.

Today's restaurants in Paris and the French countryside have changed a great deal, with the most marked change occurring since 1950. Tourists in increasing numbers, and especially those who can make demands because of wealth or position, have corrupted restaurant traditions and created chaos throughout the entire restaurant business in Europe.

In addition to this problem, there is the growing tendency to look upon working with one's hands as an inferior occupation. No longer are there talented chefs emerging through the apprentice system to take the place of the fast-dwindling ranks of the great. And the Americanization of certain French food habits adds to the decline of a glorious art.

I am inclined to believe that the starring system put into effect quite honestly by Michelin, and adopted by every magazine in America and Europe, has contributed much to the ruination of good eating. And the excessive promoting of "must" restaurants throughout Europe, which magazines are prone to do, have turned many temples of gastronomic splendor into mere tourist traps. To achieve any status at all as a gourmet these days, one *must* go to Maxim's or to Lapérouse. And "doing" the three-star restaurants is one of the current fashions for travelers in Europe. This is a rather grim phenomenon to anyone who has for many years loved certain restaurants that happen to be on the list.

In 1961 I visited all the three-star restaurants in France and a great many of the smaller restaurants, and I trekked through the restaurants of England twice in that year. In addition to my far-ranging visits to restaurants, for over ten years I have worked as a consultant to restaurateurs in the United States. I have come to many conclusions as a result, one of the most significant being the conviction that this has become an age of family restaurants—a condition brought on by the shortage of chefs. Many of those who are working in this profession go into mass production when they reach the top, and their individual talents are lost in the anonymity of frozen and processed foods. The great restaurants tend to be those which have the family integrity for their inspiration and which cater to a comparatively small clientele. This trend is especially true in Europe.

My favorite restaurant in all of France is L'Auberge de Père Bise at Talloires, and certainly this is a family affair, of three-star magnitude. Marius Bise is the presiding genius and the man whose inventiveness and keen palate have made the restaurant what it is. But everyone else in the family is there, working to maintain the standard of perfection in food and service which Marius has established.

In another three-star restaurant, Oustau de Baumanière, one discerns the imprint of the *patron* everywhere. The menu remains limited. Obviously this restaurant would rather produce five or six main courses impeccably than a larger menu which allows no time for the refinement of details.

In a smaller way, the *bistros* one finds throughout France embody this same family idea. Often the *patron*

199

is the chef, and *la patronne* is at the front of the house. This in itself almost assures one of good service and good food. Such restaurants as Aux Marronniers and Paul Chène have an honest quality about them, with an excellent choice of regional specialities, a polished style of cookery and pleasant, if not perfect, service. On my first visit to Paul Chène I remember being offered *beignets* of *brandade de morue* and a superlative *boeuf bourguignon*—not the stew version but a *daube*. I am not ordinarily fond of this dish, and when it intrigues me, it has to be unusually good. The *beignets* were so delicious and so delicate, one wondered why they didn't fly off the plate. Paul Chène has just one star in Michelin. He deserves to be awarded two more.

I was first taken to Aux Marronniers by Naomi Barry of the Paris *Herald*. On that occasion we ate delicious brioche with *langouste à l'américaine*. Another time I had their incredible lobster *pâté*, and on a third visit, the most perfectly grilled little chicken I have ever eaten, served with a richly tarragoned béarnaise sauce which was heady and stimulating. Such restaurants as this one are the hope of good eating.

Another restaurant in the family tradition, Chez Camille, reverses the usual order of things, for the *patronne* is the chef, while her husband manages the front of the house. Strangely enough, one of the great specialties here is the same chicken one finds at Marronniers, and very good it is, too. However, the mussels done in pots with a snail butter are sensational, and so is the *gratin* of mussels. I have sent many people to this small restaurant, and they have been enchanted with it.

One of the oldest examples I know of the family restaurant is that of Mme. Pannetrat of Aux Bonnes Choses in rue Falguière near the boulevard Montparnasse. Madame and her daughter and granddaughter are all part of the staff, which sometimes includes twenty people. This *bistro* is different from any other I can think of and serves some delicious food from the Périgord. Madame makes her own *confit d'oie*, buys good truffles, does an excellent *poulet à la basquaise* and also a heavy winter luncheon dish—*confit* with white beans—which I adore but dare not eat more than once a year.

In 1924, the year after I had visited the West Indies, Europe and other parts of the globe, I made my first trip to New York. I arrived in the city with no particular joy, having been quite content in Europe, and I was convinced that I could never come to love it. In this frame of mind, and without bothering to do much sightseeing, I went off to visit friends outside the city for a few days. When I returned something had happened to me. I suddenly saw the city afresh, and spellbound I began to wander along the streets of Manhattan, absorbing its grandeur, charm and excitement.

New York was much more European in feeling during the twenties than it is today. It was gay and wild, as were all the world capitals at that time. Money was plentiful, and the ways to spend it were legion. Speakeasies flourished, and they ranged from the very elegant to the joints where you asked for Joe. The fashionable ones became the great restaurants of today, and some of the joints became famous nightclubs. Patrons of the speakeasies had their own keys or knew the mode of entrance. I remember one club where a tiny ball and chain was the token of admission. Here drinks were expensive and good, and the ambiance was as elegant as the Plaza's today. I believe there were more really great restaurants then than there are now. And one ate well in many of the small speakeasies.

Once I was captivated by the city, I began to search out the places whose names were familiar to me. One of these was the old Waldorf on 34th Street, where the Empire State Building now stands. I went there for

lunch and took a table by a window, where I could
watch passing traffic. Just as I began reading the menu
and relaxing in the splendor of the dining room, I was
struck by the most painful toothache I have ever had.
By this time the captain was awaiting my order. I
explained my predicament. He was sympathetic and
promptly suggested that I permit him to choose my
food. I did, and he brought me the most perfect oyster
stew imaginable—creamy, rich and pungent. It salved
my body and cheered my soul. This was my introduction
to the Waldorf Astoria, and I have always savored my
memories of it. What a glorious old hotel it was!

I also had great affection for Sherry's small restaurant
and pastry shop on 58th Street and Fifth Avenue, across
from the old Savoy Hotel, where one lunched or dined
on the porch in summer—an enchanting spot. Sherry's
had a truly Old World quality and offered good food
and excellent service. The baked foods were superb,
and I depended on its pastry and that of Dean's, and
of Henri on 46th Street, to remind me of Europe.

Another place I became attached to was a French
restaurant and speakeasy on West 49th Street called
Eugenie, where one could lunch very well for seventy-
five cents and could have a gingerale bottle of wine for
another seventy-five cents. Dinner, which included hors
d'oeuvre, soup, fish, entree, salad, cheese and dessert,
cost all of a dollar and a half, and the wine was not
very expensive.

During my first days in New York I was taken to the
Algonquin, which was frequented by theatergoers and
actors—as well as by would-be actors. I aspired to
the stage in those days and reveled in the sight of the
theater greats and their admirers, who crowded into the
rooms there as they do still. Frank Case, the owner of
the Algonquin, was to have his best days later, but
during this period the dining room was already exciting
and provided delicious food.

Lüchow's in the twenties was magnificent—the food wonderful, the clientele fascinating always, and the atmosphere as charming as it is now under very different auspices. I have always found the little orchestra at Lüchow's a delightful and ludicrous divertissement as it pours out selections from *Madame Butterfly* or *Rigoletto* with its four or six pieces. I still make a sentimental journey there occasionally and eat the canapé with tartar steak and caviar, together with some sausages.

One cannot have lived in New York or Washington of the twenties and thirties without knowing Childs. Except for Horn and Hardart's, it was probably the most unusual restaurant operation that ever existed in this country. Unhappily, it fell upon less successful days, but at its prime the Childs chain presented food typically American and thoroughly satisfying. Who could forget their butter cakes, which were made in the window on a long griddle, their famous wheat cakes, their incomparable corned beef hash, their chocolate layer cake? These standard items brought people back time after time. Everyone seemed undeterred by the antiseptic look of the white tile, an ugly trademark through the years. What astonishing people passed through the doors of some of the Childs'! The one on Fifth Avenue at 58th, the one in Times Square and the one that opened later in the twenties between 56th and 57th Streets were rendezvous, late at night, for everyone in the arts.

New York today is still famous for restaurants. Some, like "21," the Colony and Voisin, have lived through Prohibition and the depression and remained tops in their field. Others, such as Henri Soulé's Pavillon and Joseph Bugoni's Baroque, have appeared in the last twenty years and become outstanding through a consistent quality of excellence. Still others, notably the restaurants of Restaurants Associates—the Four Seasons, the

Forum of the Twelve Caesars and La Fonda del Sol—have established revolutionary ideas in restaurant design and the presentation of food. But with very few exceptions, the average expensive New York restaurant is not as good as it was twenty or thirty years ago, because, for the most part, restaurateurs have lowered their standards; too many of their patrons are diners-out on expense accounts, who value a "chic" restaurant for its snob appeal, not for its cuisine. They no longer pride themselves on being purveyors of fine food and drink.

On the other hand much of the public has become more sophisticated in its eating habits, and these people expect the best when they go to a good restaurant. Wine lists and menus may be intriguing and well planned, the décor handsome, the service good. But it is what happens in the kitchen that makes a restaurant.

With all of my restaurant experience I have come to learn one thing, and I regret that it is so. There are great restaurants, good restaurants, and poor restaurants, but no restaurant is any better than the performance you can exact from it by knowing the chef, the maître d'hôtel or the owner. Alas, the restaurants are few where you can go unknown and unannounced and be served good food.

CHAPTER

7

Next to the mammoth preparations for winter, I
suppose our greatest activity was organizing for summer at the beach. Since we spent three to four months
there each year, including visits in spring and winter,
Mother had to be certain that things were in order for
every possible emergency. My father, who didn't enjoy
life at the beach, could be expected to join us only for an
occasional weekend.

A huge trunk plied its way back and forth from
Portland to the beach, along with an enormous packing

case of general supplies, for Mother felt there was nothing in the stores near our destination but inferior merchandise. Thus, she would make a special visit to the paper company for the sole purpose of buying a summer's supply of waxed paper, wrapping paper and toilet tissue. Then she would commence to select food to be packed and shipped—such staples as dried beans and rice, spices and seasonings, and a few jars of vegetables and jams. She hated the musty smell which linens took on when stored at the beach, so there were fresh linens to be sent, too.

Two or three days before we left, the household was in a tumult. A ham was being cooked, a batch of bread was baking, and miscellaneous tidbits were being prepared to see us through the first two or three meals. All of this was stored in a large willow picnic hamper. Then our clothes were packed, the bags were closed, and the expressman came to collect everything and check it through to Gearhart. I have gone to Europe for a year's stay with less packing and far less strain than this took, I assure you!

Finally the day arrived. In the early morning Mother fixed a luncheon to take along, although we arrived at the beach shortly after noon. You never knew what friends you might meet on the train, and a few sandwiches and cookies would be just the thing to greet them with. Usually this meant thin slices of bread with marmalade, sandwiches of sliced egg and cold chicken, and perhaps a tidy poundcake.

In the early days, Mr. McKiernan arrived to drive us to the station in a horse-drawn hack, much in demand for such special occasions. We got ourselves and the remaining bits of luggage settled inside, and off we went to the old Spokane, Portland and Seattle Railroad station.

This had a branch line along the banks of the Columbia River to Astoria, and the train tore down at the astonishing rate of twenty miles an hour or better. We rode in the same venerable parlor cars year after year, and the porters were like members of the family. Some of them were even put in charge of us children at the beach.

We had to arrive at the station early or I made a frightful scene, for it was absolutely vital that I have a certain chair on the observation platform. I usually had it. Oh, what train travel lost when the observation platform went out! I have never enjoyed trains as much as I did then, sitting in the open air getting covered with coal dust and clinkers. I had a feeling of personal contact with the world passing by. It was as if I were touring the countryside on my back porch.

Well, the train left at about 8:30 and the first stop of any importance was Rainier on the river. Mother had friends in Rainier who were advised as to the exact time of our arrival, and they always came down to the station to say how-do-you-do and pass a few minutes exchanging pleasantries with us. Then we set off again, and before long we were unpacking the sandwiches, especially if friends of mine were aboard. Children and mothers alike shared our picnic, the porters brought us ginger ale, and there was a festive air about the entire trip.

Finally we would reach Astoria at the mouth of the Columbia River, where there was a twelve- to fifteen-minute layover. Sometimes more friends were on hand to greet us here, and on we went over an endless trestle spanning Young's Bay, which thrilled me beyond words, for it was just like going to sea. Then we traveled the final lap to Gearhart.

Gearhart was on the coast about eighteen miles below the mouth of the Columbia River. It was a heavenly spot with lush timber, beautiful meadows, a wide white beach delightful for walking, driving or riding, and a tossing, roaring surf perfect for bathing. It was, and

still is, a unique little community, for its commercial life
has been kept at a minimum, and there are no amusements other than a golf course. Today it continues to
have a sort of isolated charm that attracts the same type
of people who lived there when I was a child, and many
of the houses are occupied by the families who built
them soon after the turn of the century. Our first year
there was 1908, and in 1910 we built a small house in
what was then considered a rather remote part of the
meadow. Gearhart is still not too built up. No place I
have ever been gives me quite as much pleasure. I adore
the ocean, the sand, the solitude.

Mother would have written asking the Tybergs or
William Badger to have the house opened and to meet
us and pick up the trunks and assorted packages. When
she stepped from the train, it was like the arrival of a
celebrated prima donna.

As soon as we reached the house, there was the fuss
of getting unpacked, getting a fire going, getting a bit
of lunch ready—invariably, it seems to me, cold ham
and pickles, bread and butter, and cheese and tea. Then
we set to work on the house, and by evening it was so
well organized we might never have been away at all.
We would have a long walk on the beach to see if its
familiar contours had been altered. Most likely there
would be a dinner invitation for us, and people we knew
began to drop by. Among them was sure to be the
Hamblet family.

The Hamblets were close friends of my mother's, and
their gastronomic life was so interlaced with ours that I
must pause to introduce them here. Harry Hamblet was
a New Englander, a man of medium height and stocky
build. A rounded stomach showed that he enjoyed good
food. His skin and features were soft, and he had expres-
sive eyes that lit with glee when something pleased him.
The same eyes could be very stern. He was an immacu-
late dresser, and his clothes had the look of being

brand-new no matter how long he had worn them. And Harry Hamblet was the most thoroughly generous and outgoing man I think I ever knew. Had he harnessed his energies for himself instead of others, he would have been immensely rich. As it was, he went up and down the financial ladder, leaving behind him a number of people wealthier than he. His wife, who became known to my generation of Portlanders as "Grammie," was one of my mother's intimate friends over a period of more than fifty years. And the last Hamblet—Mary—is still one of my best friends—another friendship of over fifty years.

To say that the Beards and Hamblets ate hundreds of meals together is an understatement. I suppose the greatest thing we shared was life at the beach. And what a treasure house of good food this part of the world was for us! The sandy soil was perfection for vegetables and small fruits; the evening dew and the temperate climate were good for growing and ripening. The nearby waters provided an inexhaustible supply of fish.

The Columbia River abounded with salmon, sturgeon and halibut; and the ocean into which it emptied teemed with the small turbot, grunions and a tremendous variety of smaller fish. The Pacific's greatest blessing, though, was the Dungeness crab, to my mind unequaled by anything in the shellfish world. (I will match a good Dungeness against the best lobster in America and against the best *langouste* in Europe.) In addition to the crab, there were the superb razor clams, whose virtues I have already touched on. These flourished in the days of our beaching and continue in small supply nowadays—definitely a sportsman's catch. They have a rich flavor, somewhat akin to scallops, and a delicacy of texture that is different from any other clam I know. And they are larger than most clams, with a tender digger muscle and a somewhat less tender body.

So distinctive are they that one should have them cooked as simply as possible in order to savor their natural goodness.

We also had mussels by the ton, but there is something in the water or the life cycle of this mollusk which makes it inedible in the West for a long season of the year. This greatly upset Mother, who had a passion for mussels and who looked longingly whenever we saw them clinging to the rocks.

In the rivers and streams around us there were also thousands of small crawfish, trout, pogies (not to be confused with the Eastern porgies), tom cod, catfish of a type, and other delights.

It's no wonder we hardly ever touched meat. Save for picnics and occasional dinners, we existed almost entirely on the riches of the rivers and the sea. Harry Hamblet had an interest in the first oyster beds on the Pacific Coast in which Eastern oysters were transplanted. As a result, bags of oysters arrived each week from not too distant Shoalwater Bay, and these added to our bounty.

One of my memories of this period is the sight of my mother and Harry Hamblet, in early morning, cooking dozens of freshly opened oysters in butter by the pound. There were two big iron skillets on the fire. The oysters were floured, dipped in egg and cracker crumbs and cooked quickly in deep butter till they were golden on both sides. The butter was not hot enough to blacken them, and the oysters were not deep-fried but merely sautéed just fast enough to heat them through. A squeeze of lemon and some freshly ground pepper were all they needed, except for a garnish of bacon and crisp, buttered toast. On such occasions I'm certain that more than a dozen oysters were consumed by each person. Anyone who says you should never cook an oyster has never tasted these after a long walk along the beach in the sea air. They were ambrosial, and this isn't just a sentimental memory, for I tried them again lately to see!

Sometimes after an early morning session of clamming we had a breakfast of fried clams, fresh from the sands. The razor clam spits through the sand and leaves an indentation known as a clam hole. As soon as one spotted this marker, he fell to his knees and searched through the sand until he struck the clamshell. Sometimes it was a struggle to bring a clam to the surface, so strong was its digging power, but a take of five to six dozen in a morning was not unusual.

Mother thought clamming a great sport and would arise at five when there was a good low tide, don her best alpaca bathing suit and be off to the beach equipped with shovel and basket. She would meet a number of friends there, mostly men, for few women would bother to go clamming. I often went with her in later years, but my special joy at first was crabbing. The Dungeness used to hide in deep pools accessible at low tide, and if you wandered through with a rake you could trap a fair quantity. You had to be alert, though, and early—for everyone else wanted them too.

Thus we often went home with five dozen clams and six or eight crabs. If she was in the mood, Mother would clean a dozen or so clams and remove the digger muscles, which she brushed with flour and sautéed quickly in butter until they were heated through and not particularly golden. Most people cooked the whole clam. Mother was independent enough to think that only the diggers were fit to eat in this manner; the rest of the clam could be used for other dishes. Nowadays, alas, you are lucky if you can get the clams to sauté in their entirety. I am certain that if the razor clam existed in France, the recipes for them would be classic. As it is, such people as Helen Evans Brown, Catharine Laughton and I go on singing their praises.

Mother took a dim view of the average clam chowder,

as did the Hamblets. The one we all loved was magnificently creamy and filled with the smokiness of bacon
and the piquancy of thyme. The clams and their juice
were added at the moment of serving, and this timing,
together with the seasoning, made it better than any
other chowder on the beach.

Clam broth we had by the quart. The portion of the
clams she didn't use for sautéing were tossed into a
large pot together with their shells, onions, celery, carrots, parsley and water to cover. She allowed this to
steep for an hour or so till the flavor of the clams had
permeated the broth. This was strained and served hot
in small cups or served chilled with a tiny bit of very
salty whipped cream on it. And it was also used as a
base for soups and sauces, bestowing a flavor that was
wonderfully delicate.

The same, less choice, portions of the clam were
sometimes minced and used in the clam soup I spoke of
earlier—an exquisite, simple soup which belies the notion that great soups must be complicated and difficult
to make. The minced clams were also made into the
lightest of fritters, served with a genuine tartar
sauce—not a concoction with some dill pickle and garlic
added.

Clam Fritters

Beat 2 egg yolks till light and lemon-colored and add
to them 1 cup minced clams which have been drained.
Blend this with 1½ cups toasted bread crumbs or
cracker crumbs, 1 teaspoon salt, and a dash of
Tabasco. Add enough clam juice or milk to make a
heavy batter, and lastly fold in 2 egg whites, stiffly
beaten. Drop the batter by spoonfuls into a well-
buttered heavy skillet and cook the fritters till they
are nicely browned on both sides. Serve them with
butter or with a tartar sauce.

Our scalloped clams, another delight, were made
with cracker crumbs (not cracker meal, but rather

coarse crumbs of good soda crackers), clams, butter, milk, cream, egg, and chopped parsley. They were baked in a brisk oven and came forth as light as could be and with such an aroma that one could hardly wait to attack them. Guests frequently begged Mother to fix them, and naturally her vanity always caused her to try to produce a better batch than the one before, to everyone's benefit.

Sometimes Mother would use much the same base as for the scalloped clams and added beaten egg whites to make a form of soufflé I have never had anywhere else. It was puffy, subtly flavored with clam, and as airy a dish as ever existed. And this was baked in the oven of a wood stove, which was like a pet to my mother; she could almost tell it what to do.

Scalloped Clams

Combine 3 tablespoons grated onion, 2 cups minced drained clams, ¼ cup fine-chopped parsley, 1 teaspoon salt and a dash of Tabasco.
Combine ½ cup bread crumbs and 1 cup coarsely crushed cracker crumbs with ½ cup melted butter. Blend these well. Reserve one-third of the mixture. Combine the rest with the clam mixture and spoon it into a buttered baking dish or casserole. Top with the remaining buttered crumbs, dot them with butter, and pour ½ cup heavy cream over all. Bake for about 25 minutes in a 375° oven till the top is nicely browned and crisp.
For a Clam Soufflé: Fold in the stiffly beaten whites of 8 eggs, pour the mixture into a 1½-quart soufflé dish, and bake at 375° for 35 to 40 minutes.

Clam and Corn Soufflé

Blend one 7-ounce tin minced clams or whole clams with one 12-ounce can whole-kernel corn. Add 5 egg yolks, a dash of Tabasco, ½ teaspoon salt, and lastly fold in the stiffly beaten whites of 6 eggs. Pour the mixture into a buttered 1½-quart soufflé dish and bake at 375° for 30 minutes or until the soufflé is delicately browned and puffy.

The trouble with American gastronomy is that the tradition of regional eating has been ruined during this century. Everyone thinks he must have Maine lobster in Oregon and California asparagus in New York, and so it goes. What a job it is to find a restaurant—and they are rare—where the pleasures of regional food are still respected.

Dungeness crab is now sent across the country, but to eat it freshly cooked and to eat it after refrigeration are two different experiences. And to eat it frozen after it has traveled the breadth of the country can only be a disappointing experience. There is a restaurant in San Francisco—Big Ben—where the crab is cooked and never refrigerated, merely cooled, and the flavor speaks for itself.

One can also get crab fresh from the boilers along Fisherman's Wharf and in shops in Oregon. If you allow these to cool and eat them with a rich homemade mayonnaise, good bread and butter, and beer or a very light white wine, you will have a meal that the gods intended only for the pure in palate. Or you can make a glorious dish, served by the Four Seasons in New York, by sautéing the meat with a little onion, parsley, a shred of carrot and white wine, flaming this with cognac.

Sautéed Crabmeat as Done at the Four Seasons

At the Four Seasons, crabmeat Casanova is prepared at table over an alcohol flame. Melt 6 tablespoons butter in a skillet and brown 4 small slices French bread on both sides. Remove to a hot plate. Add ¼ cup fine-chopped shallots, a few shreds of carrot and ⅔ cup crabmeat. Add ¼ cup cognac and flame. Add ⅓ cup white wine and let the crabmeat cook gently for 3 minutes. Add ¼ cup chopped parsley, ½ teaspoon salt and 4 grindings of the pepper mill. Spoon crabmeat on a hot plate with toast points as a garnish. This is one portion. Increase the recipe according to the number of persons to be served.

Another thrill at the beach was Grammie Hamblet's deviled crab! I have maintained all my life that this is the best cooked crab I have ever known. It is made with crisp vegetables chopped fine, cracker crumbs and butter, and it is seasoned well and cooked just long enough to heat the crabmeat without turning it mushy. Served with a very brisk wine—a Muscadet or a Chablis—it is indescribably good, for there is the luscious flavor of the crabmeat in a crusty exterior. Grammie Hamblet deserved a seat in the gastronomic heaven for having thought that one up!

Grammie Hamblet's Deviled Crab

Chop enough celery to make 1 cup. It must be cut finer than fine. Add 1 good-sized green pepper cut exceedingly fine, 1 cup fine-sliced green onions, ½ cup chopped parsley, 2 pounds crabmeat, 2½ cups coarsely crushed cracker crumbs, 1 teaspoon salt, 1½ teaspoons dry mustard, a healthy dash of Tabasco, ½ cup heavy cream and 1 cup melted butter. Toss the ingredients lightly and spoon them into a buttered baking dish. Top with additional crushed cracker crumbs and brush them with melted butter. Bake at 350° for 25 to 30 minutes or until crumbs are delicately browned. Serve the dish at once.

We used to have another superb crab dish which included sautéed bacon and ham, onion, parsley and tarragon (this grew extremely well at the beach) with a little rum added. This was one of Mother's bits of exotica she had collected in Panama, the West Indies, or some other place she happened to turn up one day when the crabmeat was good, and it was often a Sunday dinner entree for people visiting us at the beach for the first time. It was usually served on large slices of homemade bread toasted in front of the open fire and buttered.

Mother's Crabmeat Sauté Caribbean

Cut ½ pound bacon in small pieces and let it try out till cooked through but not crisp. Remove bacon strips, and add 1 cup fine-chopped green onion, 1 cup fine-chopped green pepper, and 1 fine-chopped garlic clove. Add 4 ripe tomatoes, peeled, seeded and chopped fine, ½ pound shredded Virginia ham, and 1 teaspoon dried basil or 1 tablespoon fresh basil chopped fine. Simmer the mixture for 10 minutes, correct the seasoning, add 1 pound crabmeat and ¼ cup Jamaica rum, and cook till the crabmeat is heated through. Add ¼ cup chopped parsley. Simmer the mixture for 3 more minutes, stir in ½ cup heavy cream and heat through. Serve the crabmeat over a rice pilaf.

Crawfish we caught with string and a piece of liver. When I was around eight, four or five of my contemporaries would set off for the day with a picnic basket and return with a large number of them. Most families didn't care to bother with crawfish, so often two or three of us would profit by the work of five. These small crustaceans were cooked in a court bouillon, sometimes to be eaten hot and sometimes chilled, with homemade bread and butter. They have an elusive flavor, and I have never been sure they were worth all the trouble.

We had salmon during the entire season. Harry Hamblet and the Peter Grants saw to that. The Grants were in the cannery business and commuted all summer between Gearhart and the plant in Astoria. About once a week they would ask if we wanted a fish, and that night a salmon would arrive, caught the same morning, sometimes sent along with a package of salmon cheeks, which the Hamblets and Beards preferred to almost anything else in the fish world because they were so tender, fat and flavorsome. The cheeks were easy to get in those days, for no one thought of cutting them out when the heads were removed. Nowadays they are as scarce as white caviar and nearly as expensive, if you can get them at all. We feasted on them sautéed in butter or occasionally grilled over the fire.

The rest of the salmon we poached, baked or cut into steaks to grill. The poached salmon was usually accompanied by an egg sauce or a parsley sauce; the baked was done with onions, tomatoes in season, peppers and a few rashers of bacon, all of which were served up with the fish. This year in Oregon I had an extremely tasty baked salmon stuffed with vegetables, covered with layers of cucumber and topped with a little garlic, dill and some bacon.

Poached Salmon with Egg and Parsley Sauce

Choose a 4- to 5-pound piece of salmon from the center of the fish. Wrap it in cheesecloth with the ends of the material extending on either side of the fish for some distance so that you can raise it and lower it into the kettle. Prepare a court bouillon in a large kettle that will accommodate the fish. You will need 3 quarts water, 1 cup white wine, a dash of vinegar, an onion stuck with 2 cloves, a carrot, a sprig of parsley, 2 tablespoons salt, a bay leaf and 2 or 3 slices of lemon. Bring the bouillon to a boil, and boil it for 10 minutes. Reduce the heat and lower the salmon into the liquid. Poach it at a feeble ebullition for about 6 minutes per pound or until the fish flakes easily when tested with a toothpick or fork. Remove the fish to a hot platter.

While the fish is cooking, melt 3 tablespoons butter in a skillet, blend it with 4 tablespoons flour, and cook for 2 or 3 minutes. Add 1 cup of the fish liquid and stir until the sauce is thickened. Season it to taste with salt and freshly ground black pepper. Stir in 1 cup heavy cream mixed with 2 egg yolks and stir until the mixture thickens slightly—do not let it boil! Fold in ½ cup sliced hard-cooked eggs and ¼ cup chopped parsley. Correct the seasoning and serve the sauce with the fish, boiled potatoes and a cucumber salad. Drink a brisk white wine—a Chablis or a Muscadet.

Rhoda's Baked Salmon

Split a 4- to 5-pound piece of salmon and stuff it with thin-sliced onion, tomato, pepper and a few sprigs of parsley. Salt and pepper the salmon lightly and add a touch of tarragon. Place 1 large or 2 small cucumbers, cut in medium slices, atop the salmon skin. Add a little chopped garlic and fresh dill. Lay bacon strips across the top and bake in a 350° oven for about 55 minutes or until the salmon flakes easily when tested with a fork.

Serve this dish with tiny new potatoes and tiny French peas.

Albert Stockli's Fabulous Grilled Salmon in the Japanese Fashion

Split a piece of salmon of about 4 pounds and remove the bones. Cut it into sections about 3 inches wide. Rub them well with coarse salt and place them in a dish, skin side up. Add about ½ cup oil and let fish stand for 20 minutes. Grill the salmon pieces with the skin side to the flame for about 5 minutes, turn them and brush them with salt again, and grill till they have a light glaze. Serve the salmon with melted butter and steamed buttered cucumbers. Superb!

Most any way you treat a fresh Columbia salmon, it is good, but it must not be overcooked. It should be moist, tender and just cooked through. Since my Gearhart days I have eaten a variety of salmon and learned a number of ways to prepare it. It is a fish with great distinction, and I feel it has never had the acclaim in this country it deserves. Too many people think of it as something that comes in cans or is smoked.

How delicious it was when I had it as the Indians used to do it, barbecued or smoked over an open fire, attached to a forked spirea branch, which won't burn, or spitted and roasted over charcoal or wood coals. And how good it was prepared with a soufflé mixture, which was poached and served with a *mousseline* sauce; or when poached and served cold with a *sauce verte* or a simple tarragon mayonnaise. And there is a salmon treat we hardly see any more—the tips, which were put down in brine in kegs. These would be freshened, poached and served with an herb sauce, egg sauce, or heavy cream for a breakfast dish. The tip is fat and tender, and with the salt overtones it made an incomparable cured fish, equaled perhaps only by fine anchovies, smoked salmon and smoked sturgeon. Harry Hamblet kept us supplied with these salted glories till they became a thing of the past. And another treat: salt salmon bellies—how often on a winter Sunday we had them for a wonderfully good breakfast, accompanied by toasted homemade bread and fine tea and marmalade.

Salmon has always been a regal fish, and it is said that in the royal courts of the past, it was considered to be the greatest of delicacies. In fact, it was served at the coronation banquet of Henry V. And Pepys refers to a most satisfactory dinner he offered friends with a "jowl of Salmon" as the first course. It was known in the very early ages both in England and in France. Little wonder, then, that when Drake and his party found the Columbia River, they felt at home. Salted salmon was carried on many voyages of early explorers.

Smoked salmon varies in quality a good deal, and as I have already said, the Scotch and the Swedes have done the best with the smoking process, to my mind, and the Irish almost as well. The salmon smoked in their countries is firm and pungent. Most of the Nova Scotia is too soft, and the West Coast variety is too salt, too pulpy or too hot-smoked, so that it resembles a kippered rather than a smoked fish. There should be standards set for fish smoking so that one needn't shop around for a reliable piece. Ironically, good grades are even hard to track down in New York, where probably more smoked salmon is eaten than in any other city in the world. I know of two restaurants where it is perfect—the Four Seasons and "21"; also the United States Line and the

Cunard Line have given me really fine Irish and Scotch salmon. And I know of one or two shops where salmon may be bought with some assurance of quality. For the rest, smoked salmon is disappointing in the extreme.

Kippered salmon, which is smoke-cooked, can be as great a delicacy as the smoked salmon if the kippering process is properly done. I think the Northwest kipper people come through with the best product, providing they do not stoop to the horror of artificial smoke. It is a delectable bit when cut thin and served with a mustard mayonnaise or a dill sauce and eaten with rye bread and beer. It is also good heated in foil and served with butter and boiled potatoes for breakfast or lunch.

There is an exciting Scandinavian salmon dish— beautifully served at Scandia in Los Angeles—called *gravad lax*. Here, the salmon is boned and treated with salt, saltpeter and sugar. Then layers of the salmon are alternated with thick layers of dill. This is pressed, stored in the refrigerator for 24 hours and then sliced thin and served with buttered pumpernickel or rye bread. Few things are as good, if you like the blend of dill and salmon, and if this marriage of flavors is unknown to you, by all means try it at once.

Gravad Lax

Split a 4-pound piece of salmon and remove the bones. Mix together ⅔ cup coarse salt, 1 tablespoon freshly ground black pepper, ½ cup sugar and a touch of saltpeter. Rub this into the flesh of the salmon.

Choose a deep bowl or dish and line it well with sprigs of fresh dill. Lay one-half the salmon on the dill, skin side down. Arrange a thick layer of dill sprigs over the salmon and top with the second piece, skin side up. Press the salmon well—cover it with foil or with a board, and place weights on top—and chill it in the refrigerator for 24 hours.

Remove the dill pieces and serve the fish raw, cut in very thin slices, with well-buttered rye bread or hard bread and fresh butter.

There were great quantities of sturgeon available in Astoria—and there still are—and if you had your own smoking arrangement, or knew someone who did, you could have quite wonderful smoked sturgeon. Small amounts of home-style caviar were done as well—some of it thoroughly delicious and the rest undistinguished. A picturesque individual came to live in the area of Astoria after the Russian Revolution, who claimed to have been tailor or *chemisier* to the Czar. His name in America was Wuori, and he did remarkably good smoking. A great deal of his product he canned, but the canning process, I found, intensified the flavor too much. Nowadays the smoked and kippered fish business has developed improved canning techniques, but a good deal of the time artificial smoke is used, resulting in fish dominated by a dreary, creosote smoke taste—unacceptable by those who like gentleness in smoking and curing.

Smoking is such a simple procedure that it seems a waste not to do it yourself if you are near a supply of good fish. I know a number of friends in both this country and France who do their own smoking. In this way, one can smoke to one's taste and the fish is fresher and much better when it is eaten.

Many verses, songs and essays have been written to glorify the trout, and I must say the trout deserves the praise it gets. In Switzerland and the Alpine section of France, live trout are tossed into an acidulous court bouillon to make a delicate and great fish dish—*truite au bleu*. This is usually offered with melted butter or a hollandaise. We seldom had trout this classic way in Gearhart, because they were generally brought to us by fishing friends who came down late in the morning from their jaunts. Thus, we would have a simple, impromptu lunch, the trout being served *meunière* or cooked in a coating of cornmeal with bacon. I have been castigated by a gourmet-according-to-the-books for even mention-

222

ing the idea of bacon and trout together. But is it any more improbable to add the flavor of bacon than to add lemon or vinegar, as in *truite au bleu?* I hope someday to have the chance to offer this critic a perfectly sautéed mountain trout with bacon. I'm certain he will eat it with gusto, protesting the while that it shouldn't be.

Truite au Bleu

The secret of a good blue trout is a live trout. It must be gutted and tossed into the sharp bouillon of vinegar and water with salt and peppercorns while it is still jumping. The proportions for the trout are about 1 part vinegar to 3 parts water, and salt and peppercorns are all you need—although you might toss in a small onion and a sprig of parsley without being called a nonclassic cook. Cover the trout and cook for 4 or 5 minutes or until the fish is just cooked through. It will have developed a delightful bluish tinge when cooked. Serve this delicacy with melted butter and lemon juice and plain boiled potatoes. Drink a light white wine—perhaps a Swiss one.

We had much company at the beach. Good friends of Mother's would come to stay for a week or two, and there would be talk fests, visits, walks and picnics. We lived informally, and there was little punctuality about mealtimes unless guests had been invited in advance or unless something very special, such as a poached salmon, was on the menu. Then, God help you if you were late.

Breakfast, Mother and I usually had together. We were both early risers. If we had already been clamming, crabbing or swimming, by seven o'clock or seven-thirty we were ravenous. We might have sautéed clams or clam fritters, sour milk griddle cakes with bacon, or scrambled eggs with bacon. If Mother was in the mood, she might make popovers, which she did with a flair, and these would be served with fresh jam and probably a boiled egg. I could easily eat three of the light puffs and was then quite happy to set out for an adventure at the beach or in the woods. Occasionally I would take a jaunt to the neighboring community of Seaside or up the beach to Strawberry Knoll; or else I went riding.

Luncheon, if we were home and not picnicking in the woods, might be just cracked crab with Mother's fine mayonnaise, or a crab salad with shredded young cabbage, a tiny bit of celery, a touch of onion and plenty of good crabmeat—two parts crab to one of vegetables, tossed with a judicious amount of mayonnaise. This was fantastically good eating and was often served as a company lunch, along with legs of crab as a garnish and thin-sliced hard-boiled eggs. We had big peach-blossom Chinese bowls for salads, and the dish looked extremely handsome as it was brought to table. With this lunch went thin homemade bread and butter or hot rolls or muffins and fresh fruit, a tart or one of Mother's quick coffeecakes.

Another favorite lunch for guests was a huge piece of cold salmon which had been pickled with vinegar, oil, bay leaves, peppercorns, lots of sliced onion and a little garlic, as well as some of the broth in which the fish was cooked. This was drained and arranged on a platter with chopped parsley and chives, thin-sliced cucumber and tomato, if in season. A mayonnaise was served with this, and it was accompanied by homemade bread and sometimes a vegetable salad, in addition to the cucumber. If good fruit was available, there would be a fruit tart for dessert, or there might be a soufflé.

One year our rich next-door neighbors, who always maintained a staff of five or six at the beach, and who frequently invited us to lunch, arrived with a fine French cook. Julie took a great fancy to Mother and gave her tips on shopping and on managing with a beach kitchen. And when she made soufflés she would often make two and have one rushed next door to our table. She made a pineapple soufflé such as I have never eaten since, and

on one rare occasion we had picked enough wild strawberries for a soufflé. This turned out to be a heavenly,
once-in-a-lifetime treat. It was Julie who, in collaboration with Mother, first produced the highly successful
clam soufflé; and another triumph in fish soufflés was
her crab and crumb creation.

Julie's Basic Soufflé

Blend 3 tablespoons flour with 3 tablespoons melted
butter, stir well and cook for 3 or 4 minutes over
medium heat. Stir in ¾ cup milk or other liquid and
stir till the sauce is thickened. Cool it slightly, add
4 egg yolks and return it to heat for 2 or 3 minutes,
stirring well. Add flavorings (e.g., ⅓ cup Grand
Marnier for a dessert or 1 cup grated cheese for a
savory soufflé) and cool the mixture slightly. Finally
add 5 or 6 egg whites beaten stiff but not dry. Fold
them in with a spatula, with the hands, or in the
electric beater if you have one with a whisk attach-
ment. If you fold by hand or spatula, fold in one-
third of the whites very thoroughly. Then add the
other two-thirds more lightly but do not leave great
chunks of white in the batter. Pour the soufflé into a
1½-quart container—it does not need to be a standard
soufflé dish—and bake at 400° for 25 to 40 minutes,
depending upon the firmness you desire in a soufflé.

The most important thing is not to have any fear of a
soufflé. It is a simple process, and if you learn once to be
casual about it there can never be a failure. Folding is important, and once you get the feel of a soufflé into your
fingers by folding by hand, you will know the quality of
batter that makes a good soufflé.

Test the soufflé in the oven by gently pressing with your
hand to determine the firmness inside. Some people like a
firm soufflé, and others prefer one that is firm on the outside
and quite runny inside.

Some soufflé recipes will vary in the number of egg
whites and egg yolks specified. This is precisely what the
soufflé's originator had in mind, for—depending on the
other ingredients used—some soufflés need more egg whites
as a leavening agent.

Julie's Pineapple Soufflé

Prepare the basic soufflé mixture above but use 6 egg yolks instead of 4, and add ½ cup sugar and cook over medium heat till it is well blended and thick. Stir in ⅔ cup crushed drained pineapple, 1 teaspoon vanilla and a pinch of salt. Beat 8 egg whites and fold them in according to the directions given above.

Butter a 2-quart soufflé dish and sugar it well. Pour the mixture in the mold and bake at 400° for 35 minutes or until the soufflé is firm enough for your taste. Serve it with a sauce of melted vanilla ice cream—an easy and perfectly delicious sauce for soufflés.

Mother's Clam Soufflé

Blend 4 tablespoons flour with 3 tablespoons melted butter, ½ teaspoon salt and a dash of Tabasco, and cook till lightly golden, stirring constantly. Stir in 1 cup clam juice and continue stirring until the mixture is thick. Cool it slightly, add 5 egg yolks and heat for 2 or 3 minutes. Add 2 tablespoons chopped parsley and 1 cup drained minced clams, and cook for 3 or 4 minutes, stirring constantly. Cool. Beat 6 egg whites till stiff but not dry and fold them into the mixture according to the directions in the basic recipe. Pour the soufflé into a buttered 2-quart mold and bake at 400°.

The summer that Julie was next door was truly a gastronomic season. I think if Mother had had the courage she would have set Julie up in business running a restaurant. In a way, it was tragic that she didn't do it, for she was never happy without some business project. Twice, later in life, she herself was offered money to go into business, but each time she decided against it. Julie also introduced *tuiles* into our lives, which became part of the permanent repertoire. They were delicious the first day they were baked, but they would not hold up longer than that in the dampness at the beach.

Tuiles

Cream 2½ tablespoons butter with ½ cup sugar. Beat in 3 egg whites, one at a time. Stir in ⅓ cup sifted flour and ¼ teaspoon vanilla.

Drop the batter in ½ teaspoonfuls on 2 greased and floured baking sheets. Sprinkle a generous amount of sliced almonds on each cooky. Bake in a 450° oven till the cookies are golden brown—about 10 minutes.

Right after removing them from the oven—while they are still soft—lay the cookies over a long stick, so that they will assume the slightly curved shape of roof tiles.

Other luncheon dishes included two steaks cut from the middle of a salmon, which were either sautéed with parsley, lemon slices and butter or baked sandwich fashion with a stuffing of crumbs and fresh vegetables. Or we had a mess of our wonderful salmon cheeks, about the size of a silver dollar and half as thick, sautéed in butter and served with a mustard sauce which had a generous amount of Worcestershire and lemon in it, and with fried potatoes and a salad. And once in a great while we would have a fine piece of sturgeon, which we braised or sautéed as a steak—either way it provided a welcome change of flavor, and when served cold with mayonnaise, it was remarkably good. With this, usually, went a good cole slaw and hot bread.

If we had a meat dish, which was not too often, it might be a meat pie with kidney and vegetables or a really good *pot-au-feu* with all the seasonal vegetables in the broth and plenty of marrow bones. Potatoes in their jackets were the proper accompaniment, and the extra beef was pressed and made into cold cuts or used in a salad. Occasionally a piece of corned beef was brought to us from Portland, and this provided a pleasant change of fare. It was ideal for picnic sandwiches or as a snack for supper. And sometimes Mother would come by a fine fowl, procured from the people who sold eggs, and this would make a rich fricassee, or it was used for Mother's special smothered chicken—a type of *daube*—in which the chicken was browned and put to simmer with vegetables, seasonings and liquid, to which cream and thickening were added. The vegetables were removed and served separately, along with boiled potatoes in jackets or rice. This dish could last for a couple of days if the weather was right; refrigeration at the beach was somewhat primitive.

Our Beach Fricassee of Chicken

Cut a large fowl into serving pieces. If it is a very large one, make separate pieces of the thigh and the leg, cut the breast into 2 or 3 sections, and have the wings separate. The back and the ribs make 3 pieces, too.

You should have an extra package of backs, necks and gizzards to make a rich broth. 2 pounds each of necks and gizzards with 2 quarts water, 1 onion stuck with cloves and salt should make a good rich chicken broth which has so many uses. We always seemed to have a great jar of it in the icebox or cooler.

Make a bed of the following vegetables, cut into matchlike sticks, on the bottom of the kettle in which you are to cook the chicken: 3 leeks, 2 carrots, 1 large onion, 2 stalks celery. Several sprigs of parsley and 1 teaspoon thyme should also be in the mixture. Arrange chicken pieces on this and add ¼ cup oil, ¼ cup white wine and enough broth to cover the vegetables and touch the chicken pieces. Sprinkle with 1 teaspoon salt and a little freshly ground black pepper. Cover the kettle tightly and simmer at 300° in the oven, or atop the stove at medium heat, until the chicken is just tender—close to 2 hours.

About 20 minutes before the chicken has finished cooking, cook 2 cups rice in 4¼ cups chicken broth —bring the broth to a boil, add the rice and bring to a boil again. Add salt to taste, cover the kettle, and put it on very low heat for 13 minutes. Test the chicken for doneness and make sure the rice has absorbed the broth.

Brown 2 tablespoons flour in 3 tablespoons butter, gradually stir in 2 cups rich chicken broth from the pan in which the chicken cooked, and continue stirring till the mixture is blended and thick. Cook for 2 minutes, add 1 cup cream mixed with 3 egg yolks, and stir until the broth is thickened but do not let boil. Taste the sauce for seasoning. Add some chopped parsley and serve with the chicken and rice.

Sometimes we added tiny green olives to the sauce, which made a spectacular difference.

For supper we might have a simple meal of eggs and cheese or a cold snack of some sort, together with tea and a sweet or toast and marmalade. If we had been picnicking on the beach at lunchtime, supper was a quickly prepared but heavy meal. Often we'd sup with the Hamblets or the Marias family, who were numerous and who would have invited a crowd of guests for an evening of food, music and conversation.

What a collection of people lived in Gearhart during the winter! All of them were eccentric, and many of them were real hermits who resented the intrusion of summer visitors. A few of these permanent residents became part of our lives. There was one remarkable person, Fred Hager, who was a German by birth. What his education had been I do not know, but it apparently had been a good one. Nor does anyone know how he happened to come to Gearhart and build a small house for himself, with a huge plot of ground surrounding it, on which he raised for sale specimens which could be prize winners at any flower show. His dahlias became famous and were much sought after.

Fred Hager had a marvelous vegetable garden, too, and he would sell to certain people of the summer colony. He and Mother had an uneven relationship during the first years; sometimes they got along well and sometimes they barely spoke to each other. In any event, Fred would usually give or sell her vegetables. He would drop by with a great bouquet of flowers and a basket of lettuces, onions and telephone peas—huge, sweet and wonderful in flavor. These peas grew better in Gearhart than in any other spot I have known, and they were even better than the petits pois of France, especially when cooked just long enough to be tender and served well buttered and salted, or cooked with lettuce leaves and a little onion or ham. Telephone peas were an annual event in our beach lives. They must still grow in that sandy soil, and I'm sure they must taste exactly the same.

During World War I some of Gearhart's misguided patriots felt that Fred Hager was a German spy and should be interned. This was when Mother came to his defense and so befriended him that he never forgot it. From then until he died he showed my mother many favors, and needless to say, a steady supply of vegetables was one manifestation of his gratitude. He died still a man of mystery and left a considerable amount of money and property to friends who lived nearby.

Two other interesting residents of Gearhart were Jean, a Breton fisherman who for some reason had been transplanted to the coast of Oregon, and Charley Hildebrand, a Scandinavian, who talked endlessly to anyone who would listen, or lacking an audience, to himself. Charley was a handyman and often did odd jobs for us, chattering all the while in his peculiar singsong fashion, never having anything sensible to communicate but seeming thoroughly happy.

Jean, of course, knew the sea and loved to fish. He was bearded and fierce-looking and lived in what had been a boathouse on stilts. He made his living clamming and crabbing, and he fished for himself when he felt like it. He and my mother were the only people in the district who would eat skate, and when Jean caught one, he would share it with her. They exchanged recipes for this strange winged fish. Mother liked the wings cold with a caper mayonnaise, and Jean preferred his hot with black butter, capers and vinegar, which is, of course, the prescribed method.

It was not everyone whose food Mother would eat. She was highly critical of the way most people lived at the beach, looked down her nose at food served in other houses, and except for meals with the Hamblet family, she usually refused invitations to eat out. "No use giving up the pleasures of eating just because you're on vacation," she would say. "Who wants to eat a lot of horrible stuff out of jars and cans and that ghastly baker's bread that tastes like cotton batting? To hell with it. I'd rather have a cup of tea and some of my own bread and cracked crab than eat all that stuff that's bound to give me indigestion!"

The Hamblets, the Beards and two or three good friends who would share our house for a fortnight or so seemed to have noses for wild berries—Mother and Grammie Hamblet, especially. They could almost scent them in the air when the wild strawberries were just right, and off they'd go with the rest of us in tow, all laden with buckets. Five- and three-pound lard pails made superb berry containers.

The wild strawberries at Gearhart and up the beach took hours to gather, but they were so good that no one seemed to mind. They grew on long stems, similar to the European *fraises des bois*, and had a sugary, wild flavor that has lingered on my palate all these years and still fills me with nostalgia. Occasionally in Spain or in the remote parts of France, one finds *fraises des bois* with the same flavor—the cultivated ones are tasteless pulp—and in the countryside and mountains of the Northwest and sometimes in New England one discovers them in small quantities. No one has experienced the real flavor of strawberries until he has had a plate of these or tasted a good preserve made with them. Fortnum and Mason have done a superb job of bottling little scarlet berries in preserve, and I urge you to send for some or buy some the next time you are in London. Incidentally, only strawberries of the wild variety grew in England until the sixteenth century, and it was an Englishman, Cardinal Wolsey, who started the fad of eating strawberries with cream. Mother was deeply indebted to him; she loved to skim heavy cream from a pan of milk and spoon it onto a plate of berries.

During our berry jaunts, we would also find yellowish-pink salmonberries. These were good enough to eat from the vine, my mother pronounced, but not good enough to carry home—too gross in flavor. The same thing went for the thimbleberry, a variety of wild raspberry.

Blue huckleberries were the most elusive of the wild berries. They usually grew in places difficult to reach, in the midst of a mountain wilderness. But once you found a patch you were in luck. No matter how they were prepared—in a deep-dish pie, which we had often, or in a strange English version of the *clafouti*, with a batter poured over the berries and baked, or in little dumplings which were dropped into cooked huckleberries, or in the famous Hamblet huckleberry cake—they were fantastically good.

Huckleberry Cake

Cream 1 cup butter and 1 cup granulated sugar together until the mixture is very light. Add 3 eggs, one by one, beating after each addition. Sift 2 cups flour and save ¼ cup to mix with 1 cup huckleberries. Add to the rest 2 teaspoons baking powder and a pinch of salt, and fold this into the egg mixture. Add 1 teaspoon vanilla and, lastly, fold in the floured huckleberries. Pour the batter into a buttered, floured 8-inch-square baking tin. Bake at 375° for 35 to 40 minutes or until the cake is nicely browned, or when a tester inserted comes out clean.

Serve the cake hot with whipped cream, or cold.

No cultivated blueberries ever tasted as good. I think it was the slow maturing and the fact that they grew in deep forests which made the wild variety so exceptional. Once years after my beach days when I was working with a restaurant, I opened a great container of frozen berries from Canada, and through freeze and all the wonderful scent of wild huckleberries reached me. How I longed for a berry patch at that moment!

There was one patch of what my father called "swale wild huckleberries" near our house, but I strongly suspect they were abandoned bushes of blueberries which someone from New England had brought long before. The bushes were very short, and the fruit was delicious in its own way, but it had none of the true wild flavor. Great quantities of red huckleberries grew around the beach, but they had little or no flavor and were considered hardly worth picking.

Another berry much prized by us was the mountain blackberry, which has now been distributed through the country by a firm—in its infancy when I was young—called Dickinson's. These wild brambles flourished in logged-over land and trailed through all sorts of terrain. Since there was a good deal of logged-out land near us, it was simple to find them. One could get rather torn and scratched gathering these tiny blackberries, but they were well worth the trouble. They were too tart to eat in any quantity from the vine, but in jam and jelly and tarts and pies they were exceedingly delicious. Here was flavor no commercial house could re-create with concentrate or artificial flavoring if they tried for centuries.

We usually had the blackberries baked with a top crust only, or we would go to the Hamblets' for a two-crust pie, which Grammie Hamblet made with great flair. Or we would feast on sour-milk pancakes for breakfast generously covered with freshly made blackberry jam. Sometimes the pancakes would be made large, buttered, spread with jam and rolled, then brushed with more butter, sprinkled with sugar and put into the oven for a few minutes.

Mary Hamblet practically lived on her horse—her sister and brother spent as much time on theirs—and the trio would come prancing down to our house to announce the discovery of a new patch of berries or the fact that there had been a good catch of crab, and how many could we use, or how many oysters? Such gastronomic courier systems are rare, and this was just another aspect of our world of food for which we were grateful.

The Dutch had settled farther down the coast at Tillamook and created what has become an extraordinarily good cheese industry. In my day, cheesemaking in that area had only just begun. There was also an English family called Waterhouse, with several farms in the district, who made a true Cheddar that was not too aged and was very pleasant to eat. We always wrote to the Waterhouses to reserve a cheese or two, and sometime later we would pay them a visit. The Waterhouse farm was a joy. The family lived in a typically English way and quite comfortably. Eventually they gave up farming, after the children chose other professions and became highly successful. But in the early days I can remember taking the train up from Gearhart to the whistle-stop of Clatsop and going to the Waterhouses, where we had a delicious English tea with muffins and jam, cakes, and little sandwiches of chicken. Mrs. Waterhouse made beautiful cottage loaves of bread, and she would also slice this at teatime and toast it in front of the fire with a toasting fork. While we were having our tea, the cheese would be discussed, and one of the Waterhouse boys would promise to drive into Gearhart with it in a few days. This was the most pleasant negotiation imaginable.

Three miles from Gearhart was a bustling resort

called Seaside, quite the opposite of our reserved community. There were shops, amusements, dance halls, restaurants and hundreds of tourists. People there lived in cottages built close to one another and without the splendid isolation that Gearhart provided. At any rate, we had many friends there and often spent the day visiting, seeing a movie, then taking the late train back, or walking the three miles at night with a spirit of adventure.

A day of Seaside was more than enough for us and we were content to remain in our less populated locale for a week or so. One place in Seaside fascinated all of us children, however, and drew us back each time we were in town. This was West's Dairy, where they made a five-cent milk shake, which resembled the *granitas* of Italy and offered twenty-eight different flavors. We always resolved to sample each of the flavors before the season was over. I doubt that we ever made it, although we'd invade West's five at a time, order five flavors, and try one another's flavor. And what flavors—claret, wild blackberry, tutti-frutti, grenadine, blue huckleberry, cherry, pistachio! I can see the soda jerks now scraping ice from a tremendous block, putting it in a mixing glass, adding the flavor and then whole milk. It was probably the biggest five cents' worth of anything I ever had, and it was good. Needless to say, it was the only time during the year I drank milk.

These days on the Oregon shore were among the most memorable in my life. I can remember several occasions when an equinoctial storm came up suddenly, catching us still on the beach. I reveled in being out in the driving rain and high winds and in watching the surf go wild. It was equally exciting to scurry home, draw the shutters and sup on good food while listening to the wind and the beating rain. When the storm had passed, it left a calm of indescribable beauty. I would rush out to the beach to see if any damage had been done to the other houses or to the bulkheads and to see what new treasures had been washed ashore.

Then for complete peace there was nothing like the week between Christmas and New Year's when we stayed at the beach. Few houses would be open, and the sense of removal from the rest of the world was even stronger. Mother kept certain items stored in the house for this off-season visit, but as always, we went to the sea for our food, and it sustained us perfectly.

CHAPTER

8

Since my earliest recollections of food, I have fancied
picnics and eating out of doors more than any other
fashion of eating. I don't especially mean formal picnics,
for I find that a plate of lunch carried to the garden or a
sandwich to the beach is just as diverting. Only last
spring two friends and I bought smoked fish, bread,
butter, cheese and beer and toted it to the beach, where
we sat on the sand, munched, drank, talked, looked at
the sea and enjoyed ourselves beyond belief. It is perfectly true that under these circumstances food tastes
better. One relishes the fresh air and the escape from

crowds, and delights in being simply oneself.

The same pleasure is possible in the countryside, and my happiest experiences of this kind have been in France and in our West. In France one can stop at a small *charcuterie* where things look delicious to buy a bit of sausage, and can then pick up a local cheese, perhaps some fruit and vegetables, bread and a bottle of wine. Under a tree or beside a stream, one enjoys his food and the landscape together. Sometimes this is the only way to discover some of the more remote regional foods. I become so curious when I look in the windows of foodshops in small towns that I must picnic in order to sample whatever intrigues me. In this way one really discovers regional food.

Philip and Helen Evans Brown and I once spent weeks doing a tour of several Western states, stopping off to buy the specialties of villages and towns. And in doing so we destroyed the notion that there was little of gastronomic interest to be found outside American cities—nothing to compare with provincial France, to be sure, but still exceptionally good things. We carried wine from the Napa, Sonoma, and Santa Clara Valleys along with us and feasted and drank rather well most of the time.

I can recall my very first automobile ride, and for this I was indebted to the Hamblets. We drove in a huge touring car, Mother and Grammie Hamblet all done up in veils, and picnicked beside the road. It was an exciting day for all of us, for picnicking in a car was relatively rare, and to drive out of town with a hamper of food was a great adventure. I remember this picnic especially, because it had been suggested on the spur of the moment, which added to the fun. Most of our food came from a Portland establishment known as the Royal Bakery. Some of its offerings were superb and some mediocre. But it did make clubhouse sandwiches so well that the memory of them lingers on my palate as a standard of perfection. Really good, fresh bread, toasted, was used, excellent white meat of chicken (never turkey), crisp bacon, ripe tomatoes and genuine mayonnaise. With the sandwiches we took Thermos bottles of coffee, fruit and cookies. It was a highly satisfying lunch and a stimulating episode; and so began my career of roadside picnicking.

From then on we drove to picnics either by car or by horse and carriage. At the beach enormous carryalls, drawn by two or four horses, took us over the hills to Cannon Beach or Ecola, to the lake at West's Farm, or up the beach to the wreck of the *Peter Iredale*.

Our lunches were not so simple on these occasions. We often took along a good ham, roast beef, chicken, and bread and butter, and we made sandwiches on the spot. Grammie Hamblet or Mother might contribute her own version of potato salad. One salad—Grammie Hamblet's—was made with boiled potatoes, onion, celery and hard-boiled eggs, dressed with mayonnaise; Mother's was made with oil and vinegar poured over hot potatoes, with onion and parsley added after the potatoes had cooled. Both versions were good. And sometimes we would tote a huge cole slaw, with extra ingredients to vary it, which had been done with a pungent boiled dressing. And there were usually tarts or pies, which Grammie Hamblet made, or else we had some sort of coffeecake or Danish-style cake; and always there was plenty of fruit.

Then Mother might make a true *pâté de campagne*, with ground meats and seasonings, baked with strips of bacon or salt pork over it in an open pan rather than in a loaf tin. This made thin, firm, tasty slices for sandwiches.

Pâté for Picnics

Wash and sauté in 4 tablespoons butter 1 pound chicken livers. Chop livers exceedingly fine or whirl them in a blender with 2 eggs, 6 garlic cloves, 1 medium-sized onion peeled and ½ cup cognac. Place this mixture in a large bowl and add 2 pounds ground veal, 2 pounds ground pork, 2 tablespoons salt, 1 teaspoon freshly ground black pepper. Blend the ingredients well with the hands and add ⅔ cup cognac, 1 teaspoon thyme, ½ teaspoon summer savory, a pinch of nutmeg and a small pinch of clove. Blend all thoroughly. Cut 2 pounds cold boiled tongue into long strips, about ⅜ inch thick, and cut 1 pound fresh pork fat into thin strips, about ¼ inch thick.

Line a shallow baking dish with bacon strips, place one-third of the mixture on the strips in an oval shape and add a strip of tongue and fat pork. Add another third of the mixture, more tongue and pork, and finally a top layer of the mixture. Form into a loaf. Top with additional slices of bacon and bake at 325° for 3 to 3½ hours. Let the *pâté* cool. Remove it to a carving board or platter. Serve it in thin slices.

This *pâté* will keep under refrigeration for a week if wrapped in foil to keep it moist.

Another picnic favorite was a chicken salad.

Chicken Salad

This was originally a recipe of Let's. He would take 1 or 2 large stewing chickens and separate the dark meat from the white. The dark meat along with the giblets, 1 large onion stuck with cloves, a bay leaf, a sprig of parsley, a few celery leaves and salt would be covered with cold water. The pot was covered, and the water brought to the boiling point. After the dark meat had cooked for 30 minutes, the white meat was added and the simmering was continued until the meat was tender. Care was taken to prevent overcooking. When it was cooled, the meat was torn from the bones and cut in fairly large pieces. This was tossed with a fine mayonnaise seasoned to taste. It was served with a garnish of black olives, capers and hard-boiled eggs. Additional mayonnaise was passed. If the salad was served at a party, only white meat was used; but for a picnic or family consumption, the dark meat was added. Sometimes walnut meats were added, or almonds. Other additives might include fresh tarragon, fresh chopped parsley or capers, but nothing to overpower the taste of good chicken and good mayonnaise.

Mother developed ideas for outdoor cooking which were ahead of her time and which were not approved of by some of her friends. As a result, we assembled an entirely separate outdoor cooking group, and we established procedures that I have used all my life.

It gave Mother great pleasure to set up grills on the beach with a driftwood fire and cook breakfast or supper for an assemblage that sometimes numbered twenty or

twenty-five people, all of whom were assigned food to bring or duties to perform. I don't know where she got the energy or how she persuaded the people to volunteer their help, but she did.

These parties were organized by Mother with the same intensity with which she had managed her hotel business years before. If it was to be a breakfast, we two and perhaps a third person would go to the beach an hour or an hour and a half before everyone else, laden with baskets, equipment and a checklist of what others

were to bring. We collected wood, got the fire going, and set up the racks for skillets and griddles. The ingredients for coffee were readied—the kind made directly in boiling water, with cheesecloth and egg shells—and if there were to be pancakes, a favorite for our beach breakfasts, the batter was given a last stir.

Then as people arrived, bacon was started, buns toasted, fruit arranged and places set on cloths laid on the sand. You sat and ate on the sand, too, and if you were lucky you might have a log for a backrest. Mother would start two griddles going for the pancakes, and after a bit she would leave the responsibility of cooking to others. The pancakes were small, light and blessed with the taste peculiar to sour-milk dough or sour dough. Sometimes eggs or ham or sausages accompanied these. And the quantities of cakes one could put away after some exercise in the fresh morning air! Following the food and innumerable cups of coffee, everyone was ready to rest, wander along the beach, fish in the little Necanicum River or merely sleep or read. It was a wonderfully lazy interval after the excitement of preparing and eating breakfast.

Sour Milk Pancakes

I am quite aware that we do not have the opportunity to get sour milk these homogenized pasteurized days. One must content oneself with buttermilk—and cultured buttermilk at that. However, it does have the same rather pleasant sour quality. If you want to quicken this process of making the batter, I find the buttermilk pancake mixes on the market to be pretty good.

Beat 2 eggs very well—they should be foamy and light-colored. Add 2 cups buttermilk or sour milk and beat. Gradually add ½ teaspoon salt, 1 tablespoon sugar, and 2 to 3 cups flour with which you have sifted ½ teaspoon soda and 1 teaspoon baking powder. Add flour to make a batter the consistency of very heavy cream, and add ⅓ cup melted butter. Spoon the mixture onto a buttered griddle and cook the pancakes until they are nicely browned on both sides. Serve them with melted butter and hot syrup and lemon juice.

Sometimes we had pancakes that did not include sour milk, but of which we were exceedingly fond.

Cornmeal Pancakes

Stir 1 cup cornmeal into 1½ cups boiling water and stir over brisk heat till the mixture thickens and boils —be careful it does not burn. Stir constantly.

Sift 1½ cups flour with 1 teaspoon salt and 2 teaspoons baking powder. Add 1 tablespoon sugar and 1½ cups milk to the cornmeal mixture and then add the dry ingredients. Lastly stir in 2 egg yolks, 1 whole egg, and ¼ cup melted butter. Beat the batter well and if necessary strain it through a sieve. Cook the cakes on a buttered griddle. Serve them with melted butter and fruit syrup, buckwheat honey, or maple sugar.

Supper on the beach changed with the seasons. We often had salmon grilled over the coals of the fire and brushed with bacon fat or butter. This was served with home-fried potatoes made in a large iron skillet. We also ate steaks and chops grilled over the coals, and we tried chicken this way occasionally.

For a beach luncheon, we frequently had sensational hamburgers of beef, onion, herbs, garlic and salt and pepper, which Mother formed into thickish cakes and cooked on a griddle instead of broiling over the open fire. It is my contention that chopped meat thus cooked has much better flavor and texture than when exposed to the coals. Most of our picnic guests agreed, for they could dispose of untold quantities of these hamburgers at a noonday feast. And that was not all we ate, for Mother felt that the hamburgers were merely a novelty. She would also provide pickled salmon or cold ham, salad, relishes and pickles and very often a pan of her baked beans boiled till tender with onion and bay leaf and then baked with salt pork, mustard and seasonings, with the addition of meat broth, sometimes, or sausage meat or spicy sausages. The beans had a rare good flavor, and eaten with ham or the hamburgers, they were superb.

Mother taught me to detest beans done with molasses or brown sugar. I remember once going to a picnic given by other people where canned beans of a famous make, thus sweetened, were served. I thought they were very chic and told my mother her beans were old-fashioned. At the next picnic of ours, Mother brought a huge mess of canned beans and insisted that I eat them instead of hers. I never complained again, nor have I ever again wanted another canned baked bean!

My Mother's Favorite Baked Beans

Soak 1 quart navy or pea beans overnight. The next morning drain them, add 1 large onion stuck with cloves, 1 tablespoon salt, 2 sprigs parsley, and cover them amply with water. Bring them to a boil and then reduce the heat and simmer till the beans are just tender and crack when you blow on them. They must not be mushy. Drain them.

While the beans are cooking, poach 2 pounds coarse pork sausages—the Swiss or Italian or French ones—in water for 12 minutes and drain them. Also poach 1½ pounds salt pork for 10 minutes and drain it.

Chop 2 cloves garlic very fine and 1 large onion rather coarsely. Make a layer of beans in a baking pan or dish and add some of the salt pork cut into small pieces and some of the sausages. Sprinkle them with some of the chopped garlic and onions and some dry mustard—about 1 teaspoon. Add a dash of Tabasco and another layer of beans and another layer of meat and seasonings. Make the final layer one of beans. Taste the broth in which the beans cooked and add salt if necessary. Give several grindings of the pepper mill to the beans and add about 1½ to 2 cups of the broth. Cover the top with strips of bacon and bake at 350° for 1½ to 2 hours or until the beans and meat have blended well and the liquid is practically entirely absorbed.

One year we arrived at the beach to find that near us—almost directly in front of us—a most unusual house had been built. We considered it a curiosity and wondered who might live in such a hideous structure. Eventually we found out, for the Marias family met the owners and introduced us to each other. They were Belgian, with the odd name of Antich, and extremely charming people. Although we continued to think little of the Antich taste in architecture, their taste in food left little to be desired. We were invited one evening for after-dinner coffee and dessert. One bite of a superb pastry told us they would make a real addition to our outdoor eating group, for it had been made by the grandmother of the family, a sensational baker.

She made delicate fruit flans and several Belgian specialties which were buttery, light and overwhelmingly delicious. What dessert feasts we had at our picnics from then on, for our new friends enjoyed taking care of that part of the meal. They would bring apricot tarts, strawberry flan or a magnificent thin cake topped with a web of melted sugar and butter. And on special occasions they would produce a deep-dish tart with a puff paste top—really luxury fare for any beach. Mr. Antich was an importer, so we were treated to good wines as well, and anchovies and sometimes a *foie gras*, much to the delight of Mother, who would compete by having some of her own *foie gras* sent down from the larder in Portland. And she also offered her best sardines for the Antichs.

Mother never cooked over charcoal, but her innate sense of cooking techniques, especially as far as meats were concerned, brought her to the habit of cooking with bark and driftwood which we found on the beach and which were unbeatable. She was able to gauge the heat of the fire and apply the meat, or whatever she was cooking, at just the right moment. And she had a sense of timing that was foolproof. When she did a steak over the coals, she used a thick, well-aged porterhouse and cooked it slowly. She felt it should have a good crust and be as rare as possible, but heated through and juicy. And, she thought, why hurry? There was nothing more important at the time than getting the steak cooked to perfection. People could wait for the steak, but she'd be damned if the steak would wait for people. She cooked a steak only when Mr. Hamblet or someone coming from Portland would bring one from her own butcher—the same was true of chops—because she held such a low opinion of most of the Seaside butchers that she would buy nothing from them but ground meat and meat that was to be boiled.

As I grew and there were more and more picnics, I learned a good deal from Mother on the subject of grilling and cooking over a fire. Once in a while I would go off on my own with one or two of my friends for an all-day jaunt to the beach, and we would carry food to be cooked and eaten there. We made many experiments. We tried grilling small fish we had caught in the rivers around us. The first attempt was a total failure; with the next we at least achieved edibility; and finally we learned the secret of slow cooking—undercooking, almost. Fortunately we had frankfurters along with us during the period of trial and error, so we didn't starve. We also played with cooking potatoes, apples and tomatoes in the sand under the fire, and they were always unpleasantly burned. (Foil has helped that form of cooking in recent years.) I can now do potatoes in this fashion with a good deal of success, but it took a lot of practice. Potatoes can be done superbly outdoors in more orthodox ways, too. It is very hard to beat a skilletful fried over the coals or a potful of small potatoes cooked in their jackets.

At times we had an evening bonfire on the beach with nothing to eat except frankfurters roasted on sticks and quantities of popcorn, popped over a low fire, with salt and extravagant dollops of butter added. Popcorn done freshly with generous amounts of butter can be completely captivating and is far different from the usual movie theater version, which has little to recommend it. We used a wire popper with a long handle in those days. Frequently two of them held popcorn while a third was being used for frankfurters.

A word about frankfurters: In my day they still had skin, and what's more, they had flavor. They snapped crisply when you bit into them, and exuded a delicious trickle of juice. And the buns they were served in tasted as though they had really been made from flour and yeast, not cotton. A very nice snack, indeed, this used to be. But to find comparable frankfurters nowadays, not to mention rolls, is almost impossible, since artificial flavors and fillers and the skinless process have come along. A mighty dull sausage we have offered to us in this country, with the exception of two or three brands. To compound this iniquity, someone has now come up with a tuna frankfurter. What a travesty!

Apart from our cooking parties, there was quite another type of picnic at the beach or in the woods. I had a group of friends whose mothers and nurses permitted them to eat only the simplest foods, so when they were guests Mother served thin, thin sandwiches of home-made bread buttered well and filled with slices of breast of chicken or tongue or just chopped parsley and green pepper with a touch of onion. There would also be jelly and jam sandwiches, cookies, fruit and wonderful stick candy, which was brought to us from Swetlands in Portland every week—long sticks of satin candy and striped clear candy, with a variety of flavors which were intriguing and satisfying. It is so difficult in this age of candy bars to find such delicate, simple, good candy. I miss it.

These picnics were often highlighted by pleasant surprises, which taught me how much fun your guests can have when you provide them with something unexpected. For example, Mother packed the sandwiches in individual baskets for each family group and put name tags on them, and in the baskets she included crazy folding Chinese and Japanese napkins, hard-boiled eggs wrapped in silly papers or a gaily wrapped fresh vegetable. This wasn't a cute Dennison festival by any means but had an element of whimsey about it that encouraged high spirits and stimulated the appetite.

Another memorable outdoor event for me came each May on or near my birthday. Mother, with someone to help her, held an enormous picnic for about twenty of my schoolmates. We all set out for an amusement park in Portland known as the Oaks early on a Saturday morning for an all-day party that was incredibly well planned. At lunch there would be a hot food dish with salads and relishes, cookies, ice cream and a mammoth coconut birthday cake (I had a passion for coconut in those days) —always an important feature of the picnic. In late afternoon there would be sandwiches of ham and perhaps tongue, followed by more cookies and cake, if any remained from lunch. Between meals the mob of children played games and rode on the carrousel, the Figure Eight, the chutes and the Old Mill. There was also a vaudeville show. At about seven o'clock everyone dragged himself home, filled with food—and, usually, good humor, providing there hadn't been a major fight.

I think this used to be the most successful birthday party of the whole year, because of the good food and the excitement of the park. There was seldom any actual rowdiness, for Mother could be an ogress if she cared to, and the children accepted that fact. But we must have been a handful, and how Mother managed to keep her equilibrium at these celebrations is something I'll never know.

When I grew away from the beach days and wandered about the world as a young man, there were few chances for really good picnics till I lived in England, where picnicking is one of the greatest of outdoor pleasures. I remember being taken to the races at Epsom and having my first introduction to a Fortnum and Mason hamper, complete with a raised pie, cold birds, wine, cheese, fruit and all sorts of elegantly prepared items which looked as if they had just left the kitchen. All of this was enjoyed at a table set with good china and glasses, and then and there my whole idea of picnics came into focus. I knew that a picnic worth doing at all was worth doing with a hell of a lot of care, and this belief has remained with me ever since. Even when I have carside picnics in Europe and in America, there are good glasses along, good forks and knives, and if possible, china plates. I would rather smuggle a few dirty plates into my hotel to wash, wherever I happen to be, than eat fine food on paper plates. I suppose the new ones with plastic coatings are all right, but there is something aesthetically satisfying about a handsome plate and a linen napkin when you are sitting beside your car, or by a stream, eating sausage and cheese and drinking a pleasant red wine of the country.

Several years ago when I was doing a lot of traveling to and from the Eastern Shore of Maryland, two friends of mine, Henry and Bettina McNulty, with whom I had shared some lovely picnics in France, decided to join me on a few of my trips. On one occasion we reminisced about our French picnics and notably one when Alice Toklas roasted as delicious a chicken as I ever ate, and I, who was settled in a hotel, had searched around early on Sunday morning for the best treats the markets offered. I had found a *pâté* of duckling *en croûte* that

Alice praised as the best she had eaten, some remarkably
good cooked ham from Milan, a selection of cheese and
salad greens. The McNultys contributed stuffed eggs,
various tidbits for hors d'oeuvre, a superb *gâteau* and
two magnums of champagne. Equipped with oversized
linen napkins and Baccarat glasses, we settled down in
a peaceful meadow about 30 kilometers from Paris and
ate with the greatest of delight for hours, consuming
both magnums of champagne. A brief downpour inter-
rupted us at one point, but we covered ourselves with a
tarpaulin, laughing heartily, until the rain stopped and
we could go back to our glorious picnic.

The McNultys and I re-created much the same kind
of picnic on our Maryland journeys, some of them, I
confess, enjoyed in stolen corners of the Howard John-
son reserves on the New Jersey Turnpike. But we had
our Baccarat, our good damask, our china, we ate filet
of beef, salad, bread and cheese, and we wondered if
people were ever puzzled by the champagne bottles we
left behind.

The Western trek I did with the Browns a few years
ago was done in much the same style. Through California, Oregon, Washington and Idaho we feasted on good
crabmeat, oysters, chicken and occasionally good
smoked sausages, which we would discover in remote
small towns. We also found good bread in many places
where there was still a local baker.

I can recall another picnic adventure in this country
which was as memorable as any I have known. I
drove with some friends on a bright fall day up the
Hudson and across to High Point, New Jersey, where
the view is absolutely breathtaking at this time of the
year. One sees three different states, I believe, and colors as ravishing as autumn can produce. We carried
Thermos jugs of cocktails and coffee and a light red
wine—a young Beaujolais, as I remember it. We had
our cocktails with some *foie gras*, then wine with cold

broiled chicken halves, onion sandwiches on homemade bread, whole peeled tomatoes, sliced cucumbers, cheese and fruit, and finally the coffee. It was simple food, and perfection in this setting.

You don't have to travel or make a lot of preparation to have a good picnic. You can do one in your backyard, and it can be as simple as you wish. I remember one in New Hampshire where we ate well of cold meat and cold soup, and for a special treat we had a great potful of boiling water ready for corn, which was freshly picked and cleaned as we needed it. No ear was more than five minutes from stalk to pot, and it was on a plate soon after that. It is not often that one is able to savor corn at its best, and thus a relatively simple picnic was made exciting.

An elaborate picnic can be fun, too, especially if you happen to be a guest! I attended a real Fourth of July outdoor party one year with a rural backdrop but in an elegant setting. This was in the garden of a handsome house in Pennsylvania. There were about thirty house guests, and about thirty more people were asked for the day. Drinks were dispensed from a bar, and most of the food was laid out in the great dining room. Guests were free to eat and drink whenever and wherever they chose. Tables were set up throughout the garden, along the pool and in the house. Nothing was planned. One could participate in a game if he wished—anything from bridge to golf—or, if he preferred, just sit and talk. Among the foods served were cold roast beef, a cold country ham and cold chicken; a hot curry and a hot sauced beef dish similar to a goulash; rice, small pota-toes, and tiny rolls; three different salads and raw fresh vegetables in ice water; and quantities of homemade Guernsey caramel ice cream that was staggeringly good.

Then when darkness fell, there was a massive display of fireworks in the pasture. What an enchanting day!

Well, picnics lead us to more outdoor cooking. I have been in the midst of a great deal of it and have written reams about it, and I think that this country's habits of cooking outdoors are in need of a complete reform.

CHAPTER

9

consider myself a pioneer in outdoor cooking. It has I been over fifty years since I helped my mother set up the little racks made for her to use over a wood fire on the beach. I have worked with three other people over the years whom I consider the greatest authorities on the subject—Helen and Philip Brown and Harold Bartron. I am not always at one with Harold Bartron but usually so with the Browns, who work daily at outdoor cooking with intelligence and no chichi.

What is wrong with outdoor cooking? Well, the trouble with most men is that they have too many drinks

before they get down to the business of cooking. Then
they lose their technique, and things get out of hand
completely. Other men are too scientific, carrying the
cooking process to a degree of perfection that loses sight
of the fun involved. A major difficulty with barbecuers,
in general, is the tendency to oversauce. Catchup,
Worcestershire, garlic powder and artificial smoke look
fine on the supermarket shelves, but when they are
combined indiscriminately they fail to improve any
piece of meat being broiled over coals. For years I have
been subjected to steaks marinated in everything from
coffee and cream to bottled French dressing, a mixture
of sugar and salt, and other indescribable horrors. I
repeat here—and I have said this often—that no good
piece of beef to be grilled outdoors needs a marinade.
But if you do want a variation of flavor there are a few
sensible things to do:

For an Oriental Touch—Marinate the meat in soy
sauce, garlic and a little sherry or Chinese wine. Or you
can substitute Maggi Seasoning for the soy. This is as
close to soy sauce as you can come and is pure vegetable
protein. It has been an additive for years.
For Steak au Poivre—Press crushed or cracked peppercorns into the steak before grilling or pan-broiling.
After it is done to the right stage, flame it with a little
cognac. When the steak is pan-broiled, sometimes the
pan is rinsed with cognac and heavy cream, which is
poured over the steak.
For Garlic Fanciers—(America has become the Number One garlic-eating country in the world.) Rub fine-
chopped garlic and coarse salt into the steak before
broiling it. This complements the beef flavor nicely and
is a refreshing way of doing steak once in a while.

We are also the greatest beef-eating country in the
world, and we have bred beef to a high degree of

perfection, changing the eating habits of cattle to suit our idea of good meat. Cattle whose meat is to be sold as prime and choice are fed on corn to fatten them for slaughter, which produces meat marbled with fat and deliciously tender—tender to the point where some eccentric has gone around the country testing steaks with a butter knife and awarding honors.

We age beef longer than any other country, which results in a certain amount of shrinkage and firming of texture, plus a definite improvement in flavor. Thus, when a steak from well-aged beef is cut, it should be fatty, tender and flavorful, and all it needs is careful cooking.

As I already explained in an earlier chapter, French and other European beef is sometimes three to five years old before it is slaughtered—whereas we slaughter at eighteen months—and for the most part is grass-fed. As a consequence, there is little marbling, the meat is firm and exceptionally chewy, and the flavor is not as pronounced as ours. And it is never hung more than a week at the most—occasionally ten days, but that is unusual.

So, if you have ever wondered why you never get a steak abroad as tender or as fatty as those in this country, the reasons should now be clear. Most of the *fines gueules* I know in France, however, are of the opinion that their beef is better than ours. All I can say to this is *chacun à son goût*, although I have thoroughly enjoyed some of the Charollais beef in France, chewy though it may be. It has fine texture and an excellent fresh, beefy flavor.

Notice another thing about French beef. It is usually served with mustard, pepper, a béarnaise sauce, or a Bordelaise sauce. Seldom do the French enjoy the simplicity of a good well-aged steak grilled to perfection and served with nothing other than salt and pepper.

In dealing with less choice cuts of meat in French recipes—such as *boeuf à la bourguignonne, pot-au-feu, daube provençale*—the differences between American and French beef are essential to remember; for again, these less choice cuts of American beef are far more tender than their French counterparts, and they will require less cooking time. A *daube provençale*, to which Elizabeth David allots six to eight hours' cooking in her excellent *French Provincial Cookery*, would be a mess of really stringy meat if done with American beef. Also, American beef needs no larding for certain French dishes, such as *boeuf à la mode*, for the plain reason that the marbling supplies enough fat.

The closest approximation to the texture of European beef we have is a flank steak. And even then, at times a good grilled flank will be tenderer than the usual French *entrecôte*.

Cooking beef over an open fire is an art that requires much practice. A frequent error is the tendency to cook over a roaring fire capable of destroying the bones, not to mention the flesh, of beef. The ideal surface temperature for broiling should be around 350°. I am certain I have witnessed fires that have been nearer 1,000°. Over such an inferno, beef becomes charred, shrunken, quickly cooled inside, and offers little except bulk. If you build a fire carefully, achieve good coals and grill slowly, bringing up the temperature at the last to sear the beef—you can brush the meat with oil or flame it with cognac to increase the char—then you will have perfect results.

I believe that thickish cuts of meat are best for grilling, unless you grill at a brisk heat. You can use the outdoor grill for minute steaks only if you are an expert. Flank steaks require quick broiling, too, and need the heat brought up to finish them off. If you have marinated the flank in some soy sauce, it will give it a good color, and you can continue to brush it with the marinade as it cooks. Beware of steaks with such names as "Delmonico Club." They can be tricky. Sometimes the first exposure

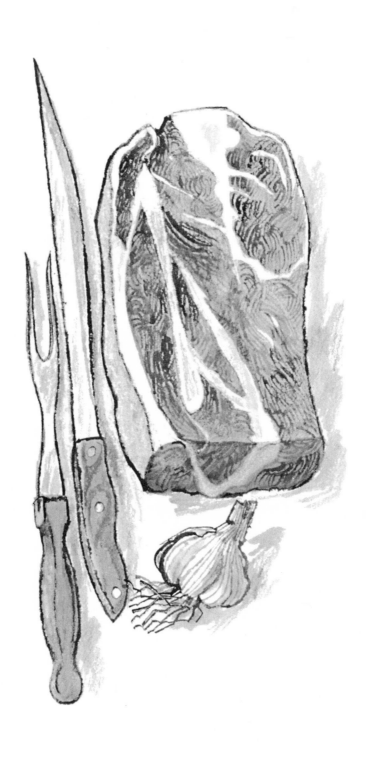

to heat will cause them to contract, thickening the meat, and you will have to adjust your timing accordingly. (This holds true for a flank steak in the ordinary broiler of your range, as well.)

Thick steaks prove much more economical for groups of people. Grilling, after all, is a quick roasting process, and if you have any steak left over, it is as good served cold as roast beef, and is perhaps even better than hot steak. If it has a crusty exterior and is nicely rare inside, it is superb for lunch sliced thin and served with a salad; or for a summer dinner, combined with cold ham or chicken, or both, and served with a salad, followed by a hot dessert.

Strangely enough, meat and certain other foods often have a truer flavor cold than hot. Many dishes are made to be eaten cold, of course—some of the classic *daubes*, for instance, and certainly *pâtés* and terrines. Here, the food has been allowed to cook a long time and cool slowly. And it is eaten cooled, not cold from the refrigerator. The dish has settled and mellowed and provides a flavor and delicacy it never had when hot.

Most city dwellers, unfortunately, have no proper cooling space. I am lucky enough to have a basement in my house, which I use in winter or spring. I can leave dishes of food there, covered, and they cool down perfectly.

If you have to use your refrigerator for cooling, be sure to take food out early enough before serving so that it will approach room temperature. Cook your food in the morning and serve it at night. If you wish to serve cold steak for a dinner party, broil it either the morning of the day you plan to use it or the night before. If you are doing a roast of beef, and if you have a spit, try roasting a large rib roast—four or five ribs—letting it stand for the afternoon and serving it in the evening with its juices intact and at a temperature that is cool but not cold. The beef flavor will be at its best.

One great fault of many restaurants in their service of hot roast beef is that when they have an order for it, they heat a plate, place cold beef on it, and then douse it with that horror know as "*jus*." This superficially heats the beef, and at the same time robs it of its flavor, making it as interesting to eat as a piece of watersoaked cardboard. Give me cold beef any time!

Filet of beef has been badly mistreated, and the usual roast filet with vegetables that one gets at all too many formal dinners is a boring dish. But a well-spitted filet, brushed with soy and salt and pepper, and turned over a brisk fire till it is extremely rare, is a morsel worth eating. It can be served with a *sauce diable*, a *sauce moutarde* or a good Bordelaise sauce, together with marrow on toast. Again, it is a wonderful snack when sliced paper-thin and served on small thin rounds of French bread, pumpernickel or toast. And it is easy to do, for it takes only twenty-five or thirty minutes to roast and no time to slice.

Right here, I think, is the place to write about the universal popularity of the hamburger—chopped beef, chopped steak, or what you will. It has now become an international dish after shuttling back and forth between continents. It was well known in Europe centuries before America took it over—first in Rome and then later in Middle Europe and England. When beef was too tough to cook as steak, it was hashed and grilled, or cooked in a skillet. In Germany it was, and still is, often served with a fried egg, and the same is true in Switzerland and certain sections of France. In this country, of course, it is a mainstay of the American diet. Many children, I am told, do not know there is any meat but chopped meat.

Well, it can be a delicious morsel if the beef is good and contains a certain amount of fat and if it retains its juices as it cooks. Sautéed with butter, it can be luscious indeed, and grilled over coals by a master, it can have real distinction. Too frequently—and especially in restaurants—hamburgers are grilled over excessive heat, which chars and coarsens the meat on the outside and leaves the inside dry and without flavor. There are some good steak restaurants where they use the trimmings from the short loin and the filet for chopped meat. This is well-aged, excellent meat, and when it is grilled properly, the taste of ripe beef comes through. With some mustard or coarse pepper, this can be a succulent treat.

Most of the hamburger sandwiches we find nowadays are hardly memorable gastronomic experiences. We have all seen and eaten those tasteless pieces of chopped beef which are waiting in stacks, separated by waxed paper, to be cooked on a greasy grill. If only we could encourage the use of good meat, good buns and tasty relishes throughout the land, we might have another golden age of the hamburger, which we last saw in the twenties. But one hears few protesting voices.

I have no quarrel with those who season their chopped meat before cooking it, providing they season it sensibly and cook it well. Mother's seasoned hamburgers were superb, and I have had others containing a good deal of garlic which I found delicious. It is a treat to mix coarsely grated Cheddar cheese, chopped garlic, chopped shallots, a dash of Worcestershire and some mustard and Maggi Seasoning with chopped beef before grilling it in butter. The cheese melts within the meat and imparts a delicate flavor—purely U.S.A. and excellent eating. Prepared with coarsely cracked pepper, and flamed, as in a steak *au poivre*, chopped meat becomes *haute cuisine*. And combined with a little tomato sauce, chili sauce, or catchup and mustard, it achieves a pleasant pungence. I have also had hamburgers with a real Mexican chile sauce over them, which I like immensely, and *sauce diable* can be a wonderful addition too.

If the treatment given to hamburgers in this country is a matter for concern, what is done to the meatball is a criminal offense! The thought of eating little balls of chopped meat mixed with various inappropriate additives and then cooked in some vague sauce for minutes or hours is the ultimate in culinary nightmares. And to accuse Italy, which loves good food, of having inspired some of the Italian meatballs served in the United States is to insult that country. As for the "Swedish" meatball, I am not a devotee of Swedish meat cookery, but of this I am certain: No cook in Sweden would ever have concocted the frightful, overcooked, overseasoned, coarse-textured balls of meat I have had served to me at buffets as "Swedish."

I do not say that tiny meatballs cannot be good. The Lebanese make them with lamb, pine nuts and parsley—and they are not cooked to a tasteless lump. The Austrians and Germans do dainty meatballs of veal. The French do their chicken quenelle, which is, after all, nothing but a highly refined chicken ball. And some of the steamed meat mixtures of the Chinese tea lunch have the quality of a quenelle, although they are coarser. I have eaten at least two hundred different versions of these tiny steamed dishes, in or out of paste—some prepared with pork, some with chicken, and others with a mixture of seafood and pork—and I usually find their delicate flavor completely enchanting.

Your choice of equipment is important for cooking outdoors. Unless you have a good grill with a firebox which can be elevated and lowered, such as the Bartron, you might as well give up the whole idea of grilling. Most other grills are just toys that will successfully char a piece of steak or broil hamburgers but are not for the man who wants to do some superlative eating after careful preparation. You are better off

broiling your meat in the kitchen and carrying it outdoors.

Outdoor cooking is not an inexpensive pursuit. A
good grill with a firebox of generous size will cost you
around a hundred dollars, and if you want a fine spit,
electrically operated, you will have to add much more to
the cost. But you are not investing in something for a
season; this is an item as durable as a kitchen stove and
almost as useful. I have cooked outdoors on a grill for
weeks at a time and feel it is a way of life, not a novelty.
As a matter of fact, if I were building a house I would
certainly include a charcoal grill in the kitchen setup,
for it is a comparatively simple thing to install. If you
are tempted to do this yourself, be sure to get a good
basic grill, and if you wish to supplement it with a spit,
you can do so later. Or you might want to consider a
doner kebab from Turkey, which is quite a piece of
machinery to set up in a kitchen; but if you are an
enthusiast for this type of meat cookery, no trouble is
too much.

The *doner kebab* is a perpendicular grill with three
or four small fireboxes at the rear for charcoal. It has a
rather formidable swordlike spit which extends the full
length of the fireboxes—about four feet—and a highly
decorative brass top. In Turkey this is used for lamb,
which is boned, pressed together into a large cone-
shaped piece and hung on the spit to revolve before the
fire. As it cooks, meat is sliced off when it is wanted into
a small crescent-shaped container with a handle, which
holds a generous portion and catches the juices. It is
called "the ever-turning spit," and you can always have
rare lamb. This is an ingenious piece of equipment, and
why it has not become part of the American outdoor
fad, I do not know. Perhaps too few Americans have
had the courage to eat in small restaurants in Istanbul
where delicious lamb is prepared this way, or perhaps
Americans don't go to Istanbul at all.

I have discovered that birds can be cooked on this spit

also; one doesn't need to have twenty-five or thirty pounds of lamb turning on it to make it a useful piece of equipment. The *doner kebab* is a far cry from the original custom in the Near East of cooking lamb on spears, swords and sticks over a fire of camel dung, although I imagine it was very good done in that manner, too, for camel dung is supposed to be a very efficient fuel.

The next best spitting device for your kitchen, and for your garden as well, is a Town and Country grill. Frank Dieterich in Culver City first perfected this wonderful grill for restaurant use and has since made a great many of them for home use. And while they are expensive, they are absolutely without peer for roasting meat. Dieterich has invented another joy-giving device—a spitless spit! This clever and temper-saving piece of equipment may be made to fit almost any grill. It used to be—and this is still true of most electrically driven spits—that you had to achieve perfect balance of whatever you were roasting before the spit would operate properly. Dieterich's basket spit, which cradles meat and birds, finds its own balance as it adjusts to the motor that turns the spit. It is practically foolproof, and for those who have in the past seasoned roasts with curses and four-letter words, it is a real blessing!

When you buy a modern spit, you are supposed to be in possession of equipment with a precise self-basting tempo. I have noticed, however, that some spits change pace slightly and show a little unevenness. So while you are told it is not necessary, I think it is a good idea to baste now and then with melted butter and white wine or with oil and vermouth. Just get yourself a collection of good brushes, and keep them in fine condition. I hate swabs, cornhusks and dishmops for this purpose.

If you like fish grilled, there is a French gadget which I think you should have, available at a number of shops in the United States. It is a grill, as old as time, which is fish-shaped and set on four legs to permit the turning of the grill while the fish is kept in proper position, and the wire of the grill is fine enough so that you may surround the fish with herbs or ferns if you wish. It is so novel that you will find yourself using it a good deal when you have guests.

In my opinion fish lends itself to charcoal cookery as well as, or better than, meat. There is a flavor from the slightly charred skin which brings the superb hint of smoke to the fresh taste of the flesh and intensifies the overall flavor. The perfect example of fish flavored as it grills is the *loup flambé aux aromates*, which is served all along the Mediterranean and in Mediterranean restaurants in Paris. The *loup* is a close relative of our bass. In this dish it is grilled and placed on a rack with dried fennel or occasionally with dried parsley and other herbs. Then it is flamed with a touch of spirit, and the perfume of the herb fills the air. My own judgment is that most of the flavor is enjoyed by the nose in this case. The fish itself has a wonderful flavor and a tasty char comes through to the palate, but the nose sustains the dominating perfume of the *aromates* throughout the eating. Or so it has always seemed to me.

Whether the nose or the mouth is primarily responsible for the pleasure, this dish is a classic conception of charcoal cookery. And if you have never tasted it, you don't have to wait for a trip to Europe. You can do it yourself, using salmon, salmon trout, large trout, whitefish, striped bass, sea bass, black bass, or practically any fish you care to use. Broil it well over charcoal, then place it on a rack or platter with dried herbs *en branche*. Fennel is the herb generally used with fish, but you must dry your own. (You can buy fennel in the market a good part of the year, and it is simple to grow if you have a garden.) Cut the feathery tops and then dry them in the sun, or in the oven on foil, which is my trick. You can use instead, if you wish, a branch of thyme, rosemary or marjoram, for a more pungent, herby flavor. Do not use sage; it will overpower the flavor of the fish.

You can, of course, grill fish without herbs. You will need some sort of device to hold the fish properly, and if you can't have one of the French grills, you can use a toasting-type grill which folds and locks. (Fish is so fragile that when it is turned on the ordinary grill, it falls apart.) Don't overcook it. Most people do. If the flesh flakes easily when you prick it with a fork or toothpick, it is done. Nothing is less palatable than overcooked fish, which has become soft and mushy, losing both texture and flavor. Good raw fish is better than this.

Whereas fish is delicious when its skin is grilled to a crisp char, the opposite is true of chicken. I have been served too much blackened, dried-up chicken from grills, and I have come to the conclusion that few people know that chicken can be juicy and flavorful. For one thing, they believe in the superstition that if any blood shows in chicken it is not cooked and should not be eaten.

You must have underdone dark meat to have perfectly cooked white meat. Therefore, you should quarter your chickens and cook the white and dark meat separately—or learn that a little pink in the leg is not going to harm you.

At any rate, charring does not improve the flavor of chicken. I recently ate the best grilled chicken I have ever encountered, and it had not a trace of char. The skin was crisp, the flesh was soft, tender and juicy, and there was a trace of pink at the joint. A béarnaise sauce, heavily flavored with fresh tarragon, went with it; and it effectively masked the pinkish juices.

Roasted and spitted chickens are usually overcooked too. Neighborhood rotisseries coat tender little birds with paprika and roast them till both flavor and texture are gone. Such dull, desiccated specimens these are! And what a waste when one knows that a plump pullet turned on a spit in the correct way can be as toothsome a dish as you can find.

Buy a three- to four-pound bird, have it trussed, butter it well and rub it with salt and freshly ground black pepper. Then spit it and allow it to turn for about an hour to an hour and fifteen minutes. Brush it several times with melted butter and white wine or a little oil. Transfer the chicken to a carving board, cut it, and eat it while it is hot. All this needs as accompaniment is a vegetable, a salad and a glass of good wine. Simple though the meal may be, you will find yourself eating superbly.

I have had a good deal to say about roast wild ducks, but I think that when they are prepared on a spit they are an interesting departure from the usual oven methods. They should be marinated in oil with an onion or two sliced thin, a few juniper berries and a few sprigs of parsley for about six to eight hours. Spit them perpendicularly, run long steel knitting needles through the tops and bottoms and start them rolling. Roast the ducks for exactly twenty-four minutes. Bring up the heat, anoint them with additional oil and some cognac and flame them. Remove them from the spit, let them rest for a few seconds, then split them. Serve them at once. Serve sautéed potatoes with these; perhaps petits pois prepared with a bit of lettuce, ham and a tiny onion or two; and a fine Corton or a Chambolle-Musigny. You will have a really beautiful blending of flavors. It seems to me that the final flaming of the duck adds the fulfilling touch and no sauce is needed. It is my conviction that good raw material, properly seasoned and well cooked, needs no saucing.

Wild geese, especially the small variety one gets in

California, can be spitted and cooked to perfection in the same manner as the wild ducks. Goose needs something strongly grainy with it, however—wild rice, if you must, but I prefer the flavor of barley cooked in chicken broth with mushrooms added. And I think a sharp mustard sauce or a mustard hollandaise provides a complement to the goose. Neither sauce is too rich, for wild goose is not nearly as fat as the farm goose.

Shish kebab has become a popular addition to American outdoor cookery. For my own taste, I feel this dish is usually overseasoned or overly marinated. Most people, I know, think that the longer the bits of lamb soak in a mixture of herbs, spices, wines, juices, etc., the better they taste. I disagree. I believe that the true essence of the meat is by far the most important flavor, and therefore I prefer to enhance it simply—with some olive oil, salt and pepper, and a bit of thyme, rosemary or oregano, depending upon my mood. Sometimes I settle for fine-chopped tarragon and a touch of lemon juice. Whatever you choose for flavoring lamb, the meat should be marinated for only about two hours, I firmly believe. And never should vegetables be put on skewers with the meat. For the meat cooks quickly, and the vegetables take varying lengths of time. It is better to skewer the meat separately, with a little distance between pieces. The vegetables, if they must be skewered, can be grilled by themselves, or broiled in the kitchen. But I take a dim view of skewered vegetables generally.

My own suggestion for an accompaniment to shish kebab would be thin-sliced raw onions in a vinaigrette sauce and grilled tomatoes—an excellent combination. If you can supplement this with some Syrian bread or Armenian *lavash*, all the better. And a good red wine—a Fleurie or a Moulin-à-Vent—will provide the finishing touch for a really sensational outdoor dinner with no work but the grilling.

269

Lamb takes little enough time to grill, but one must be careful to turn it often and brush it occasionally with the marinade so that it becomes nicely colored while it remains deliciously underdone.

Apart from kebabs, grilled lamb makes extremely good eating when it is spitted. A boned shoulder of young lamb or a boned leg is ideal for turning. Baste it with a mixture of butter or oil, a little white wine, and fine-chopped or crushed tarragon, and you will have an extraordinarily good roast. Or if you like the flavor of dill—and I do with many different meats—substitute fresh dill for the tarragon when you baste, and add a good dose of garlic to the lamb before you roast it.

For a very special company dinner, a saddle of lamb (or two, if you are entertaining a large group) done on the spit makes a spectacular offering. The saddle should be cut and trimmed so it can be tied into a compact and good-looking joint. Before spitting it, brush it well with salt and pepper, rub it with a bit of garlic, and tuck a few pieces of garlic into the flesh. Roast it rare with an occasional brushing of melted butter, and carve it in thin slices down the sides, parallel to the spinal column. In this way, you get long, delicate slices with a tiny edge of fat on top.

With saddles on my mind, I can recall doing a saddle of venison this way only a year or so ago when I was lucky enough to have a young one sent to me. I gave it practically no marinating, for I had the feeling it was right without it. I simply rubbed it with a little thyme and a good deal of coarsely ground black pepper, then I spitted it and basted it frequently with red wine and melted butter. I served it daringly rare—about 120° on the meat thermometer—with a *sauce poivrade*, a purée of chestnuts and a fine Château Ausone of considerable age. The venison was cut in thin, bloody slices, and the sauce provided a complementary blanket of flavor, while the purée of chestnuts gave a suitable contrast.

Pork is a meat much neglected for the spit. But if one has two loins of pork boned and tied together, rubs them well with thyme and salt and pepper and spits them, cooking them slowly and basting with a little melted pork fat blended with a touch of Dijon mustard, the resulting meat will prove sensationally good. Serve it with a *sauce Robert* or merely a mustard sauce; apples sautéed until crisp and buttery; and fresh cabbage sautéed with champagne or white wine. Drink beer along with this, or champagne, and you will have a meal that is a masterpiece.

And why use a spit instead of an oven? The principle of exposing meat to the air as it revolves and cooks is an old one. Supposedly the air develops a better skin and flavor, while the turning gives an evenness of cooking one can't achieve in the oven. You can certainly circulate some air around a roast in an oven, and that is the point of placing the roast on a rack. There are V-shaped or X-shaped racks on the market which are ideal for this purpose. If you have been using the old-fashioned type of roasting pan, you may have noticed how your roasts cooked nicely on top and either overcooked and stuck to the pan at the bottom or became rather stewed. A rack (even the broiling pan will do) will also help you to achieve a more evenly cooked roast or bird.

It is my opinion that charcoal has nothing to do with the success of cooking meat. The electric spit, such as the Town and Country, will give the same flavor. And I know that if I roast in an electric oven on a rack, with the joint lifted completely out of the pan, it will be as full of flavor as any spitted roast. I have made comparison tests with beef and lamb, using the electric rotisserie and the oven, and I have found that there is little difference in the results if the same principles of cooking are applied.

* * *

The French have now started a fad of the barbecue and of copying our barbecue dishes for their parties. How sad to find in a French food magazine a recipe for frying chicken dipped in flour seasoned with curry and dry mustard and garnished with ears of corn! This is called "Virginian," but I'm certain that we could never, even at the height of the fried-chicken craze, have perpetrated this dish. I also found a recipe calling for a fine Virginia ham to be covered with millions of cloves and then glazed with pineapple, too. (In another magazine, I discovered recipes for peanut butter sandwiches and sandwich mixtures made with cream cheese—a deplorable effort to imitate what the service magazines in America consider American taste.)

But aside from these errors of judgment, there is a superbly done chapter in one of the food magazines, *Arts Ménagers*, on the subject of barbecuing, which offers an international barbecue menu. No one in the realm of modern gastronomy could get through this menu at one sitting, but the international idea is so good that I would like to repeat some of it.

It begins with a salute to the United States with hot dogs in buns as an hors d'oeuvre. Well, that is just when they should be eaten, for the pungency and delicacy of the combination make them a good accompaniment to drinks.

The second item is something of which I highly approve—*rougets* grilled over the coals. They are done in the Greek manner, rubbed inside and out with garlic-flavored olive oil and a dash of Tabasco, stuffed with tender vine leaves, and then wrapped with vine leaves and salted, to be grilled over "*une braise lente*" for about seven to eight minutes and turned once. The outer leaves are discarded, but the inner ones remain and have a lovely flavor. The recipe doesn't call for lemon juice, but if I know my Greek cuisine, plenty of it should be used.

The *rouget* is followed by a Caucasian recipe whose

directions are not according to the rules, for the French are trying to be so very American. However, if you blend together about half a cup of olive oil, three fine-chopped garlic cloves, a touch of thyme, a little paprika and some cayenne or Tabasco, and rub well with this mixture three small chickens cut in half, you will have the basic idea. The chickens should be grilled and then served with a Caucasian sauce, which can be made in a blender or the electric mixer. For the sauce you will need three cloves of garlic, two medium-sized onions and six or eight dried apricots or some apricot leather (sheets of dried apricots, which come from Turkey and Lebanon, superb for cooking). Lacking dried apricots, you might use apricot preserve, with a little lemon juice added to cut the sweetness. All of this should be cut very fine or blended, and mixed with a cup of tomato sauce, a third of a cup of olive oil, and salt, pepper, paprika and Tabasco to taste. This, by the way, is a truly traditional sauce of the Caucasus and is served with shashlik (kebabs).

It is a curious development that cooking *à la broche* or on the spit should be called an American specialty. This happens to be the oldest form of roasting and has been used for thousands of years. No doubt it began soon after man learned to eat meat, though the first attempts at cooking over fire must have proved far from palatable, for the meat was neither fattened, nor cured, nor seasoned. The taste of char must have done some-thing unusually stimulating to the dull, primitive palate, and the surprise of first smelling smoke and then tasting it probably created the first step toward *gourmandise*.

The Egyptians and the Greeks, like the Persians and the Chinese before them, used the *broche* and the idea of hanging meat in front of the fire (the Chinese dan-gled meat in an oven contraption) all centuries ahead of Europe.

The Romans followed with elaborate *broche* systems

and spits, used largely for the ever-popular young
pig—the most fashionable of meats in many Roman
banquets, loved for its crisp, tender skin and the juici-
ness of its meat. The Romans, by the way, obtained the
blood of the pig for sauces and other mixtures by
running a red-hot spit through the live animal—an
unnecessarily cruel practice, as horrible as the Chinese
monkey dinner, outlawed only recently, where the
brains of a live monkey were eaten!

The Romans also liked to cook tiny birds on spits and
had them carried that way to the banqueting rooms.
And later the broachboys in England carried birds and
joints on broaches or small spits to the guests, who
helped themselves by cutting meat or fowl directly from
the broaches—without the aid of a fork, incidentally, for
there were none.

I have several times attempted to re-create the atmosphere of an early English feast by serving my guests a
baron of lamb—a cut of meat much used in those days.
If you are able to get a good young lamb for spitting,
you can have the most dramatic presentation and most
toothsome bit of eating imaginable. The two legs, together with the saddle, constitute the proper cut for this
roast. Once, in Mexico, when I planned to cook a baron,
the hind quarter of the animal arrived practically as it
had left its hide. It took me two hours to eviscerate it,
and while I had a fine anatomy lesson that day, my
appetite was decidedly reduced.

Since I first became interested in the history of eating,
I have tried to visualize a baron of beef being roasted.
This, of course, would mean the two legs and some of
the loin. It was served at great banquets in England
from Norman times on. I have seen a few of the kitchens
dating from this period and now understand how such a
mammoth roast was accommodated. And I wonder if I
could ever have a large enough establishment to warrant

such a great fireplace and spitting arrangement. Of course, I would not attempt to make a spit large enough for our present-day barons of beef. One must remember that the process of fattening steer is a comparatively recent development and that the beef cattle in the days of English banquets were pretty small and unimpressive animals from our point of view.

Helen Brown and I were once invited to visit a working kitchen in France where the *broche* or spit could easily have taken a baron of beef. It was operated by wheels attached to a cable, which extended across the huge kitchen in order to protect the broachboys from the heat of the fire. These lads must have turned the spit for hours, endlessly, to roast a whole animal, a baron, or a line of birds.

Some spits were worked by pulleys—many of these are still in use—some by clockwork, and some by a contraption in the chimney, operated with ascending and descending currents of air, which were, in effect, smoke-driven.

Other spits used to be driven by dogs—bassets were preferred. And it is said that some of the animals would go for hours without a halt, they so loved the warmth of the room and the tidbits tossed to them. There is a story about a sea captain in Bristol who was not socially acceptable because of his rough language and uninhibited behavior, and to avenge himself he stole all the dog turnspits and hid them, leaving the kitchens of Bristol bereft and in a state of crisis.

I also read an account of *geese* having been trained in France to run spits, and I have always envisioned the grisly picture of a goose running a spit on which another goose was cooking!

If you are interested in spitting as it was done in the eighteenth and early nineteenth centuries, you will find a treasure, indeed, by visiting the Brighton Pavilion in Brighton, not far from London. The great kitchen there in which Carême held sway for many years for the Prince Regent is in good working condition. And although they are artificial, you can see animals turning on spits. The entire *batterie de cuisine* of the Duke of Wellington is on display—the Prince Regent's and Carême's having been auctioned off when the city of Brighton turned this priceless relic of the period into a recreation center. Thank heavens, the Pavilion has been completely restored now and is a perfect memorial to one of the last of the great *bons vivants* and his exquisite Morganatic wife, Mrs. Fitzherbert.

It is little wonder that the English have always been considered good meat and fowl cooks, for it was they who used the spit and its variations to perfection. And it was the English who imported all the greatest names in French cuisine to work for them at one time or another. Furthermore, these "greats," such as Carême, Soyer, and Escoffier, who spent many years of his life in England, adapted a number of the old English habits of eating for their own repertoires. Thus, meats prepared *à l'anglaise* are simply roasted or spitted or broiled.

Barbecue cooking was first introduced in America by the French who settled in Louisiana. The original idea was to feed a large outdoor gathering by roasting an animal, perhaps a whole sheep or goat or pig, in front of or over a fire on a homemade spit which pierced the animal from *barbe à la queue*—literally, from whiskers to tail. Thus, the word came into our language through the South and from there spread all over the country. Great community barbecues were held where whole hogs, steer, sheep and dozens of chickens were roasted and consumed by a festive populace. On national holidays large numbers of people all over the countryside gathered for the pleasure of eating outdoors.

My father was able to tell me something of this

tradition, which he remembered from his trip by covered wagon from Iowa to Oregon. As a child of five or six, together with his brothers and other boys of the same age, he would shoot birds, while his elders hunted small animals. These were usually cooked on wooden spits over a wood fire. The cooking, according to my father, invariably led to a great dispute among the members of the wagon train, for there were varying ideas as to how the cooking should be done. I can only imagine that the dispute was settled by a division of the food so each group could cook in its own fashion—in other words, this was regional cookery standing up for its rights!

As outdoor cooking developed throughout the country, there were great chicken fries for church benefits, and in the South, of course, there were the famous fish fries, where the meals were prepared by the servants or slaves after a hunting or fishing party had returned to the plantation. These fish fries were supplemented by enormous hampers of food from the main kitchens, and a huge supply of tin plates and other simple tableware came from a separate storehouse on the estate.

Although enormous barbecues still flourish, outdoor cooking is generally done on a small scale these days. The custom has grown to the point where when you drive through the suburbs you can smell more beef and chicken being charred, scorched and burned than in all previous history!

So now the barbecue returns to France—to the whole Continent—which knew it well before it came to the United States, but it returns with an American accent—very chic at the moment. Where *barbe à la queue* will go from there, we do not know.

CHAPTER

10

I suppose that everyone who has ever become interested in food has nursed dreams of one day owning a small restaurant. I know that I did, and for years drew up elaborate schemes, worked out menus, and imagined ideal locations. Fortunately I never came closer to being a restaurateur than managing Lucky Pierre's one summer on Nantucket. My professional career was destined to begin in quite another way.

In 1937, after spending several years on the West Coast, I came to New York determined to find a place somewhere in the food world. It was a bleak year. I was interviewed by every New York executive associated

278

with food. While I held out for the perfect job, my savings were running low. I found that friends and acquaintances liked my cooking, so I began the rounds of "cooking for my supper." I enjoyed myself, and I ate well. Also, in return for my services, I was invited with great regularity to parties, the theater, and the opera. You might say that I was a gastronomic gigolo.

While biding my time thus, an old friend, Mary Houston Davis, asked me to teach at a country day school in New Jersey—not home economics, but English, French and social studies. I accepted, and at about the same time another good friend, Jim Cullum, offered me a home in his large New York apartment. So the fall of 1938 started off in great style. I lived in Manhattan and commuted to New Jersey, but I was still no closer to the food business. A cocktail party in November changed my luck.

I have never really enjoyed large cocktail parties. I find them a bastard form of entertaining. One gets a drink, tries all the little dabs of food (I have coined a word for them: doots), spends some time chatting with one group, then says to himself mechanically, it's time to move on and circulate. Often I get stage fright, walk through the room, bow or speak to those I know, and deposit my drink and leave fifteen minutes later. Smaller parties can be fun, but when social debts are paid in the form of an annual crush, the guests can only feel oppressed and bored. We are all doomed to attend and to give a certain number of cocktail parties each year, but whoever started the vogue has a lot to answer for!

Well, the party on this occasion was quite pleasant. I had been there for a while when I was introduced to Bill Rhode, a handsome, witty, thoroughly disarming man. His background, I was to learn, was Berlin, good schools, and a full social life on two continents. He knew all the smart spots of those days from Le Touquet and Deauville to Hollywood and Palm Beach. I have never known anyone who so flourished in the limelight and so loved seeing his name in print. And he saw to it that he made good copy wherever he went.

Bill, like me, was passionately interested in food, and that evening we fell into a long discussion which made us forget the party around us. Afterwards I went to his apartment to meet his sister Irma, another remarkable Rhode. Irma had attended the famous school of the Grand Duchess of Baden and had learned, as did all young ladies of her social position, the ground rules of good housekeeping, including truly elaborate cooking. Although she became a petrographer and did a fine job during the development stage of the TVA project in this country, Irma's heart as well as Bill's was in good food. We three talked far into the night. I soon found that both Bill and Irma had also dreamed of getting into the food business, and we developed plans that would astonish the bellies of New York. Something, we agreed, should be done about cocktail party food. We had eaten too many pieces of cottony bread soggy with processed cheese, anchovy fillets by the yard, and dried-up bits of ham and smoked salmon. The ghastly potato-chip-dip invention had only begun to spread across the country.

There were, we gauged, at least 250 cocktail parties every afternoon in Manhattan in the area bordered by 96th Street, 51st Street, Fifth Avenue, and the East River. Of these, probably half were catered (this was before the war, when people had full-time help). We felt certain that all we needed was the "better mouse-trap." We would open a catering business and present, at first, only hors d'oeuvre and sandwiches. I remember Mother's saying that a good sandwich at teatime was hardly to be found anywhere. It would be a good idea, I thought, to offer New York perfect tea sandwiches, also larger ones for evening entertaining—"reception sandwiches," I believe they are called officially; we called them "highball sandwiches."

As soon as we had the encouragement of wise friends and a few professional people, we set about looking for a place to set up business. We found a shop on 66th Street between Park and Lexington Avenues, near the Cosmopolitan Club and across from the Armory. It seemed a good center from which to operate. Our furnishings and equipment had to be modest; we had little capital. The reception room was tiny and contained a desk and a chair or two. Behind was a huge assembly room with a gigantic icebox (Bill disapproved of refrigerators: he said they didn't keep foods moist enough), a slicer, a worktable, and a wide shelf for utensils and mixing bowls. In the basement was the kitchen proper, where Irma and I cooked. We gave our enterprise the name of Hors d'Oeuvre, Inc.

Next came the chore of preparing our bill of fare. We assembled all the hors d'oeuvre recipes we had, put our imaginations to work, and began to experiment. Some creations we discarded at once; others we tried out on our friends. One thing was certain from the first. Aside from our tea sandwiches, we would not use toast or bread if we could help it.

We shopped in foreign sections of the city for unusual items. On one of these forays we found an almost year-round source of artichokes hardly larger than a thimble. We discovered the trick of using various smoked sausages and meats as cornucopias and developed a dozen stunning ways to offer stuffed eggs. We also stuffed tiny tomatoes, slices of cucumber, radishes and other vegetables. We even tested infinitely small aspics, although we saw immediately that the labor was too great.

The pot boiled day and night, until finally we assessed our experiments and made a few choices. For general use and for attractiveness the cornucopia ideas were best. For these we used salami, bolognas, the specially cured pork loin called lachsschinken, hams, and smoked salmon. We also made rolls—of salmon, tongue, and the rarest roast beef; and there were sandwiches of veal.

The cornucopias are still a good idea. If you wish to try them, get large cake racks with fairly big holes in them. Cut slices of salami or bologna in half and wrap around a finger to form a cornucopia. Press firmly, then slip into the rack. Lachsschinken is rolled the same way but with pressure applied at the ends. Smoked salmon is the most difficult of all to roll. It must not be sliced too thin. Chill the cornucopias well before filling them.

The fillings we created were appetizing and varied. For the most part, the base was a mixture of cream cheese and sour cream. This, with additives, could be forced through a pastry bag, which speeded the work considerably. I remember well that I became the squeeze-bag artist. The salami filling contained *fines herbes*, with the addition of dill and sometimes a bit of garlic; the lachsschinken filling included horseradish and perhaps a little mustard, if customers liked their food piquant; the salmon filling was flavored with a combination of onion, capers, freshly ground black pepper, and a touch of lemon juice. As for the rolls, the beef was spread with a very hot kumquat mustard and the ends dipped in chopped parsley, while the tongue was spread with a Roquefort or mushroom butter and sometimes garnished at either end with a sprig of watercress. Our veal sandwiches—two thin slices of veal cut in rounds—were filled with an anchovy butter or a herring butter, both of which were tremendously popular.

Among our vegetable specialties were the tiny artichokes stuffed with *foie gras* or caviar (they sold for a good deal of money) and thickish slices of cucumber, hollowed out with a ball cutter and filled with a lobster or crabmeat mixture, highly spiced and dressed with a good mayonnaise. Another specialty was our thin rolls of bread (one of our few uses of bread), stuffed with a very highly seasoned veal, ham or chicken paste, and chilled before being cut into rounds. These were incredibly delicious—I can say now; because after two weeks in business, the sight of an hors d'oeuvre caused me to lose my appetite completely!

To fashion the tea sandwiches, breads were bought all over New York and sliced on the machine as thin as possible. Butter for them was fresh and ample, and again the fillings were carefully prepared. In those days one could get freshly killed chickens and turkeys. The skin crisped as they cooked, and the meat, moist and delicate, made beautiful sandwiches. We also used good tongue, country hams, *foie gras* (for a handsome price), and sometimes cream cheese mixtures and Strathborough paste. The paste was something of Mother's which I have never encountered anywhere else nor found a recipe for in any book. She made it in five-pound lots, put it in crocks, covered it with melted butter, and kept it under refrigeration for quite some time. This is how it was made.

Strathborough Paste

Take 4 pounds of beef as for *pot-au-feu*—cross rib, short rib, chuck or rump. Place the meat in a deep pot with 2 or 3 leeks, 2 carrots, 1 onion stuck with cloves, 1 teaspoon thyme, 2 or 3 sprigs of parsley, and a little salt. Add water to cover, bring it to a boil, and remove any scum that rises to the top. Cover the pot, reduce heat, and allow the meat to simmer for 3 to 4 hours or until it is very tender. Cool the meat, then chop it exceedingly fine. It is best pounded in a mortar or put through the blender with a little of the broth. For each cupful of beef add approximately 2 teaspoons anchovy fillets, also pounded fine, 1 tablespoon cognac, and a touch of Spice Parisienne (Spice Islands). Blend, correct the taste, and add a little broth. Place the mixture in a saucepan, and bring it

to a boil, stirring constantly. Then add, for each cup
of the mixture, ½ stick butter. Blend again. Spoon
the paste into small crocks or jars, and cover with
melted butter; seal the jars with foil. The mixture
should be moist, with a heavy overtone of anchovy
and beef—a savory combination.

We made cucumber sandwiches so delectable that I
still occasionally make a batch to assure myself it was
true. First of all, the cucumbers were peeled and seeded,
and salted for half an hour. Then they were washed,
combined with a touch of well-flavored mayonnaise, and
marinated again for an hour. Finally they were drained
and placed on bread which was spread with a lightly
flavored chive butter.

Our tomato sandwiches were good too. These con-
sisted of coarsely chopped ripe tomatoes, which had
been peeled and seeded, and combined with salt, freshly
ground black pepper, and a touch of fresh basil, when
available. We also did some chopped green pepper and
parsley sandwiches, blended with a touch of olive oil
mayonnaise. They were wonderfully crisp, served on a
rather delicate brown bread called Bauernbrot, which
we bought from a German baker.

The favorite of all our offerings was something we
named "onion rings." I have never known any hors
d'oeuvre to catch the fancy as this one did. And if I serve
onion rings nowadays, they are eaten by the hundreds. I
have given the recipe many times, but I guess it is well
to do it once more. I warn you, they are tedious to make
but worth the trouble.

Onion Rings

Make brioche into a loaf, or get a good baker to do it
for you. As a substitute, you can use hallah, the
Jewish egg bread. Chill the loaves well in the refrigerator before slicing. For a party of about twenty
people I generally use two large loaves. Chop 3 large
bunches of parsley, and slice some small white onions

quite thin. You will need one onion slice or so for each little sandwich. Cut the bread in ¼-inch slices, and then, with a small cutter, cut the slices into rounds (about 1¼ to 1½ inches in diameter). Arrange the rounds on a board or table, and spread them with mayonnaise. On half of them place a slice of onion. Salt the onions, top with a round of brioche, and press gently. Have a plate of mayonnaise and a plate of parsley ready. Now roll the edge of each sandwich first in mayonnaise and then in the parsley. The parsley should make a fairly heavy wreath. Arrange the sandwiches in a box or on plates, and chill, covered, before serving. If well packed, they will hold in the refrigerator for hours, or even overnight. I guarantee they will disappear faster than anything else you can serve!

While Irma and I spent our days organizing the kitchen and trying out recipes, Bill was busy raising money and getting publicity for our opening. He was a great favorite of Danton Walker and Lucius Beebe, and we had a certain amount of interest built up by the time the first of several publicity parties was given. We sent out one of the most beautiful folders New York had ever seen at that time. We were horribly in debt. But we opened.

The notices were wonderful. Beebe devoted one of his marvelous Saturday columns to us (giving credit for the brilliant food creations to Bill), and Clementine Paddleford took up the banner, as did many others. Thereafter Danton Walker mentioned us with regularity. The ladies of the Cosmopolitan Club stopped by to inquire, as well as many passersby. And we showed at a tasting of the Wine & Food Society with great success. Soon our heavily parsleyed and watercressed trays were known throughout the city, and we had standing orders for tea sandwiches.

An old friend, Mack Shinn, who was between jobs, came to help us out, and it was good he did. Without him the business could never have gone on. Mack had been trained for the theater and afterwards started a career in merchandising. He had flair, speed, and a flashing wit which saved the day many a time. He was active in every department of Hors d'Oeuvre, Inc., from kitchen to delivery, and he was unfailingly loyal to the end.

Fortunately he was with us on our most frenzied day. A new store had opened and ordered hors d'oeuvre to be supplied every hour on the hour for ten consecutive hours. That day was a milestone; 1,950 onion rings alone rolled out of our kitchens!

At Christmas we expanded our list with the recipe for Mother's delicious white fruit cake. We sent out almost three hundred pounds of it. Irma and I folded egg whites and batter in great wash boilers till the smell of rum and fruit grew nauseating. Irma also made stollen, and we found good country hams and sold those.

Early the next year we attempted more elaborate catering ideas, for suppers and dinners—some beautiful aspics and *boeuf à la mode en gelée*, and such things—but the demand for this fare was limited. Our greatest venture came in the spring. We borrowed the idea from Louis Diat. His famous Vichyssoise was then the rage in New York, but it had not yet been imitated in cans, in powder, and by every other restaurateur. We turned out our own Vichyssoise and sold it at the then astonishingly high price of two dollars a pint. But it was really a good Vichyssoise, done with rich chicken broth, leeks, potatoes, a touch of nutmeg, cream—sometimes half sour cream—and plenty of chopped chives. We made it by the vat. Alas, here is another dish I will never be able to enjoy again. Even the sight of it can send me running from a room.

Another favorite recipe of Mother's became part of our repertoire that second year—corned beef hash, which was made with freshly cooked corned beef, chopped by hand and combined with chopped potatoes and a little onion and nutmeg. This sold by the tubful to those going to their country homes for the weekend, or to those who liked to entertain at Sunday lunch.

Came Easter, and Irma decided that koulitch, the Russian Easter cake, and the pashka that goes with it, should be offered in celebration, as well as butter lambs. We were inundated with orders for butter lambs and had to stay up nearly all one night, molding them and standing them up *en parade* inside the icebox. What a sight! All of us had to help with the deliveries that next day, and I believe it was on this occasion, for the first time, that someone dared to tip Mack. He swallowed fast and took it, and I'm certain he still has the money in a frame.

By now we were accepting all sorts of commissions—from preparing salads to cooking roasts for those with limited kitchens. We had gone far beyond hors d'oeuvre, and we were thriving. All went well, until I began to get some publicity. The spotlight, of course, had heretofore shone on Bill alone. It did not help matters when I announced early in 1940 that I was to do a book on hors d'oeuvre for M. Barrows and Company. About then I had to go to the West Coast to be, during her last days, with that incredible woman who was my mother. I never returned to an active part in Hors d'Oeuvre, Inc.

Mack stayed on with Irma until the business was sold and then swallowed up by the war. It could have remained a booming enterprise. There was a need for it, and there still is. Bill Rhode went on to become one of the editors of *Gourmet* and did a splendid job of public relations for them. This was his forte. He married, very happily I think, and died of cancer in the early nineteen-forties. His amusing book, *Of Cabbages and Kings*, is occasionally found in rare-book shops. It is worth reading, for it has Bill's charm.

Irma has produced several books and done a fine job

in the food business. We often see one another and laugh over the days when we literally had to call in our friends to slice bread and sausages and the like so we could fill an order. I can still remember Irma early in the morning making coffee in a blue polka-dotted pot. We'd munch fresh rolls, drink quantities of coffee, and go over the day's orders. We'll never forget one titled Englishwoman who always asked to have her richly filled sandwiches spread with nonfattening butter! She was particularly fond of pheasant, and ordered more birds from us than anyone could have thought likely. One pheasant recipe we did for her is perhaps worth recording here.

Ballotine of Pheasant as Done for Lady W.

Ballotines are prepared in many different ways. Some are eaten hot, and some are cooked in a broth, chilled, glazed with aspic and eaten cold. This one is of the hot variety.

Have the butcher bone a good-sized pheasant and give you the bones as well. Marinate the bird in 1 cup red wine, ¼ cup cognac, 1 teaspoon salt, ¼ teaspoon black pepper, a pinch of nutmeg, ½ teaspoon thyme, a bay leaf and a sprig of parsley.

Prepare a stuffing for the bird with ½ pound ground pork, ½ pound ground veal, 1 slice salted pork diced, ¼ pound smoked ham diced, 1 or 2 cloves garlic chopped fine or ground with the meat, 2 eggs, ¼ cup cognac, ½ teaspoon thyme, ¼ teaspoon freshly ground black pepper, 1 teaspoon salt, ¼ teaspoon ginger, and ¼ teaspoon nutmeg. Blend these ingredients, remove the pheasant from the marinade, and dry it well inside and out. Place half the stuffing inside the bird, and then add 3 or 4 truffles and cover with remaining stuffing. Sew up the pheasant, reshape it well, and tie it securely.

Line the bottom of a casserole with thin strips of salt pork. Add to this 2 carrots sliced thin, 1 or 2 shallots sliced thin, 10 to 12 sprigs of parsley, and 1 or 2 ribs of celery cut in thin julienne strips. Place the pheasant on this mixture, cover the casserole, and place it in a pan of cold water. Cook in a 375° oven for 40 minutes. Uncover. Pour over the marinade, and cook gently for another hour. Remove the pheasant, and keep it hot. Pour off the sauce. Reduce it quickly by one third, and skin off excess fat. Correct the seasoning. Return the pheasant to the casserole. Pour the hot sauce over it, and return it to the oven for 15 to 20 minutes.

Serve the ballotine hot with a garnish of sautéed mushroom caps and tiny white onions glazed in butter. Decorate the pheasant with truffle slices, and serve the sauce apart.

Twenty-three years after my publishing debut, when Narcisse Chamberlain and I were going over the revision of the hors d'oeuvre book (*Hors d'Oeuvre and Canapés*, revised edition, 1963, M. Barrows & Company, Inc.), we remarked how little of the book had to be updated and how many of the items developed in Hors d'Oeuvre, Inc. had remained caterers' standbys. Not infrequently at cocktail parties a tray of snacks is passed before me, and there among the canapés I see old friends.

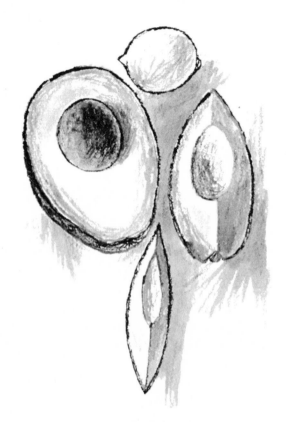

CHAPTER

11

In 1942, after writing my second cookbook for Barrows, the first ever done on outdoor cookery, I faced the probability of leaving my kitchen and my desk for a long time. The war was on, and when I tried, without success, to get into various branches of the service, I then sat back to wait for the draft. By the time my call came, there were several people with influence working on my behalf who assured me that I would have a spectacular career in the Hotel Management Division of the Quartermaster Corps. Where their testimonials went, I'll never know. I languished at Fort Dix from September to December and then found myself in the

Air Corps, in Miami, undergoing eighteen days of basic training. I can recollect one event from that period—Christmas.

It was not surprising that a dozen of us should have been assembled on Christmas Eve. Our outfit was constantly being told that we were "the cream of the crop," and it was possible that this was a gathering of the cream of the cream. What special assignment were we to undertake? Had my influential friends finally been heard? We were marched off to the messhall, and there I found my answer. Between midnight and dawn we twelve chosen people carved almost four thousand pounds of roast turkey! I thought I would never get the odor of turkey off my hands or out of my head. As a matter of fact, I couldn't eat turkey for almost two years afterwards. While the rest of the Air Corps feasted on a traditional dinner that Christmas Day, I was in Miami eating steak tartare.

Following this display of carving prowess, and after endless tests and interviews, I was told that I had been selected to attend cryptographic school. This I did, behind barbed-wire entanglements in Pawling, New York. But at the completion of an intensive six weeks' course, I learned that there was no chance of my going overseas. I was over thirty-eight, and under a new Army ruling I was considered a bad risk. Under the same ruling, I could be released from the Army. Rather than sit in the Pentagon for the rest of the war, I decided to try my luck elsewhere. On Washington's Birthday, 1943, six months after my induction, when the temperature in Pawling was fifteen degrees below zero, I was released from the Army—a graduate cryptographer. There was not a cipher in sight except my own future.

What I did first was far removed from the war. I went to a farm in Reading, Pennsylvania, run by Jim Cullum's brother, who had a prize Guernsey herd, a flourishing dairy business, and a shortage of labor. I

292

settled in, worked on the records, made butter, checked the milkings, and cultivated a huge, thriving vegetable garden. This continued through the summer and into the fall, when I returned to Portland to settle my father's estate. He had died there several weeks before.

I returned to New York, and one day, quite by chance, I met a friend who was with the United Seamen's Service. He had been trying to locate me for months; he thought his organization could provide the perfect job for me. A series of interviews was arranged, and finally I was accepted for training.

The United Seamen's Service was part of the War Shipping Adminstration Service for the merchant marine. It still exists and is one of the most worthy organizations I know. During the war, because other service organizations did not recognize the merchant seaman as a serviceman, he was without recreational and welfare facilities in ports of call. The U.S.S. clubs were created to give the seaman what he needed—a place to sleep in case he was "on the beach," food, drink, and good company. These clubs eventually spanned the world.

My first assignment took me to Puerto Rico. All we had there initially was an office and a place to interview seamen. As the result of frequent torpedoings, it was not unusual to have a pack of thirty or forty men on our doorstep. A club had to be opened, and in record time. We found an old bowling alley and fitted it up as best we could to make dormitories, recreation rooms, and a small kitchen.

I have always felt that food in the Caribbean is perhaps the worst in the world, and this experience did nothing to change my opinion. Try as we might, we could not get the cooks to produce anything but medio-cre fare, and often it was poor. Fortunately we had available *lechón asado*, the traditional barbecued pig with its crisp skin and deliciously tender meat, together with many fresh fruits and vegetables, and meat came to us through the Navy. Along with good bread, coffee and beer, we could offer basic nourishment. The club was attractive, and the men adored it, as they did Jane Gallagher, who came down to replace me. Jane was a marvel. She had understanding and great presence of mind, and she could roll a drunken seaman as well as anyone to save his money.

I was next supposed to go to France, where I wanted to be, above all places, but a replacement was needed in Rio. I found myself heading farther away than ever from Paris. But Rio is a glorious city, and we had a superb club there—a beautiful old mansion, handsomely furnished and equipped for every possible need.

In the kitchen I inherited a restaurant chef of doubtful talent, who was sending out filet mignon, potatoes stuffed with potatoes, and other *pièces montées*, which would have been fine for a smart restaurant. The waste was appalling. I fired him, exterminated a bumper crop of roaches in the kitchen, and hired a woman named Manuela, who cooked magnificently and could hold an ash on a cigarette longer than anyone else I have known.

Soon the kitchen was running in great style. We fattened our own turkeys in the garden (I could face them by that time) and gathered a variety of fresh foods from the Rio markets. The native fruits were luscious, and I kept large bowls of them around the club. Manuela made a dessert with bananas which was so popular with the men that it had to be on the menu every day. It was called, in translation, "Dirty Face," and it is simple to make and thoroughly delicious.

Dirty Face

Caramelize 1 cup sugar in a heavy skillet, and with it line a shallow 9-by-9-inch baking pan or a 9-inch pie tin. Cover the surface with whole peeled ripe bananas, and brush them with the caramel. Beat 2 egg whites till very stiff, add ¼ teaspoon cream of tartar and a pinch of salt, and gradually beat in

½ cup sugar, adding it a tablespoon at a time. Beat well after each addition. Cover the bananas with this meringue, and bake at 350° for 15 minutes. Then bake for another 30 minutes, gradually reducing the heat to 200°. Turn off the heat, and leave the bananas in the oven with the door open for 1 hour. Cool the dessert before eating. Whipped cream is excellent with this.

Another interesting Brazilian dessert was made from ripe avocados.

Avocado Purée

Combine the meat from 3 avocados with 3 tablespoons lime juice, and mash it well with a fork. Beat in sugar to taste, then chill. Serve the purée topped with chopped pistachio nuts.

These two desserts were among our most popular offerings, although fresh banana and fresh mango ice cream were also favorites.

The club functioned nicely until a shift in the war left Rio out of the mainstream. Now, I felt, would come my opportunity to go to France. But I had just begun to close the club and dispose of its furnishings when a plea came from our regional director in New York, asking me if I would take over the club in Cristobal until a permanent staff could be chosen.

I toured through South America on leave and arrived in Cristobal at the beginning of December, 1944. Here the club building was new and beautifully designed for the tropics. It was well equipped, and what it lacked the Canal Zone stores could supply. At this crossroads, naturally, the club was bustling. We often had hospitalized seamen under our care, and occasionally our boarders were men who fell for the charms of the Cash Street girls and missed their ships.

The club was not without its headaches. I had to deal with a committee of women who, although they were charming, understood the problems of management as little as I understood baby care. And then there were constant encounters with the color caste system, more rigidly observed in the Canal Zone than anywhere else in the Western Hemisphere.

Fortunately my kitchen gave me no trouble. I had a jewel of a cook, Margaret Tingling. She came from the Cayman Islands, and not only could she cook, but she was stunning as well. Every woman in the Zone would have given anything to have Margaret as a cook. Luckily for me, Margaret hated women. When I discovered her, she was in all-male company, cooking for the local jail.

Every day fresh bread and rolls and cakes issued from the kitchen. Margaret's fresh coconut cake was unbelievably wonderful and had to be eaten almost the minute it was baked. And it was.

Margaret Tingling's Coconut Cake

Cream 1 cup butter in an electric mixer, with your hands, or with a large spoon, until it is light and fluffy. Gradually beat in 2 cups granulated sugar, beating after each addition. Add 1 teaspoon vanilla, and beat again. Measure 3¼ cups sifted all-purpose flour, and combine with 3½ teaspoons double-acting baking powder and ¾ teaspoon salt. Sift the dry ingredients onto foil or waxed paper. Add the flour mixture to the butter mixture alternately with 1 cup milk in small portions, beating after each addition. Beat 8 egg whites until stiff and glossy but not dry. Fold them very gently into the batter. Pour the batter into four 9-inch layer-cake pans which have been buttered and lined with waxed paper. Bake in a pre-heated 375° oven about 15 to 18 minutes or until the cake surface springs back when pressed with your finger. Remove the layers to a rack and allow them to stand about 5 minutes before they are turned out onto the rack. Remove the waxed paper, and let the layers cool.

Frosting

Place 1 cup sugar, ¼ teaspoon lemon juice and ½ cup boiling water in a saucepan and bring to a boil. Cook until the mixture forms a soft ball when tested in cold water. Pour it in a thin stream over 2 slightly beaten egg whites, beating until the mixture is light and thickened.

Spread the frosting on the cake and between the layers, and sprinkle with grated fresh coconut—this requires 1 to 1½ coconuts.

Margaret added 10 to 12 fine-chopped marshmallows to her frosting, but I like it better without them.

Christmas came. I decided to have a whale of a party, despite the protests of some Baptists on the staff. Margaret fell in with the scheme. We decorated and prepared for days, and invited everyone in port, the boys from the hospital, and many others from town. Our guests numbered over two hundred. We served eggnog, a cold buffet, and all sorts of holiday cakes. It was without doubt the pleasantest Christmas I have ever spent in my life.

By spring the club had assembled a staff, and I finally set off for New York en route to Europe. At the beginning of May, 1945, on a day of torrential rain, I boarded a plane bound for Casablanca. I will never forget that trip. Each person aboard was given a box lunch which contained egg sandwiches and hard-boiled eggs as well. In Newfoundland we stopped to refuel and were given bacon and eggs. From there to the Azores we once again had egg sandwiches. Not until we reached the airport restaurant in Casablanca were we able to elude the hen.

After having eaten thousands of little snails in the bars of Casablanca and waited interminably, we took off for Tunis and Naples. I had my only wartime encounter with bucket seats on those hops. I arrived in

Naples on V-E Day and spent several restless days getting my papers cleared for Marseille. It was revolting to see what the Italian cooks in our Naples club produced out of good Army food—frequently greasy fritters of Spam covered with a thickish tomato sauce. At great cost to my diet, I kept a diplomatic silence. What the Italians did with the meat the Army issued only God and the black market know.

Marseille was a seething port at the end of the war. The old section of the city had been razed by the Germans, and there had been some bombing around the port and in the harbor itself, where many ships lay damaged, resting at every angle, some pointing a course toward the sky. Thousands of Army and Navy personnel were concentrated in Marseille, and more were to come; this was to be a port of embarkation for the United States and the Pacific.

Of all Mediterranean cities, Marseille is one of the most picturesque, and at this time it was also the roughest and most exciting. We had taken over the Hotel Continental, close to the old port, and were running it with French personnel. I had a good housekeeping staff and an excellent chef and kitchen help. The sole exception to the high level of proficiency was the manager of the dining rooms, who was using his position to prosper in the black market. My arrival put an end to his petty deals, and he reacted with a thinly concealed hatred of me. I loathed him heartily in return but for politic reasons could not fire him.

Seamen came to the Continental in droves. We had a good snack bar staffed by attractive French waitresses, and we served wonderful food in our dining rooms. I had made an arrangement with a baker and with a *patissier* to supply them with flour, sugar, butter, and other items, from which they agreed to produce bread and pastry on a share basis. This gave us the only good bread in Marseille and pretty much the only good pastry. I am certain the bakers' share went into the black market restaurants, for I recognized my products more than once.

We drew food from both the Army and the War Shipping Administration, which allowed us a great variety of staples, and we also were able to obtain fresh fruits and vegetables as they came into season. Often we entertained brass, who had helped us in one way or another, in our small staff dining room, and they were always amazed when we told them our food supplies came from the same source as theirs. Our chef, Eugene, made the difference. He did beautiful trays of hors d'oeuvre at lunchtime and a wonderful Bordelaise sauce served with *entrecôtes*. But his *blanquette de veau*, made from Army issue, was superb. He did the unusual by simmering the veal in chicken broth with an onion stuck with cloves and a touch of fresh tarragon, which he could find with no trouble. The broth was thickened with a little *roux* and egg yolks and flavored with a dash of lemon juice. The dish was served with tiny onions braised in butter, and when they were procurable, with fresh mushrooms—occasionally the yellow ones called *girolles*.

Eugene also made a wonderful stuffed eggplant, the most abundant vegetable in those days. French eggplants, as you may know, are smaller than those grown in this country. Eugene would halve them, scoop them out, and chop the meat very coarsely. This he would sauté lightly in oil—olive oil, if we could find it—adding a great deal of garlic (about 4 or 5 cloves for 6 eggplants), salt and pepper, and some rosemary, so dear to the Provençal heart and palate. He then sautéed fine-chopped beef or beef and pork—the remains of a roast or of a *pot-au-feu*, perhaps—added seasoning and a bit of tomato paste. The meat and eggplant were combined, bread crumbs and an egg were added, and the mixture was put into the eggplant shells, covered with more crumbs and dotted with butter. This was baked in white wine and water for 25 to 30 minutes. It made an outstanding luncheon dish.

I had a chance to wander around in the vicinity of Cassis and found some good wines for us there, and I also discovered a cache in Châteauneuf du Pape, where I could get a limited amount each month. All in all, we were magnificently provisioned.

During this Marseille period, I would save up three or four days of leave and get permission to travel into sections of France I had never seen or had not seen for over twenty years. And in October of that year I went to Paris, somewhat apprehensively, but was relieved to find it bristling with spirit and exceedingly lively in places. The visit, begun anxiously, turned out to be memorable. One thing I learned during that trip and my tours of the countryside: The French can make even the most meager food into something appetizing if they have the will to do it. I was invited to homes where rationing provided little variety of food, and yet I sat down to a table of tasty dishes. Some of my friends, especially in Provence, said they would sooner starve than face another eggplant. I knew exactly what they meant, but I also know they found the means to turn out wonderful dishes on occasion.

I can remember visiting a tiny village in the Alps near Grenoble, which had been more or less a summer resort in earlier days. One of our chauffeurs took me there to see his mother-in-law and two of his children, whom she had cared for all through the war. We were served a superlative dish—a huge bowl of *écrevisses*, or crawfish, like the ones I so often dragged from the Necanicum in Oregon. They were cooked in a wine-and-water court bouillon with thin slices of carrot, an onion, a bay leaf, a leek, and a sprig or two of wild thyme, and served barely cool with some of the rough bread of the country. We all sat breaking the shells and enjoying ourselves in a most messy fashion. A rather poor white wine accompanied the food, but who cared? And then we had a tiny leg of lamb, from the black market behind the church, which we ate with new potatoes of the season, dressed with butter we had brought with us, and finished off with a piece of cheese of the region—a rarity for those times.

I also recall a pleasant experience while traveling with a friend en route to Paris. We had eggs from his farm and thought we could have a meal by stopping at a tiny *auberge* we knew to ask them to make us an omelet and give us whatever else they could spare. It turned out they had a catch of young partridge and were delighted to feed us the partridge in exchange for the eggs!

When the time came to return to New York, I did so with great misgivings. I had done a job worth doing, and I had enjoyed it. The renewal of everyday life held little attraction for me. My third book, *Fowl and Game Cookery* (now out of print), had been published in 1944 while I was in Brazil, and I had no urge to begin another. I couldn't have been more rootless and without purpose than on that December 23rd when we sailed into New York Harbor, after a frightful sea voyage of thirty-six days.

But as has happened so often in my life—and in fact had happened only two years before—a chance meeting set my course for me. Four weeks after Christmas I was stopped on the street by an old friend who thought I was still away in the wars. He announced that NBC wanted to see me as soon as possible. They had plans for me to appear on television (then in its infancy), doing the first commercial food program to be televised in America. I had had a stage career earlier in my life. At last—a chance to cook and act at the same time.

CHAPTER

12

I have always enjoyed teaching, and my television experience was the beginning of a professional teaching career that has kept me in touch with interesting people to this day.

The program was presented once a week and was the precursor of today's family programs, with shopping hints and diversion for the children; and Harriet Van Horne interviewed various personalities and commented on the state of radio and the theater. It was sponsored by the Borden Company and was called *Elsie Presents*. The producer was an attractive young lady named Pat Kennedy, now Mrs. Peter Lawford.

I appeared during the second half hour. Bil Baird had made an enormous Elsie puppet, which announced: "Elsie presents—James Beard in 'I Love to Eat'!" Elsie disappeared after the first year when Birds Eye Frozen Foods took over, and the show continued for another year.

I can especially recall the night that Jan Struther was my guest. I was barbecuing a turkey, with the aid of a hidden electrical device to prevent smoking. Unfortunately the device was set afire by dripping grease and in turn set the turkey ablaze. It was a disaster. Generally my show ran smoothly and met with great success. This was before the time of TV sets in every home, and most people saw their favorite programs in bars and other public places. *Elsie Presents* followed the boxing matches. Once I received a round-robin letter from twenty-six signers in Peekskill, New York. They watched the boxing matches every week in their neighborhood bar and found my show so enjoyable that they left me on too! And another time a phone call came in the middle of a program while I was barbecuing spareribs. It was Charlie Berns of "21," calling to say that everyone at his restaurant was in the bar watching those spareribs and refused to go into the dining room and eat. These were compliments dear to a performer's heart.

Since that program I have appeared as a guest on many television shows in this country, in France and in England on B.B.C. I have also given countless food demonstrations across the country—benefits, "Cognac Galas" for the French National Association of Cognac Producers, and "Champagne Galas" for the French champagne industry. Sometimes these demonstrations are before women's clubs that are relatively small, and at other times they are part of huge social events, in hotel ballrooms and country clubs, and may include tastings and formal dinners.

It was not until 1955, however, that I seriously considered starting a cooking school. Again, the impetus came from meeting someone interested in the food business—this time André Surmain. André now owns the small, superexpensive Lutèce restaurant in New York, which is still pleasing patrons after more than a year of operation—a courageous venture for someone beginning in the restaurant business. Something of André's courage sparked our enterprise. We were both startled, I think, at the encouraging response to our first publicity and mailing piece.

From there we began to put together our lesson menus. Neither of us had taught a full cooking course before, and so we had to rely on our intuition and taste. We had successes and failures, but I'm afraid I was largely discouraged at the end of the year. We lacked a cohesive plan. In black moments I thought perhaps the whole idea of a school had no merit. Even so, our course opened up a new world for some people, like Paula Peck, who went on to establish a name for herself in the art of baking; and others from our first class still come to me and Ruth Norman in our present cooking school.

One of the students I recall from that beginning year was a woman who was determined to master a certain lemon soufflé made without flour, which had been part of a lesson. Subsequently, she struggled through twenty-one dozen eggs before she perfected it! She has been making lemon soufflés ever since.

Lemon Soufflé

Beat the yolks of 4 eggs till thick, and gradually add ½ cup sugar by spoonfuls. Beat in 3 tablespoons lemon juice and 1 tablespoon grated lemon rind. Finally beat the whites of 5 eggs till stiff. Blend one-fourth of the whites with the yolk mixture very well, and fold in the remaining portion lightly. Pour this into a buttered and sugared 1½-quart soufflé dish, and bake at 400° for 15 to 20 minutes or till the soufflé is nicely risen and puffy. Test it with the finger for firmness. The soufflé should be firm on the outside and slightly liquid in the center.

After reflecting for some weeks on the shortcomings of the previous year, I was ready to begin again—with Ruth Norman, a friend since the early days of Hors d'Oeuvre, Inc., as manager of the school. Joe Baum had given us permission to hold classes in the experimental kitchen of Restaurant Associates, in the Lexington Hotel, and Albert Stockli, the executive chef of Restaurant Associates, was to be our guest teacher, as he had been the year before. The new arrangement worked quite well. We were centrally located, we could buy our food supplies from Restaurant Associates, and we had a dining room adjacent to the kitchen where we could sit and sample our food, with help in serving and cleaning up. Unfortunately, the kitchen was available only during the day, and we had only one great institutional stove and one oven. We had commuters from Boston that year and a man from New Haven, who would arrive for the ten o'clock class and work through to the end of the lunch period.

This is one of the recipes Albert Stockli presented to the class:

Whole Brook Trout Grillade

Clean, wash, and dry 12 or 14 ounces brook trout and immerse, head and tails on, in 1 cup milk for 8 or 10 minutes. Then dredge the trout in ½ cup flour, and sauté gently in 2 tablespoons butter for 5½ to 6 minutes. Place the trout carefully on a broiling rack over a platter containing 2 cups rock salt, warmed and spread evenly. Sprinkle ½ to ¾ teaspoons rosemary evenly over the rock salt, and pour 2 ounces orange extract around the edges of the rock salt, taking care not to get any of it on the fish. Light a match and ignite the orange extract, which will flame around the fish. Before the flame dies down, turn the fish to expose the other side.

As soon as the flame is out, remove the fish to a plate and bone it, from the tail upward. Serve it on a hot serving plate and pour ginger sauce, hot, over it.

Ginger Sauce

Sauté 1 chopped onion in ¼ pound butter until it is golden. Add ¼ to ½ teaspoon powdered ginger, 2 ounces white wine, salt, and pepper. Simmer the sauce for 6 or 7 minutes.

The following year the enrollment increased, and we began to look at lofts and apartments with large kitchens but found that our overhead would increase so much we could not afford to teach. We had despaired of finding other quarters when Helen McCully, then the brilliant food editor of *McCall's*, came through with a generous offer of *McCall's* beautifully equipped kitchens for night classes. We had only to pay part of the gas and electric bill and leave the place clean. It was a magnificent break, and without it I doubt if we could have survived for the next two or three years.

At the end of the third year a change of management at *McCall's* terminated our "lease." I realized that a dangerous hiatus would occur if new quarters for the school could not be found. And then Agnes Crowther, the well-known New York decorator, whom I have known since my youth in Oregon, came up with a great two-story building which could be rented in its entirety and made over into living quarters and a school. I had almost decided to take the building when the house I now own came on the market. That settled it. Both Agnes and I thought it would be better to buy this property and make a permanent working kitchen, suitable for teaching as well as my personal use.

I moved in during the fall of 1959, and the kitchen was ready just in time for the first class. It is an ingeniously designed room, dominated by a U-shaped counter containing six electric stove units; a double oven and broilers are built into the wall. The space comfortably holds twelve students, Ruth, me, and a helper. I can stand behind the counter and use the stoves while the students surround me. When there is a single student, it provides the luxury of working with several burners, with the teacher on one side of the counter and the student on the other.

Classes have continued here for almost four years now. Students arrive at six o'clock and leave around nine. At seven-thirty they have an *apéritif* and often an hors d'oeuvre of their own making. Around a quarter to nine, they sit down to eat the food prepared for that lesson and discuss it. There is always one wine with dinner, and this comes under discussion as well. Occasionally a wine expert is on hand, and we have had guest teachers from time to time. Leon Lianides of the Coach House has offered Greek specialties; Paula Peck taught with us for several years, specializing in pastries and breads; and Albert Stockli, of course, our visiting chef at every session, has provided some fabulous evenings. This past year Julia Child was with us for a week to teach pastry making, and Helen Evans Brown came from California and did a week of hors d'oeuvre.

Our students are people who find in cookery a fulfillment of their creative needs, just as other people find it in painting or in music. Many of the men who come have worked all day and consider cooking a means of relaxing. Some students come to add to their repertoires, some for the sociableness of group cooking, some for professional reasons. But no one comes who does not want to cook.

We have a class of veterans who attend what they call "dinner classes." For these we choose a series of complete dinners. The students prepare the food and sit down to correct settings of silver and glassware, as they would at a dinner party, cooking between courses. These evenings are good fun, and often I leave the

company and go to bed knowing they will argue over coffee and cognac for some time.

Once in a while someone will turn up for a course who, I will sense in a flash, does not belong there. Both Ruth and I have told people to go to other schools in New York. I have disliked several students with a passion; so has Ruth—but not necessarily the same ones. As any teacher knows, it is very difficult to instruct a class in which there is one person who is hostile or whom you find obnoxious. Sometimes a class can be disrupted by a person whose know-it-all aggressiveness is a form of shyness, which wears off after one or two lessons. But there have been a few students for whom I would not have wept had they mistaken a flagon of hemlock for the *apéritif!*

We have been attacked by one or two people for not being classic. We're not; but I'd like to know what classic means today. It can't mean *haute cuisine*, for that is gone with Carême, and neither I nor anyone else in this age will be able to recapture those architectural gems. We have our Dumaine and Bise and Thuilier, but these men are not perpetuating the cookery of Carême; they are creating variations of their own on his themes. What we teach is good cooking, simply, most of it classed as *cuisine bourgeoise*. But who wants anything better?

To quote Raymond Thuilier, in his charming booklet called *Gastronomie:*

Un simple gratin de pommes de terre peut être une merveille culinaire s'il a reçu tous les soins attentifs qu'il réclame et qu'il exige, mais il peut être aussi dans beaucoup de cas, la plus détestable des ratatouilles.

L'art culinaire, voyez-vous, ne se reflète pas seulement dans l'exécution d'un mets somptueux; non! Il peut être atteint magnifiquement dans le plus banal et le plus simple des mets.

Croyez-vous qu'il soit facile d'exécuter un oeuf sur le

plat sans que le blanc soit frit, le jaune chaud et sans être cuit? Avez-vous souvent mangé des pommes frites, dorées à point, moelleuses à l'intérieur et croustillantes? Et le banal pot-au-feu de nos grands-mères, l'avez-vous souvent apprécié, comme naguère? C'est-à-dire parfumé, moelleux mais ferme? Car le triomphe de la cuisine c'est dans la simplicité qu'il se découvre, et les choses en cuisine doivent toujours avoir le goût de ce qu'elles sont.

A simple gratin of potatoes [scalloped potato with cheese and cream and egg as M. Thuilier does it] can be a culinary marvel if it receives all the attention and care it should have, but it can also be in many cases the most miserable of stews.

Culinary art is not solely the making of a sumptuous dish; not at all! It can be magnificently achieved in preparing the most common and simple dishes.

Do you think it is easy to prepare a fried egg without the white being tough, the yolk heated but not overdone? Have you often had fried potatoes golden brown to a turn, creamily soft inside and crusty? And the ordinary *pot-au-feu* of our grandmothers, have you often tasted it with appreciation and surprise? That is when it is deliciously perfumed, soft and juicy but still firm. The triumph of cooking is to be able to produce the simple things so that they taste as they were meant to.

We have taught our pupils great French dishes, great Italian dishes, some English and Oriental dishes, and regional dishes of America. During the preparation of these, the pupils learn how to make the mother sauces and variations of them; how to roast, broil, poach and bake; how to use their hands and function efficiently. Most important of all, they begin to develop an instinct for the preparation of food and imagination for creating new dishes.

The first night of a class continues to fascinate me. The students eye one another, and there is a chill in the air. It is very much like watching dogs stalk each other at a show. In my first speech I usually ask people to relax and enjoy what they are doing. The first lesson is on the making of crêpes. This may seem strange and a bit difficult for a first lesson, but by the time the twelve have cooperated in making batter and in cooking the crêpes, learning to turn them quickly by hand, all the chilliness has disappeared. Crêpes also make a good beginning lesson because they provide the students with a basic and highly versatile food. If you don't have crêpes in your repertoire, you might try this lesson for yourself.

Crêpes

For unsweetened crêpes, use ⅞ cup flour, 3 eggs, ¼ teaspoon salt, 1 to 1½ cups milk, and 3 tablespoons melted butter.

For sweetened crêpes, add to the ingredients above 2 tablespoons sugar, 2 tablespoons cognac, and the zest of a lemon or 1 teaspoon vanilla.

Mix the crêpes with a whisk or in a blender with just enough milk to make a batter the consistency of light cream. The batter is best if it is allowed to stand for an hour or two before baking the crêpes.

Crêpe pans 5 to 6 inches in diameter are ideal for baking, although you may use a flattish skillet. Heat the pan until it is fairly hot, and brush it with butter. Hold the pan while you pour in, or ladle in, the batter, turning the pan to cover the entire surface. Immediately pour the excess back to the container of batter. Cook, shaking the pan gently, till the crêpe is bubbly; then shake the pan sharply so the crêpe slides to the edge of the pan. Grasp it with the fingers, and turn it deftly. Allow it to cook to a light brown on the other side. Do not overcook the crêpes lest they become too crisp. Stack them and keep in a warm place, or if they are to be used much later, let them cool and place them in the refrigerator. They may also be wrapped in foil and frozen.

Crêpes with Chicken

Poach a 3 to 4-pound chicken and giblets in 1 quart water or enough to barely cover the bird. Add 1 onion stuck with 2 cloves, a sprig of parsley, a leaf or two of celery, and 2 teaspoons salt. Bring the water to a boil, and turn down the heat. Cover the pan, and let the chicken simmer till it is just tender. Remove the chicken and increase the heat to cook down the broth, reducing it by half. Skim off the excess fat and strain the broth. Remove the meat from the chicken, and cut it into good sized pieces.

Prepare a béchamel sauce with 3 tablespoons each of butter and flour cooked together in a heavy pan for 2 minutes. Stir in 1 cup chicken broth, and continue to stir until the mixture is thickened. Taste for salt, and correct the seasoning. Add a dash of nutmeg, a dash of Tabasco and 1 tablespoon cognac. Now gradually stir in 1 cup cream blended with 3 egg yolks, and heat till it thickens; *do not let it boil.* Stir constantly. Mix the chicken with two-thirds of the sauce, and correct the seasoning once more. To the remaining sauce add another tablespoon of cognac and a dash of lemon juice. Roll the chicken mixture in crêpes, and arrange them in a *gratin* dish. For variation, blanched toasted almonds, chopped black truffles with a little of their juice, or lightly sautéed mushrooms can be added to the chicken before rolling. Top the crêpes with sauce, and sprinkle them with a little grated Parmesan cheese. Heat them in the oven at 375° for 8 to 10 minutes, or until the sauce is glazed.

Our first lesson also includes crêpes with *duxelles* (p. 74). Layers of crêpes are alternated with the *duxelles* filling and are topped with fine-cut creamed mushrooms. The stacked crêpes are cut in wedges. Served as a main dish, this makes a dramatic presentation.

We also teach crêpes filled with a spicy purée of spinach and served with hollandaise sauce; with a soufflé batter folded in and puffed in the oven; with caviar, herring, or smoked salmon and sour cream, as in blinis; and many other versions.

The sweet crêpes are sometimes rolled tightly with raspberry jam and flamed with eau-de-vie de framboise; or again they are stacked with a rich chocolate sauce filling, to be cut in wedges and served with whipped cream. And then there are the eternal crêpes suzette.

Crêpes Suzette

There are enough recipes for this dessert to make a separate cookbook. However, I find that the greatest results come from being as simple as possible.

Place 12 to 14 cubes sugar in a crêpes suzette pan or other serving dish, and set the pan over a spirit lamp or other low heat. When the sugar has all but melted, pour over it ¼ cup cognac and ignite it. Stir rapidly to blend the two ingredients, and add as quickly as possible ¼ pound softened butter and the zest of an orange. Sprinkle this lightly with sugar, add the juice of an orange, and stir the sauce until it is rich and syrupy. Add ⅓ cup Grand Marnier and then the crêpes, folded in half and then in thirds. Let them cook in this rich sauce, and turn them once. Add ⅓ cup heated cognac, and ignite it at once. Spoon the flaming sauce over the crêpes, and shake the pan to sustain the flames. Serve the crêpes at once on heated plates.

You may also roll baked banana halves in crêpes and flame them with a sauce made in the same way. Just before serving, sprinkle them with chopped nuts.

I am an old hand at making crêpes, having given many food demonstrations with them. I once flamed an enormous crêpe on the Gary Moore show with the aid of a blowtorch. The size of that crêpe was exceeded only by the one I flamed on the Jack Paar show. To bake it, we had to have a tinsmith construct a special pan about six feet long and three feet wide. The crêpe filled the pan, and it was without doubt the biggest crêpe suzette in the world.

We have had a great cross section of people in our classes—theater people, restaurant owners, home economists, architects, Wall Street brokers, and one ex-ambassadress, who was as good a pupil as I have had. Sometimes when I am teaching classes in the kitchen Agnes Crowther designed for me, I think back to another collaboration of ours during 1931–32 in Portland.

As an adjunct of Agnes's decorating services, I went to clients' houses to teach them how to cook complete dinners, usually international in flavor, and what to drink. I guess the design of my life has not changed much over the decades after all. This year I went into the hinterlands of Pennsylvania to teach and so, after thirty years, find myself an itinerant teacher once again.

CHAPTER

13

I have eaten in restaurants all over the world, but when I come home to my kitchen, I realize it is there that I can best satisfy the eccentricities of my own palate. After endless luncheons in smart restaurants, endless tasting, endless talk about food, one inevitably develops a certain apathy toward elegant cuisine. How I have longed, after a week of rich and complicated foods, for the exquisite pleasure of a simple piece of broiled meat!

Somehow I have never minded dining alone. Instead, I find it is a rare opportunity for relaxing and collecting my senses, and I have always made each occasion something of a ceremony. A nicely set table and time—these are as important as the food. The menus I plan for myself would shock people with an Edwardian background, the seven-course-dinner set—and the nutrition experts as well. Often I order a squab chicken from the market, split and ready for the broiler. This weighs usually about a pound. I rub it with oil and butter and sometimes soy, garlic, tarragon or rosemary, according to my whim. The chicken takes about twelve minutes to broil and is completely rewarding. I like to enjoy each course by itself, so nothing is served with the chicken. Afterwards, if it is in season, I will have asparagus, either boiled quickly till tender but still crisp—and this with no embellishment save salt and freshly ground black pepper—or cut in paper-thin diagonal slices and tossed with butter and soy for two or three minutes in a hot skillet, which gives it a delightful texture.

At other times the accompanying vegetable may be a purée of parsnips, mashed yellow turnips or cabbage braised in white wine and butter. If I have potatoes, of which I am inordinately fond, there is no need for a second vegetable but perhaps some watercress or plain cherry tomatoes. And again, I may dispense with vegetables and have a salad dressed with olive oil and vinegar—Bibb lettuce, romaine, or endive, or a combination of these.

For a final course I am likely to serve myself fruit in some form—a fresh pear, maybe with cheese; berries, when they are good; sliced oranges with a touch of Grand Marnier and powdered sugar; mangoes or lichee nuts when they are in season; or a ripe melon. Occasionally a good cheese follows, but not too often, and from

317

time to time there is a bottle of wine or a glass of beer, which I feel complements certain dishes nicely.

I am not always eating squab chicken, of course, and the main course varies according to my appetite. Sometimes I find myself wanting veal kidneys more than anything in the world, roasted in their fat, then sliced, flambéed with cognac and eaten with salt and freshly ground black pepper; or a tiny squab, broiled or roasted; or a flank steak rubbed with soy, sherry and garlic, broiled blue-rare and sliced thin—blissful eating, because for my palate the flank, in the realm of beef, is the kindest cut of all.

One of my greatest pleasures is having six or eight people to dinner and serving a simple but elegant menu with carefully chosen wines and handsome table appointments. I usually do a modest first course and a main course, followed by cheese—usually no salad is served—and a dessert. The meal is accompanied by two wines, sometimes after champagne has been served as an *apéritif*. These events are relaxed and casual, for I'm afraid I am not fond of formal entertaining.

I try to establish a theme in the menu, and if I happen to be entertaining friends from abroad I feature dishes they do not have in their own countries. Last year, for example, I had two friends from England to dinner who wished to sample the best of American beef. After a first course of razor clam bisque, made from the canned clams from Oregon and heavy cream, I served some succulent, grilled beef with tiny braised new potatoes and tiny French peas, which are now sold frozen with butter in bags, and delicious they are. The dessert was a skillet soufflé—just eggs, sugar and liqueur turned out of the skillet and flambéed at table—delicate in flavor, light in texture and a perfect ending for such a dinner. That night four of us drank a jeroboam of Pommard while we lingered at the table.

On another occasion when I had English guests, I

served them Grammie Hamblet's deviled crab and then a baron of baby lamb with an anchovy and garlic sauce, leeks Provençal and potatoes Anna. Next came cheese, which was perfectly aged, followed by a superb fresh raspberry frozen mousse. We sat at table from eight-fifteen until twelve-thirty—eight of us—enjoyed stimulating conversation and drank a Chassagne Montrachet and a Château Pichon Longueville. Cognac, a bottle of chilled Mirabelle and a sampling of a new tea liqueur accompanied coffee.

When I am experimenting with new dishes, I frequently have two or three old friends in to taste with me. Whether the dish is successful or not makes little difference in their pleasure, for people enjoy being behind the scenes of my profession and are usually fair and constructive critics. I recall one evening recently when I tried out a new kidney dish, which received a favorable reaction, a shrimp dish with a most unusual Oriental sauce, which turned out to be a major discovery, and a dessert which was pretty bad, though edible. Thus the experiment ended with a score of two to one in my favor.

I have vivid memories of the period when Helen Brown, her husband Philip and I were making tests for the book Helen and I did together, *The Complete Book of Outdoor Cookery*. We spent almost three months over the grill and invited all our friends in to feast with us.

Naturally, in the course of my work, I must entertain a great deal and on a larger scale than the intimate type of feasting I have just recounted. I enjoy having many people around me and often have a buffet for thirty or forty in my rather small house (although it is large compared to the one-room apartment I lived in for sixteen years, where I dispensed food to as many as twenty guests at a time, working in a kitchen the size of a closet). The physical arrangement of this house is perfect for large parties, however. The horseshoe-shaped construction in the center of my huge kitchen—I call this my grand piano—has Formica covers designed for it which fit over the cooking units, and thus the entire setup is converted into an ideal buffet, providing space for someone to work within the horseshoe, if need be. Tables are set in the kitchen, the living room and sometimes upstairs in my bed-sitting room if it is an exceptionally large gathering. I like to serve the first course at table because so many people make such a mess of buffet plates.

This course often consists of small ramekins of cheese or deviled crab or shrimp, with a sauce of nuts, Pernod, garlic and oil, served in small shell dishes. When the dishes for this course are cleared, the buffet is ready for the main course—never more than one meat dish and usually a vegetable and a relish or a salad. I abhor plates piled with a conglomeration of food, so I provide plenty but limit the variety. The main dish might be a *cassoulet*, for example, with a salad that can be eaten with the fingers. Or it might be a boiled boned leg of lamb with a brisk Provençal sauce and a rice dish. At times I do a Mexican dinner with some inventions of my own—*seviche* to start with, and *guacamole*, followed by a dish of pork and veal, with a sauce of chiles, nuts, sesame seed and a bit of chocolate as thickening (in effect, a combination of a chile dish and a *mole*). Frijoles with cognac and sour cream accompany this, together with tortillas—sometimes giant ones of wheat toasted in the oven. And still another favorite buffet dish of mine is an enormous *choucroute garnie*, containing five or six kinds of sausage, thin slices of ham, and sauerkraut cooked in champagne or white wine. With this go boiled potatoes and a cucumber salad or a crisp and pungent onion salad. Good wine in generous quantity is served with these buffets, as well as the best bread I can find—usually French or Italian.

I like to linger over a meal and believe others do too, so I allow a lot of time between courses. After the main course is over and the tables are cleared, a cheese board is passed and sometimes another wine. I shop for two or three varieties of cheese in their prime and serve them with bread, crackers and biscuits and butter. Nothing seems to stimulate more comment in my house than a good cheese. After cheese comes a simple dessert—fruit with a liqueur, a mousse, or homemade ice cream or water ice. A coffee mousse is one favorite and another is fresh preserved-pineapple water ice. Sometimes the dessert is nothing more than delicious *petits fours* served with coffee, liqueurs and cognac.

Planning such dinner parties so that served courses are alternated with buffet courses does away with a great deal of the mess of an unattended buffet and still permits an air of informality. For a large party I have two or three people to assist me and do some serving myself.

Frequently I do a cocktail buffet, which is neither buffet nor cocktail party. For this sort of affair I sometimes have as many as seventy guests. Occasionally the potable is champagne, sometimes sherry, and at other times mixed drinks, and I prepare three or four substantial dishes to be eaten throughout the party. I say substantial because my conception of entertaining at cocktails has changed completely since the days of Hors d'Oeuvre, Inc. No longer do I worry about having hundreds of little bits and pieces of food, trying to be original with them. I loathe the precious tidbits that are passed on trays at so many parties. These little creations are messy to handle and are either so tailored or so fancy that they cannot possibly intrigue anyone with good taste—and the more decorated the doots are, the more they revolt me.

Nor do I turn people out in the dinner hour half full of food and quite filled with alcohol. I now ask guests for six-thirty or seven and let them know there will be ample food—enough so they can forego a dinner later on.

I frequently have a large roast beef, just warm so that it slices paper-thin, together with a variety of breads and several mustard combinations, including one of Dijon, English and German mustards blended with fine-chopped gherkins, which seems to be exceedingly popular. Sometimes I make a great *pâté de campagne* or a *pâté en croute*, and with it serve vegetables—essential for any party—and a *tapenade*.

The *tapenade* is a Provençal dish, which varies from town to town in Provence just as *salade Niçoise* does from section to section. It should be pounded in a mortar, unless you are fortunate enough to have a blender.

Tapenade

If you use a blender, blend a little olive oil, together with the oil from the anchovies and tuna, with 14 anchovy fillets, a small tin of tuna (or half a 7-ounce tin), and 2 cloves of garlic. Set aside this mixture, and pit 2 dozen of the soft black olives (Italian, Greek or French); blend them with ¼ cup brandy, 1 tablespoon capers, and a little more olive oil. Combine the fish and olive mixtures, and taste for seasoning. This is best if it stands a day before using. You may vary the amounts of each ingredient to suit your own taste. I know spots in Provence where the *tapenade* is quite black and other places where it is rather a mustard color. It is extremely good with bread and raw vegetables, and it can also be used with eggs in a salad or as a sauce for an hors d'oeuvre of eggs *mollet*. Under refrigeration, it will keep in a jar for some time.

Recently I entertained seventy guests at a cocktail buffet, and for this I prepared a huge *pâté de campagne* with pistachio nuts, tongue and all manner of things in it; an even larger Virginia ham glazed with apricot; and two giant garlic sausages, which I poached in the oven for two hours before slicing and serving with very thin pieces of French bread.

For a gathering of this size I very often serve whole rare filets of beef, marinated in soy, sherry, garlic and olive oil and roasted for twenty-five minutes. Another good meat dish is perfectly cooked corned beef, sliced and served with mustards and raw vegetables. You have no idea how popular this is.

At other times I offer an enormous platter of all sorts of smoked fish, with onions, cream cheese, and breads; and also, perhaps, thin, well-filled chicken sandwiches and a few vegetables. Or I gather together in a great basket every type of sausage I can find in New York—and the number is rather large—which can be carved as people choose. Rolls, bread, wonderful pickles, and a huge cheese board make this the easiest and often the best way of all to entertain at cocktails for people you know well. And then there are occasions when I serve a ham and perhaps a ballotine of duck or chicken.

For one of the best parties I ever did I made huge, wonderful hamburgers and frankfurters and a very special chili.

Chili

Sauté 4 fine-chopped large onions and 4 fine-chopped garlic cloves in ¼ pound beef suet. Add 3 pounds fine-ground lean beef (round steak is best) and brown it quickly. Add 1 teaspoon oregano, ⅓ to ½ cup chili powder, 2 dashes of Tabasco sauce, 3 tablespoons tomato paste, and 1½ cups beer. Cover, and simmer the chili for 45 minutes. Uncover and correct the seasoning, adding more liquid if necessary. Cook the chili down for another 15 minutes. Add fine-chopped parsley or fresh coriander.

This is better made the day before and reheated. It may be varied by the addition of whole-kernel corn during the last 15 minutes of cooking, or ground peanuts or almonds. I sometimes serve toasted almonds with it.

I use this chili as a sauce for the frankfurters and hamburgers and have bowls of chopped green chiles and chopped onion and chopped peanuts at hand for those who want them. Naturally plates and napkins are in order for this dish.

None of the dishes I have mentioned entails a serving problem, and if you want, you can even ask a good restaurateur to do the beef for you. As a rule, beef trimmed for the restaurant trade is best for carving, and a "whole rib," as they call it, will give you a few meals after the party. You can send someone for it as soon as it comes from the restaurant oven, and it will be perfect for your party when it arrives. Do not refrigerate it, for you want the feeble warmth to hold the crispness of the outside surface.

Good Virginia hams and country hams from various sources around the country can be bought ready to eat and are easily shipped. They are a great boon to any cocktail party, for they stretch wonderfully well if carved properly.

In addition to such hearty fare as the meat dishes, I generally provide a large tray of hard cheeses—Emmenthal and Gruyère from Switzerland, Cheddar, and Cantal from France—together with a few dishes of nuts, placed here and there for those who can't seem to drink without them.

Whenever I do a cocktail buffet, I usually have a tray of coffee and cognac brought out around nine o'clock as a hint that the party is over. The guests are usually very content by then. It is surprising how much more pleasant this type of cocktail party is than the old, familiar ones. Even the host has a better time.

It goes without saying that the appeal of food is greatly heightened by the way it is served, by the dishes and color used with it. While I am not basically an exponent of the *pièce montée* school of presentation, I like food to look smart and appetizing when it reaches

the table. For that reason I have collected pieces of
serving china and porcelain from all quarters of the
globe. These have unusual shapes and glazes, and so I
have a houseful of what some people might call horrors
and others might consider amusing whimseys. Nothing
is quite so dull in my mind as the traditional set of
dishes, paraded doggedly through course after course.
And in my opinion an unusual plate provides an interesting enough background for food to obviate such
decorations as the little orange cup, the lemon frill or
the fluted mushroom—and I loathe, with few exceptions, pastry tube decorations on platters of food.

To entertain successfully, one must first of all pay
attention to his cookery, but food should look as well as
taste good. Then be certain to provide good wines. Have
comfortable chairs at the table. Gather around you
guests who are stimulating to you and who will amuse
each other. Put on a fine show! Like the theater, offering
food and hospitality to people is a matter of showman-
ship, and no matter how simple the performance, unless
you do it well, with love and originality, you have a flop
on your hands.

Whether you are serving one person or a hundred,
entertaining at a dinner or cocktail party should be a
pleasure, not a chore. I often think of my mother's
remarkable ability to put guests at ease, which must
also have accounted for her success in business. She
could make the most insignificant person feel important,
and whether she was presiding at the tea table in her
own house with twelve ladies she didn't particularly like
or directing a beach supper for forty friends, she had
the graciousness that marks a successful hostess. She
was never very formal in her entertaining, and her
uninhibited style may sometimes have been thought
shocking. But no one left our house without feeling
happier.

There was something about sitting over a cup of

morning tea or "elevenses" with Elizabeth Beard which made it a special occasion. And when childhood friends came to dinner with me they would soon fall under her spell, respond to her warmth and find themselves talking about their problems without shyness. Even when Mother offered you nothing but cold meat and home-made bread at the kitchen table, she served it with flair, and you felt she was doing it with thought and love for no one but you.

I can remember Mother's pointing out a woman to me one day and saying scornfully, "She has no right to those airs. She doesn't know a thing about a home and less about food! She's clothes-crazy."

More and more I think about Mother's small wood stove at Gearhart and the dishes that issued from the tiny kitchen. I still wonder at her technique. She could even do popovers in that stove, and without iron pans. Her hand was her infallible oven gauge, and I often wonder what she would think about our oven and meat thermometers and our myriad gadgets and electric appliances. It would amuse me to see Mother and Let confronted by my kitchen with its rather laboratorial battery of ovens and burners, controls and timers. Mother would probably scorn the whole affair!

I remember how quickly she would start a fire on the beach with fine kindling, adding split wood and then bits of bark. In no time she would have breakfast going. And it was even more incredible to see her produce dinner or lunch for six to eight people from her trusty wood stove. Those busy days on the Oregon coast left their mark on me, and no place on earth, with the exception of Paris, has done as much to influence my professional life.

In the spring at Gearhart, when the meadows were purple with violets and bluebells and the woods filled with new skunk cabbages and the first shoots of ferns, life was at its most tranquil. One could wander alone for

hours on the beach, gaze at Tillamook Head and watch
the surf. Only last spring I spent a weekend there with
two old friends, and we did these same things—only
instead of walking, we drove in a jeep!—going far up
the beach to the jetty, searching for the Japanese floats
we remembered from our youth. At night, when it was
raining and blowing slightly, we went out once more in
the jeep and drove along the beach, reminiscing about
berrying, clamming, picnicking. Then we parked and
sat a long while in silence, looking at the surf, longing
for the floats to come tumbling in.

Lausanne, 1961
New York, 1962
St. Rémy-de-Provence, 1963

INDEX

(AN *INDEX OF RECIPES* FOLLOWS)

INDEX OF RECIPES